THE DETOUR

Turning the Tide

Ben. J. Harris

Grosvenor House
Publishing Limited

This book is published by
Grosvenor House Publishing Ltd
Link House
140 The Broadway, Tolworth, Surrey, KT6 7HT.
www.grosvenorhousepublishing.co.uk

A CIP record for this book
is available from the British Library

ISBN 978-1-83975-213-1

About the Author

Ben was born in London, England. He would say "into a middle-class family with working class values".

He made it clear from an early age he was not going to university or into a traditional profession but wanted to get on with life as soon as possible. He was diagnosed with Dyslexia, permanently bored at school, and often suspended for weeks at a time. He left at 16 hoping to be a stuntman but after some research decided it wasn't for him and took the next option to become a diver. This career has taken him all over the world and his epic 2005 journey reinforced for him that happiness and contentment came from exploring new places and "living free".

When not volunteering for Sea Shepherd Conservation Society or Parley for the Oceans in the fight to save our oceans, Ben runs and operates his own company – The Other Panama. He lives on a small island off the Pacific coast of Panama.

In memory of Stevie Reeve

Dedicated to my Mum and Dad, for letting me follow
my own path in life.

Contents

Preface

This book came from witnessing the devastation of the 2004 Tsunami in Thailand.

Mother Nature was angry with us, but I was angry with her for the loss and destruction all around me.

After weeks of helping where I could in the Ground Zero that was Khao Lak, I decided I couldn't return to England just then to face questions from people who wouldn't understand. So I picked up my few belongings and began the long trek home overland, hoping to find a better understanding of why.

I was 19 and it was a long way to go...

Prologue

I have no real idea of how many miles I travelled, it's difficult with no well-planned route, mobile phone to record my steps or guide my way. My route relied on my sense of direction, my compass and the kindness of others. Maps were difficult to find and so were often drawn or shared by fellow travellers or copied from hostel walls.

I left the shattered shoreline of Thailand, my home for the last year, and travelled initially into the slightly familiar territory of Myanmar and Laos but then sneaked my way into the confusing and hostile world of China, illegally crossing the forbidden plains of Tibet from east to west. I traversed the slopes of Everest, became the guest at a Sufi ceremony in a graveyard in Pakistan, swigged beer with opium dealers in the tribal lands of Afghanistan and then drank tea with the traders in Iran. Eventually, I arrived at the White Cliffs of Dover one very dark night having crossed 11 countries in 8 months.

It all began with The Wave...

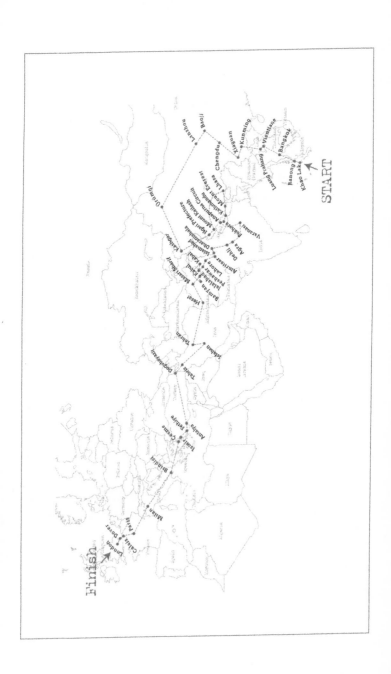

START

Finish

1

The Wave

January 2005

Panic spread! Car and truck horns blared as vehicles screeched and swerved like rally cars in a race to gain higher ground. Those on foot were screaming. A month before, this scene would have included tourists dressed only in their swimwear, clutching infants, dragging children; their beach bags, towels and half-finished breakfasts abandoned in restaurants and resorts along the coast line, but now those fleeing were the rescue workers, the remaining locals and those now in the area trying to rebuild what had been lost here.

I was sitting on the steps of a derelict shop, but did not move. Not this time. It had been nearly a month since the tsunami had struck, and almost every day since, there had been false alarms, often triggered by the simple changing of the tide. It only took one persons' fears to get the better of them staring out at the quivering horizon, and no one would stick around to debate. But I wasn't going to keep running uphill; it was far too hot for all that. And anyway, a part of me didn't care anymore. If it came, it came.

For the past few weeks, I had helped where I could with the recovery in Khao Lak, a small village on the west coast of Thailand, where I had worked for the past five months as a freelance dive guide.

As someone with relatively little dive industry experience at that time, I'd been told there was plenty of work in Thailand – plus, the flights were cheap, the diving was amazing and there were lots of good times to be had on land. I hadn't been disappointed. Khao Lak, could only be described as a bubble; a tropical paradise where bamboo huts sat on sandy beaches, small resorts and a dozen restaurants made up the little community here surrounded by luscious green hills with a backdrop of jungle.

The view from the beach across the milky green water took your eyes to the bumps on the horizon that were the Similian Islands, a national park 60km off land. The home of world class diving and picture post-card white sandy beaches.

It was here that I led three to four scuba dives a day. My days were spent swimming in the Andaman Sea, amidst its immaculate coral reefs and incredible boulder formations, alongside Hawksbill and Green turtles, Leopard sharks and Manta rays with six-metre wingspans. For a 19-year-old guy, from a grey and drizzly south west London, who had left school at the first opportunity with no GCSEs to his name, it was a life that dreams were made of.

On the 26 December 2004, it happened that quite by chance I was nowhere near Khao Lak, but out in the islands in deep water. Less than 24 hours before, I'd been sitting on the beach, wearing a Santa hat, drinking beer, having just turned down a job leading a dive on a local wreck just off the coastline. I was a bit gutted, because normally I'd have jumped at the chance to lead this particular dive and with that particular dive shop, but my hands were tied since a few hours before I had agreed to go out on a day trip to the islands for another company.

I didn't witness the tsunami in the way you might imagine. Most people have a vision of it like in the movies – an enormous tower of water, curling towards the gentle waves lapping the beach. But I've learnt that, if I had been unlucky enough to have been on the mainland that morning instead of out at sea, that's not what I would have seen. First, there would have been the rapid changing in the tide, as the sea was sucked out towards the horizon. It would probably have caught my attention; I'd have headed down to the waterline with scores of other onlookers, curiously inspecting this mysterious phenomenon. But then, as we stood there, shaking our heads, frowning out at the horizon, we would have noticed that the sea had now swollen in height from right to left, and before we had time to shout, scream, run, it was returning to where we stood, with the full force of the Indian Ocean behind it, ready to decimate everything in its path.

Instead, I had left the mainland with the customers and other crew members in a speed boat around 9am, and by the time I had arrived at the islands less than an hour later, we could sense there was something amiss. We'd arrived by speed boat with around 30 customers on board, a mixture of families, backpackers, a few solo dads who'd left their wives and kids on shore for a day of snorkelling or diving.

About a 100metres from one of the islands a bigger two-storey boat was waiting for us with our dive tanks and food and drinks, and it was this that we then transferred onto.

I began going through the motions of preparing the dive gear, making sure the people had all the equipment they needed and started presenting a safety and diving brief to everyone aboard. I was just getting into my stride when one of the customers, interrupted me.

"There's been an earthquake in Indonesia," he said, his eyes focused intently on the little Nokia screen. "I get alerts."

There were a few mutterings, there might even have been the word "tsunami" thrown about, but it wasn't something I'd ever really heard much about, and acknowledging him politely, I impatiently carried on with my brief. But after a couple of minutes I broke off again. Something strange was happening. The sea had inconceivably changed around us. We watched, wide-eyed as the sea level dropped dramatically, and the reefs we had planned to dive among that morning began to protrude above the surface. People broke away from the briefing area and walked over to the sides of the boat, holding onto the railings as the boat gently rocked from side to side in waters usually sheltered from any water movement or wind by the natural bay the island created, the very reason the boat was anchored where it was.

A moment later the sea level began to rise, until it engulfed the surrounding islands, swallowing the beaches so that just the top halves of the palm trees poked out. The videographer for the company began filming the events and following his lead the tourists began snapping photos with their cameras and chatting excitedly as they witnessed this bizarre phenomenon.

4

This happened three more times, and myself and the crew watched in stunned silence, and then very slowly the boat started to spin in circles, and the surface of the sea began to foam. I later found out that this was the tsunami passing below us, heading for land.

Unnerved, but not overly concerned, we decided to delay our first dive of the morning, and instead of providing them with wet suits and tanks, we equipped all the customers with lifejackets as a precaution – against what, we were still unsure. The customers had a few questions and were a little unnerved by the appearance of life jackets but we reassured them it was only a precaution and standard procedure. People were starting to realize something was wrong though, the feelings of excitement and curiosity had passed, people were starting to want answers as to what was happening around them.

After a while, aware we had a boat of paying customers and time was ticking, I began to grow impatient, aware that the customers had paid for three dives that day and we were now falling behind on a tight schedule to provide that service, so half in a bid to test the water conditions, but really because I was itching to get into the water myself and feel what was going on, in I dived with some snorkel gear. It was a mistake. As soon as I broke the surface, I felt myself being dragged along in an undercurrent, and by the time I was able to find air once more I was 20m from the boat. The Thai crew, who clearly thought I was stupid were laughing but moving with some urgency, threw me what they call, a "Jesus line", which in this instance was a football in a mesh bag attached to a rope. They dragged me towards them, and I clambered back aboard.

"We may want to wait a while," I said with a sheep-ish smile. A few minutes later, a tent floated past. We fished it out and hauled it up onto the dive deck, shaking our heads and joking about being washed away in your sleep. It was 10 minutes after that we received the first tsunami warning over the radio. It ordered us to stay out of the water, and I don't know why, but none of us really took it very seriously. We were in paradise after all – anything that was not beautiful or fun simply didn't happen here. Even so we moved the boat into deeper water to shelter behind one of the larger islands as instructed, and as nothing happened over the next four hours or so, we slowly relaxed even more, began using our lifejackets as pillows as we napped on deck, and even began a back flip contest off the side of the boat. We had no idea. So many laughable things hap-pened when you lived in Thailand; so much corruption, mismanagement, odd rules and bungled situations, that we assumed this was just one of those. A false alarm, a waste of time. We were still thinking this, even when a few more tents floated by. I don't know why, but it never occurred to us that thousands of people – whole families and villages – had been wiped out while we lay sunbathing on the deck.

Suddenly, a huge Navy frigate came in to view, and over a loud speaker, ordered us aboard. I felt sick to my stomach now as we did as we were told. On board, we joined a couple of hundred other day boat trippers, all sitting in their bathing suits and rigid with shock. I realized something was very wrong. We spent the next few hours on the metal deck in full sun, with no shade or food and very little water. Rumours of what might have happened passed from crew to crew like Chinese whispers, and we began to learn that people had died – some were saying it was a few hundred, others thousands, and as the information filtered through from the crew to the customers, a strange stillness stole over the boat. We forgot about how hot and thirsty and uncomfortable we were, and instead began to fear for those left on dry land.

When we were eventually allowed back into the speed boats to return to land, we witnessed just how cruel and powerful Mother Nature could be. As we approached Thap Lamu Pier, the sea was thick with debris from land and the resorts that had been washed away. Larger objects like fridges, coolboxes, plastic chairs and beach umbrellas jutted out like little icebergs among the multicolured swamp of plastics and rubber flip-flops. Someone shouted they had seen a body float past but I didn't look and we didn't stop to confirm the claim.

The true force of the tsunami really struck home, when we saw that a Navy boat that was as long as 10 buses and permanently docked offshore, was now lying on the beach, having been picked up and lifted over the Navy base wall like a floating piece of polystyrene. The pier itself was slightly wonky, but we were still able to tie up, and once we were loaded off, all our passengers were urgently herded into the back of open trucks and driven 5km inland from the harbour.

It had been more than six hours now since the waves had struck and survivors and rescuers had ploughed a rough road through the carnage.

The harbour area was totally unrecognizable from that which we had left that morning. Cars lay upside down on their roofs, the interior sodden with silt, windows and doors crushed and mangled, wheels ripped from axles.

Where shops and restaurants had stood that morning now there was just rubble 6ft deep, in the air hung the smell of damp and decay. The place which was normally bustling with life was now eerily quiet. To one side of the public harbour was a Navy base and to the other were unoccupied fields and a school. Between the two ran the only road back inland, this was the road we had been evacuated down in the back of the trucks. As we hurtled down the long road we looked out from the back of the trucks at the surrounding area. Torpedoes littered the land, of the now quiet waterlogged Navy base, on the other side, the school football pitch was identifiable by the one remaining goal post now crooked but somehow still standing above the waterline of the flooded field.

Our group was kept together – and I was grateful to be with two familiar faces – Maria, an English divemaster who I had been working with that day, and my sort of housemate Nigel, the onboard videographer, in whose garden I pitched my tent. The military trucks took us to a large café on the corner of the main road, which appeared to be feeding the 5,000. While we gratefully received food and water, our eyes were glued to the horrific images of destruction being broadcast on a small television showing BBC World News. At the time, the news seemed to be all about Phuket, an area 100km south of Khao Lak which was far larger and more crowded with tourists, although it would later emerge that it somehow suffered far fewer casualties than where we were.

We were told that no one was allowed back in to Khao Lak, and a checkpoint had been set up on the main road into town, only giving access to army and medical teams. I found this frustrating at the time as I was keen to get back and find my friends and see what was really going on, but I later realized that the last thing they needed were hysterical civilians adding to the chaos. It also helped stave off the looting that had already begun.

As we sat watching the news, still unable to fully absorb what had happened, a truck full of service men came screeching around the corner. They were screaming at us in Thai, "It's coming, it's coming!"

No one needed a translation. Chairs were left toppled where they stood as everyone jumped from their seats and ran desperately in all directions. Some were scooped up into military trucks and driven up into the mountains. Many headed for the nearby Buddhist temple where an aid post had already been assembled.

Our group became separated, and Nigel, myself, a middle-aged Italian man, and a Finnish woman with her sobbing young daughter who had at some point become separated from her father, ran for the nearest high ground. We spotted a white-washed building with three floors and made for it as fast as the slowest of us could manage. We banged frantically on the door for them to let us in and up on to their roof. When there was no answer, we ran around the back, and started piling random objects up against a tin shed beside the building. The customers just stood there in shock, waiting for orders from Nigel and me, as though this were all in a day's work for your average dive guide. The roof of the tin shed was only corrugated plastic, but from there we would be able to reach the main structure of the building. Nigel climbed up on to the fragile roof and I stayed on the ground and began to push the customers up, shouting at them to keep to the edges as we knew it was never going to hold all our weight.

Suddenly, there was an almighty cracking noise followed by a loud thud as the Italian man fell right through the thin roof. We shouted to him but there was no response, so I ran around the building to see if I could get in to where he had fallen, but found no entrance. Then to my amazement, I saw him pull himself up through the jagged hole he had just created. His legs and back were badly cut and bleeding. "Oh my God! Are you okay?" we shouted, helping him up and over to the edges. He shrugged his shoulders, "What next?" he said.

Over the next five minutes or so we managed, child and all, to scale the next two floors. I've no idea how we did it – it's amazing what you are capable of when you are fleeing for your life. But, when Nigel and I returned to the building a week or so later, we couldn't fathom how we had scaled those last two floors – or how we had got back down. It simply didn't seem possible. Finally, all safely on the roof, we sat and waited. I had a small first aid kit in my daypack, and so dressed the Italians' wounds as best I could. Now the adrenalin was wearing off he was in a fair amount of pain. Everything around us was silent. We tried to maintain some normality, asking questions, talking about everyday things, trying to raise a smile, even though we were scared and tired ourselves.

After about an hour it became clear that the wave wasn't going to come. We clambered down the side of the building and made our way along the main road towards Khao Lak. The Italian was limping and he had to walk legs spread apart to avoid his wounds rubbing but he managed. The child in the arms of her mother was tired and in and out of sleep.

We hadn't got far when a green military truck pulled over, and we were again herded into the back with a dozen other strays, before we were driven far off into the mountains to an aid camp that had been established there.

It was like a scene from a war movie. People with horrific injuries lying on stretchers and makeshift beds, writhing in pain; some were worryingly silent, while others were simply crying. We were continuously stopped by terrified foreigners asking if we'd seen their husbands, wives, sons, daughters. Two young German children were sobbing and begging for their parents, a middle-aged man stood leaning against a pillar – every limb wrapped in blood-soaked dressings, his face expressionless, his eyes empty.

Around four the next morning, the dive staff we had become separated from managed to find us, and came to collect us in the company four-wheel drive. We said goodbye to the Italian, the mother and daughter wishing them luck before heading back to Khao Lak. Thanks to a couple of our rather more persuasive Thai staff members, we were waved through the checkpoint. None of us were prepared for what we found on the other side. Our truck bounced along a rough route that had been pushed through the debris by army vehicles and emergency services, banks of rubble were piled high on either side. The sun had not yet risen, but in our car headlights, we saw the remnants of the exclusive resorts that until yesterday had dotted the coastline. But even worse we saw bodies. Everywhere. Teams of volunteers were marking their final resting places with bamboo sticks topped by plastic cups pushed into the ground beside them. We headed for the dive shop, which having been on higher ground and sheltered behind a resort down below on the beach, was in a parade of small shops which had remained standing.

Feet from the doorway, a blanket was covering something on the floor.

In the half-light of morning we squinted at it, took a torch and lifted the blanket. It was a woman. Her lifeless eyes stared up at us, trickles of dry blood ran from the sockets, her nose, mouth and ears. The stench of death hit me hard and I turned away and swallowed the bile that had risen in my mouth. It was four more days of summer before her body was removed.

Once the sun had risen, and after a dozen cups of coffee, Nigel and his girlfriend Bee and myself got back in the car, and made slow progress through town, along the wet track of compressed debris which covered the road. We were still trying to get home, even though we were convinced that our house would be gone; after all, we had seen a Navy patrol boat lying in a field, 2km inland, and our little house was much closer to the sea.

The air smelt stagnant, and nothing was left untouched by the horror the wave had brought. Overturned cars balanced on roof tops; a body was wedged in between the branches of a tree 15ft off the ground; one shell of a building still had its iron security shutter attached, but the metal lattice had been buckled into a perfect curve, illustrating just how much force every inch of the wave had carried.

Shell-shocked people, barefoot and covered in blood, staggered along the side of the road, searching for their families among the semi-clothed bodies that lined the route. I looked away from an obese white woman, still in her swimsuit, her breasts exposed, her arms out-stretched, her legs broken. When we passed the local market, we found long lines of corpses instead of stalls, and people pacing up and down searching for loved ones, friends and neighbours.

Some attempt at preserving the modesty of the dead was being made, and pieces of paper were being laid across their faces, but dusty gusts of wind were blowing them away far quicker than they could be replaced. We watched in grim fascination, as rescue workers and vol-unteers loaded body after body on to waiting trucks. But no sooner than one body was removed, than two more would be pulled from the rubble to take its place. But not everybody I saw was working to help with the recovery. I watched in disbelief as two men found a handbag, and split the wet money it contained. But the further we trav-elled, I realized there was no shortage of opportunists with no qualms about stealing from the dead.

As we drove past yet another collection point, I spotted the corpse of a skinny man with a ponytail and realized I knew him. I recognized him as a German guy who ran a bakery and whom I bought fresh bread from often. I didn't say anything to the others in the car, as it didn't seem the right time, I was sure we were all seeing people we recognized as we crawled along that road, but we were all silent and that felt appropriate.

Of course, the phone lines were all down and our mobile phones weren't working, but as we made our funereal progress through the town, all of us had our phones out, desperately trying to call people and establish who had survived. After 30 minutes we finally reached the house and were shocked to find it was still standing – a few hundred metres further down the road, the neighbours and their homes were gone. However, the forest of picture postcard palm trees, which had previously blocked our view of the ocean, had all but been flattened, and obviously therefore had taken the brunt of the wave.

When we climbed out of the car and stood on the sodden grass in the front garden, we saw that the water had stopped just feet from the doorstep. We stayed there for quite some time, just staring out at what was now nearly a sea view. The sight of the ocean, so flat and innocent once more, made me feel quite sick.

I had only lived at that house (or in the garden of that house) for two weeks. Up until then I'd spent months living in a tent on the beach. When I first arrived in Khao Lak and was still looking for work I had very little money, and after spending my first few days strolling alone down the long, almost empty beach, I had been taken in by a group of women who ran a very basic, but professional massage parlour a stone's throw from the sea. For a small fee, they let me set up camp within the grounds of their business and allowed me to use their toilet and shower. So, I pitched my tent under a massive old tree that grew up through the sand on the beach. Unfortunately, the tree gave no shade, and I could never sleep for more than an hour after the sun had risen since my tent became a sauna. So, before my eyes were fully open, I'd simply get out, run down the beach and dive into the breaking waves to cool off.

The girls who worked at the parlour were lovely. They lived a happy, care-free, day-to-day life on the beach, and when work was over for the day, they would sneak off to karaoke bars behind their boss's back (apparently, she didn't approve of them drinking on a work night). I think it was because I kept this secret that I was often invited along to the gaudily-lit bars, where they'd spend their evenings unwinding and laughing at each other's terrible singing. My favourite one of the girls was a bubbly, big-boned lady, who always wore a multicoloured hat, so I nicknamed her Rainbow. Rainbow loved food, and would often bring me back little snacks she wanted me to try from the market. When she gave me anything that was too sour or spicy for my English taste buds, she'd laugh so hard. Every time I went out for the day in search of work, Rainbow would call after me, "Good luck to you, Ben!"

"I was born lucky," I'd reply.

A few days after the tsunami, I went back to my old campsite. I wasn't expecting to find the girls for I was sure they all would have perished, as the wave had struck around the time they would have been giving their first massage of the day. Even so, I just felt I needed to go down there anyway, whatever I might find. The landscape of the beach had changed so dramatically I had trouble finding where it had been. Then I spotted the tree I used to pitch my tent beneath. While few other trees remained standing, this one, so thick and sturdy unlike the palms, had survived, although its trunk was deeply scarred. I sat down underneath it among the debris and tried to remember where everything had been. Its leaves had fallen and gently settled on the remains of my former home, and I felt as if it was trying to tell me, 'Life goes on.'

The beach area was left almost untouched for the first week, as it was deemed unsafe due to the armed gangs who were running riot along the coastline, looting what they could and threatening to hurt anyone who tried to stop them. But I had nothing to fear from them, they could see I was too lost in my own thoughts to be a threat or a rival. So, I continued down the beach unbothered by them, passing rigor mortis-set limbs that poked up through the rubbish in the sand. Bodies rolled back and forth in the surf, and bobbed in the water that was still thick and dark with flotsam and jetsam.

I came to one of the luxury beachfront resorts, and stepped cautiously among the remains of its waterlogged bungalows. A camera lay in the mud, its lens cracked, condensation filling the viewfinder, and I wondered what story that soggy film might tell. I stepped into what was once the spacious reception area. Glimmers of lavish marble floor peeked through sodden soil. The information desk was still in place, but its polished oak surface was now stained with salt marks. Incredibly, the clock was still mounted on the wall behind it. Water lay trapped in the lower half of its housing, and its hands were stuck. The time read 10.22am – its ticking having ended as abruptly as the lives of those who had been standing below it.

A few days after the tsunami, the government tried to evacuate everyone from Khao Lak for fear of a Typhoid epidemic breaking out as a result of all the unrecovered bodies. They threatened to put all who remained into quarantine, and so as instructed, I left for a week, and went to Koh Phangan, an island off the east coast.

There, with friends, I experienced the most surreal New Year's Eve celebration of my life, since it was followed by another full-scale emergency when the bungalow resort next to where Nigel and I were staying, caught fire late one evening. The island didn't have the roads for a fire brigade, so everyone came running to help, including Nigel and myself. A whole night was spent throwing buckets of water over the flames to contain the inferno. At one point we found ourselves at the very front of the chain of rotating buckets and in our enthusiasm to get more precise throws, we ended up entering the building. With the humidity, the heat was fierce inside, and realizing the danger, I began backing out, shouting over and over for Nigel to do the same. He eventually backed out just as one of the thick wooden ceiling beams came crashing down. By morning, all that remained of the resort was a pile of smouldering ash.

Despite this drama, I found it hard to be around people who hadn't experienced the impact of the tsunami, and after about a week, I returned to Khao Lak. Over the next month, the things I saw and experienced will never leave me. How can you forget the stench of a bloated corpse, or the last expression frozen on a dead child's face, or bodies so twisted and deformed that you can only pray their owners drowned first? And the people who for days and weeks after the wave, continued to search for their loved ones, even though they knew in their heart of hearts they were gone. They would come up to you, hand you a photo taken from their family album, and desperately ask if you had seen them. Over and over I'd say, "No I haven't," knowing their loved ones may never be found, and almost certainly not alive.

On one occasion we went to the hospital with a friend who was searching for his missing wife and mother of his child. Along row after row we stared into blackened, distorted faces struggling to identify if it was someone we knew. The hospital was drastically under-equipped to deal with such a catastrophe. Outside, coffins were being filled quicker than they could be put together. Inside, bodies were stacked on top of each other on beds and floors. The smell was overwhelming and sickening, and I was horrified to see that as the bodies swelled in the heat, the dead flesh formed into bubbles which would burst and spill rank body fluids all over the hospital floor.

The first week after the tsunami, several charities, international brands and other organizations had arrived in the area to help, and while many did a lot of good, it was frustrating to see how much of the desperately needed aid was mismanaged and wasted. Piles of winter clothing sent over by well-meaning European organizations and charities, lay discarded by the side of the road – apparently, they had forgotten that you don't need coats and jumpers when it's 35 degrees in the shade. A popular English supermarket donated more than 200 pushchairs, which sat unused and unopened in a pile beside the main road for weeks where they had been unloaded – the Thais in Khao Lak never used push-chairs, but carried their offspring on their backs.

So much aid money was being wasted, and yet there were so many in need. As Nigel, Maria, Bee and myself walked around one of the refugee camps, where hundreds of huts on stilts had been built for displaced families, we noticed everyone appeared to be living and cooking outside their shelters rather than inside. When we asked why this was, they explained that the tin shelters became ovens in the day and were still too unbearably hot to sleep in at night, meaning the only real use they had for them was for storing their few remaining belongings out of the sun. We went off and bought a dozen fans, and handed them out to as many families as we could, this was paid for with money that Nigel had collected in a fund he had established from friends and family abroad. I also bought some tooth-brushes and toothpaste – a small contribution, but I felt that if I had to endure such terrible conditions, I'd at least want to start the day with the simple luxury of clean teeth and fresh breath.

But it wasn't just the locals who were suffering. I also began to hear about the hundreds of illegal Burmese workers who were rumoured to be hiding in the hills where they had escaped to after the wave. They were still there, but now not only for their safety, but for fear of being rounded up and sent back to Myanmar. Too scared of the authorities and the sea to come down from hiding, they were starving up there in the mountains with no aid from the Thais and little help from the aid agencies. Some people had attempted to take food to them and coax them down, but they had only retreated further into the jungle. While the Thai government was undoubtedly extremely good to its own people, the Burmese were left to fend for themselves in a country where they weren't welcome. Having escaped an evil regime in their home country, and survived a tsunami in their adopted one, it saddened me to think what might become of those workers and their families.

Other things just made me angry. Like the religious charities that flooded the area and used this humani-tarian crisis to recruit people to their cause, often using the most distasteful and disrespectful tactics. A Christian group hung a huge banner declaring "JESUS LOVES YOU" across a road, below which the largely Buddhist population of Khao Lak scrabbled together what was left of their lives. At the refugee camps, Hare Krishnas handed out food, but then hassled the grieving with promises of a happier life if they followed their beliefs. While another well-known charity refused to let homeless people move into their newly-built shelters, unless they first agreed to convert to Christianity.

The custom in Thailand when moving into a new residence is to place a small spirit house outside the home. The spirit house, which resembles a brightly decorated birdbox, is to give the spirits of the land somewhere else to reside, and prevent them from getting angry over their eviction and haunting the new residents. So, I was shocked that many of the religious charities refused to allow the Thais to erect these small structures outside the newly-built shelters, particularly considering the amount of unsettled spirits the locals now believed to be in the area.

I am not a follower of any organized religion or believer in any god but during that time I certainly experienced things that could not be explained, and I could not help but think of poltergeists.

One very still and airless morning I was out pegging laundry in the garden, when I went back inside to drain the scrubbing buckets and fetch more pegs. There was no one around – there never was where we lived; we were too far out and people only ever visited by car or motorbike which we'd hear approach from a mile away. On the rare occasion anyone did come on foot, the five dangerously territorial dogs that lived on the property would alert us to their presence immediately. But when I came back out in to the garden a few minutes later to finish the job, the dozen or so items I had securely attached to the washing line, were now strewn all over the garden. Pants hung from the roof edge, T-shirts and shorts were scattered in all directions over the grass and tangled in bushes. It could have been a prank, but I knew in my gut that it was something else. We didn't have a spirit house outside in the garden. Perhaps we should have had.

The aftermath of the tsunami weighed heavily on me. And so, sitting on the stoop of that abandoned shop a month after the tsunami, once again watching the panic spread around me, I knew it was time to leave Khao Lak. I had given what little I had to offer there, and I needed to focus on myself for a while. I needed to go somewhere different, away from all the constant reminders of the tsunami and take some time to process it all, to work out what had just happened and where I was to go from there. How I would move on from it all, some time to grieve for those who had been lost and the magical world I had known that was now lost, the memories of which would be forever scarred.

I wasn't ready to return to England yet and the hundreds of questions from concerned family and friends. I thought I'd wait until the tsunami was just another old headline that everyone was bored of hearing about. I suppose I had reached the conclusion that all this had happened because Mother Nature was angry with humans, and so I decided I wouldn't anger her further by defying gravity. Instead, I thought, I would return to England, but by any means other than flying. No matter how long it would take.

2

Fleeing The Scene

Growing up had always seemed like a terrible idea to me. I just never wanted to get a conventional job, and I think I'd told my mum that I wasn't going to university when I was still at primary school. At 15 years old I wanted to be a stuntman and loved the idea that on Monday I'd be jumping off a roof and Tuesday I'd set myself on fire. Then I found out that, as a stuntman you train in one discipline and do that over and over again. Since setting myself alight every day didn't appeal, I looked for inspiration from the careers test we took at school instead. Everyone else returned with at least 10 job suggestions, but I was just given two – a fireman or a diver. Funnily enough I had quite fancied becoming a fireman anyway, but as it turned out I was practically blind as a bat in those days (although thanks to laser surgery that's no longer a problem), and so diver it was. I'd only ever seen police divers before, who were pulling out a suicide from beneath Kingston Bridge, and since that didn't exactly appeal, I did a bit of research and decided that oil rig diving sounded more up my street. Yes, it was pretty dangerous, but it was also lucrative and as long as I survived, I could retire in 10 years. The problem was, I couldn't start the real training to be a commercial diver until I was 18, and rather than wasting time going to sixth-form college, I decided to travel and volunteer abroad, funded with in between stints at home, working as a labourer, and serving tea and cake to old people on a cruise boat that sailed up and down the Thames between Westminster and Hampton Court close to where I had grown up.

By the time I arrived in Khao Lak aged 19, I was a certified Divemaster and had several solo travelling trips under my belt, in Africa and India, and a stint diving in Fiji and the States, the latter of which was so expensive that I had to resort to a few nights sleeping rough in an arcade. In the previous four years I had realized that you don't have to be loaded to travel to exotic untouched paradises; in fact it's better if you're not. You see far more renting a room from a local than from the balcony of an expensive hotel. I also knew I didn't want to work 49 weeks of the year, earn loads of money but have no time to spend it on anything other than a new watch. Lucrative oil rig diving was now definitely off the cards – having spent several months working for a reef monitoring conservation group in Fiji, I now knew that the oil industry was the marine-life devil and not something I wanted to be part of. In fact, Fiji changed everything for me. I always thought life was about working hard and earning money. I never saw anyone work harder than Fijians. Surviving on limited resources meant they were far from lazy and every day survival was a struggle, but you also saw them relaxing a lot, because they figured life was too short not to be spent living.

So, although I was 19, and certainly a lot greener than I am now, deciding to travel essentially the long way home from Thailand with not a lot of money or resources, was exciting rather than remotely concerning for me.

Coincidentally, not long after I had decided it was time to leave Khao Lak, Darren, an old school friend of mine, appeared in town, having travelled down from China where he was working as a golf instructor. It was quite fortuitous timing really, because having made the decision to go, I had then started to feel guilty that I was able to leave the aftermath of the tsunami behind me, when so many others couldn't. Having been through secondary school together and getting our first jobs at a local members' club near to where we grew up in Middlesex, Darren was a close friend, and his arrival gave me the push I needed to finally bid my Thai home an emotional farewell.

Darren was not your conventional traveller. In fact, at 19 years old he was more like a 45-year-old Brit abroad, scarlet with sunburn, in his socks and sandals, sweating profusely, and maintaining a continuous background grumble about how hot it was. Having left home at 17 years old to move to a four-star hotel in Hong Kong where he taught golf to rich Chinese kids, roughing it wasn't really part of his vocabulary. Luckily, I found his old-man mannerisms funny, and it felt good to have someone around who knew me well, and me him.

By now, it was more than a month since the tsunami, and first I needed to get a new visa. This meant Myanmar, or Burma, was to be our first stop, 200km away, and it was time to introduce Darren to the wonderful world of hitchhiking! Trusting that I was the 'traveller one', Darren agreed to go with the flow with minimal grumbling. From Khao Lak it took a day to travel to

Ranong, the crossing point into Myanmar, slightly more than sun-kissed and our hair severely windswept from hours in the backs of trucks. From there we hired a long-tail boat to take us across the expanse of water that led to Myanmar, which for Darren, who was not much of a seaman, was pretty terrifying. The long-tail boats had a habit of crisscrossing each other's paths, skimming bows, with propellers swinging through the air, often causing passengers on other boats to duck to avoid decapitation. Long-tail boats are called this because the propellers are attached to a long pole/shaft that sticks out the back of the engine, often half the length of the hull of the boat itself.

The captains, when manoeuvring around other boats or objects, often lean down on their engines like a seesaw to pivot/lift the propeller up over things in order to make a quicker turn or to get themselves out of a tight spot/ parking space. This results in a sharp spinning propeller suddenly bursting out the water and swinging 90 degrees around before being dunked back into the water beside you. In crowded marinas/docks where the boats are crammed in against each other, it's not uncommon to experience a long-tail boat whip its prop up and over your boat as the captain skilfully steers around you. There was much swearing from Darren and laughing from me, as he gripped the side of the boat for dear life.

The immigration office was a dilapidated hut on stilts, and we had to stop just outside the port while the young boat boy took our passports and jumped across the bows of a dozen moored up boats to show the waiting official. He stamped us out of Thailand without even bothering to look out of his window. We could have just returned back to mainland now we had our stamps, but I thought Darren might like a little bit of a Burmese experience, and so we went on to the border town of Victoria Point – about the only part of Myanmar you can get to without a load of advance visas and permits. So, when the boy returned to our boat, we motored on noisily across international waters towards Myanmar, past fisherman and their huge nets that were scooping up the jellyfish which drifted along inches below the surface.

I watched the military-controlled land approach through narrowed eyes. Gold stupas (like bulbous minarets) dotted the mountainside and glistened in the sunlight; a sign of the wealth that this country possessed, but of which the people, whose thoughts and movements were so heavily controlled by the military junta, saw none. A life without persecution was all that most of them could hope for. Few have any understanding of politics and they cannot grasp why all these nations, who profess to care about their suffering, don't step in and do something to help them. Trade embargoes have no meaning to them; they only hear empty promises and a world that has lost sight of right and wrong. This is what you see in the people's eyes as you walk around Victoria Point, and it made me feel guilty. Guilty that this was a former British colony that we'd left with little thought or care of what would happen to its people. But contrarily, it also made me feel grateful that I was British and could float across borders simply because of the little red and gold book I carried. These feelings were nothing new to me. I'd visited Victoria Point a few times already, since at the time, a Thai visa was only good for a month which meant every month I had to leave the country just to be let straight back in. We didn't stay long on this trip, since our driver was waiting impatiently for us in the boat, so I gave Darren a quick 15-minute whistle-stop tour.

First, we headed for the bottle store which sold dirt-cheap cartons of Burmese cigarettes called 'Falling Rain', bottles of Johnnie Walker, Smirnoff Red and more surprisingly, three flavours of Pringles. As we were leaving, the owner stopped us and attempted to sell us a huge bag of Viagra, which we declined, despite his many hand gestures and actions to illustrate its incredible effects. We then walked back through the stalls selling fake designer sunglasses, and once I felt Darren had seen as much as he was ever going to legally see of Myanmar, we returned to our boat and headed back to Thailand, where we were granted another month-long visa. We then began the tiring task of finding a lift back in the direction from which we had come.

We were heading for Koh Sok National Park. I'd been there six months before during the monsoon season, and walked nine of the main trails within the park, spotting snakes, gibbons, monkeys and what in my night vision I think was a wild boar. The park seemed a lot tamer this time round, since the waterfalls had all practically dried up. The fast-flowing rivers were now gentle streams, and the trails and ground had become dry and cracked, rather than the marsh it had been on my last visit – which had resulted in countless leech bites (that made me look like I'd survived a nail gun attack), and a battered and bruised body from continually slipping over. In fact, the last time I was here, one of the trails had nearly killed me, when an unexpected rainstorm swelled the streams to torrents, and turned the narrow rocky ledges of the trail into ice rinks. I only made it out of the park alive with the help of a couple of lost Germans, without whose support I could never have made it across the fast-flowing rivers. I led them to the exit, but they had already returned the favour in triplicate by rescuing me from a deadly fall. I survived that trail with a bruised back, a lumpy head, swollen hands and feet that looked like they'd been run over by a lawnmower. So needless to say, when Darren suggested we take the same trail that day, I told him where to go!

Instead we spent the next few days swimming in the river a short walk from the park entrance, and enjoying cold bottles of Chang Beer at the guesthouse, where happy hour lasted an extraordinary eight hours. Strangely the smell and sounds of the jungle felt like such a safe environment now, after the smell of raw sewage and death I had left behind me in Khao Lak. It also made me realize how good it felt to finally be away from the threat and panic of another tsunami. Even so, it was not something I was ready to talk about, which was something Darren accepted. It was nice to think and chat about other things, to start to relax and feel refreshed.

One memorable day, we took a trip to a nearby Buddhist temple close to the foot of a mountain where the monks looked after packs of stray dogs and mischievous monkeys. Accompanied by an apprentice monk and a dozen of the curious primates, we climbed up a steep metal staircase, which took us into a cave system leading deep into the mountain itself. The floors and ceilings were covered in stalactites and stalagmites. The rocks sparkled with veins of precious stone I assumed to be quartz and bats flew around our heads. When we got back to our camp, Darren confessed that he'd been a little scared of the monks due to the computer game Tomb Raider II, in which vicious monks attack you. "And they say computer games aren't harmful," I joked.

After a few days, we continued hitchhiking the 750km or so to Bangkok, riding in the back of numerous pickup trucks and in the cabs of enormous and painfully slow lorries. At one point we were stopped by the police, but they only gave us a bottle of water each and wished us luck on our travels. Hitching is by far my favourite mode of travelling, because although it's not always the cheapest or quickest way, you meet so many different people and have the freedom to move on, anywhere and anytime.

Wherever I've travelled, one thing I have found to be a universal truth, is that those who appear to have less wealth will always be the ones to offer the most and ask for the least in return, and this was certainly demonstrated on our 48-hour journey to Bangkok. Twice, the drivers of our hitched lifts, pulled over and insisted on buying us lunch, accepting nothing in return when we parted ways. While we were wandering down the highway, an elderly lady with a safety pin holding her dress together, hobbled over from her fruit stall to offer us a bag of bananas for the road. A few hours later, as we stood after getting soaked in the rain, and unsuccessfully trying to flag down cars by waving our hands, palms facing down (the thumb gesture is not understood in Thailand) a Mercedes pulled over. I was immediately suspicious, as expensive cars rarely seemed to stop. The window rolled down to reveal two men in suits who, before I'd even had the chance to utter a *'sawadi kup'* greeting, asked for 4,000 baht (at the time about $100) for a lift. This was a ridiculous sum of money, as the bus would have been around 300 baht. We declined, despite the fact that Darren's bald and burning head could have done with a roof, and winding the window back up with irritation, the men drove on. We continued on our journey on foot for a few more minutes, when a pickup truck began reversing a few hundred metres down the highway towards us. When it drew level, a young man in his 20s hung out the window and offered us a lift. We climbed in the back and were on our way, Darren clutching a bandana to his head to prevent further sunburn. Our driver spoke just enough English to tell us his name was Art, and after our over-night drive to Bangkok insisted we had tea with him and his family. Art lived with his parents and brothers in a narrow, high-ceilinged terraced house, right opposite a noisy overpass. The moment we stepped inside we were greeted by the homely smell of sweet and sour pork and ushered into a living room with kingfisher-print wallpaper covered with family photos. There was a mish mash of furniture, and the chairs all had lace covers over the arms and backs, like you see in old people's homes. His mother offered us tea, which sadly was Lipton's, and asked Art to ask us lots of questions – she was clearly excited to have two *farangs* in her home. Before we left, she gave each of us a tiny golden Buddha pendant for luck which I kept with me for months, until it was stolen from my bedside table at a hostel in India.

Afterwards, Art dropped us off on the Khao San Road, and would only accept a coke for all he'd done for us. The Khao San Road is pretty famous among tourists, and a place with which I have a love–hate relationship, since it's full of money-hungry touts and first-time student travellers immersing themselves in the 'culture' by getting drunk and buying pairs of fisherman pants. Nonetheless, I always stay there, amidst the neon signs and stalls selling wooden frogs, knives, fake designer T-shirts and photocopied Lonely Planet guides, as it's the only place I know in Bangkok where you can get a bed for 60 baht and have easy access to internet facilities and budget travel agents.

Bangkok always takes a while for me to adjust to. It did feel good to be back, given all that I had experienced over the last few weeks. In many ways, cities are designed to separate you from nature and reality, and since I was none too happy with Mother Nature at that moment, the horrid humidity, swerving chaos, honking tuk-tuks and clouds of billowing black smoke, didn't bother me too much at first.

For a nation that operates on fairly laid back 'Thai time', Bangkok is a city that is always in a hurry, and the first thing I always notice are the incessant car horns. Bangkok is the definition of organized chaos, and as you pass through streets of guys selling soot-covered fruit and moped mechanics squatting in the street at a game of checkers using painted bottle tops, there is a real sense of community.

Nevertheless, by the next morning, I was ready to leave. Despite growing up around London I'm not really a city person, and after so long away from the hustle and bustle of city life, the crowds freaked me out a bit. I phoned the Chinese Embassy to see about getting a visa, only to be told that it would be closed for at least another week due to the Chinese New Year.

Darren was approaching Bangkok like your typical first-time traveller, and consulting his Lonely Planet

Guide book on everything. My opinion is that guide-books should be used as a reference and not a bible. They have some useful maps and addresses, but are often out of date by the time they go to print, and it's far better to explore on your own. So after I had success-fully stripped Darren of his (i.e. thrown it in the bin when he wasn't looking) I showed him some of the true sights of Bangkok: cruising up and down the river on the local ferry and visiting the free university museum where animals, human organs and even foetuses are on display in jars.

The following day was Election Day, and to keep the people of Thailand clearheaded therefore, there was a complete 48-hour ban on the sale and consumption of alcohol. Seeing this as more of a challenge than a problem, we declared a two-day drinking session to signify the end of our travels together, after which we would part and go our separate ways, me on to Laos, and Darren back to his job in Hong Kong.

To do this, we would visit some of the most seedy and disturbing bars and brothels that I had ever heard of, let alone seen. We headed for Patpong because if anywhere was going to be selling illegal alcohol it would be there, and it didn't take long before, with the help of a few dodgy rickshaw drivers, we were entering illicit bars through thick, steel-backed doors. In an area within the city where girls perform X-rated tricks with ping-pong balls and wrestled in foam, you can wander among streets that cater for homosexuals, bisexuals, transsexuals and trisexuals (apparently those who will try anything) and enjoy the compliments pouring in from either side of the road as the different hosts try to entice you inside their particular dens of vice. We entered through side-alley doorways, more often than not with some kind of special rhythmic knock, or a nod to a pair of eyes peering through a hatch from our rickshaw driver. Inside the fully soundproofed bars, more alcoholic beverages were on offer than in most of the bars on the Khao San Road.

Inside, we found overweight, middle-aged Europeans, surrounded by skinny little Thai girls with fake eyelashes and fake smiles, competing for these pathetic mens' attention and money. Some girls do this by choice, as there's good money to be made. Others have a drug habit or pimp to pay off and have no other option, and I must admit I did feel a little guilty supporting their pimps by buying the booze in their bars. The girls don't all work as prostitutes though; rather like on-site escorts, they are there to make the men feel wanted and keep their bar tab going. Most have the choice whether to return to a room with them or not, however, while some girls do only work in the bars, many will offer sex for 1000 bahts (US$30), a small price for the rich businessmen on holiday, but nearly a week's wages for the average Thai. Prostitution is not as frowned upon in Thailand as it is in many western countries; despite it being illegal, it seems to be viewed far more as a trade than a crime. Most girls will of course still tell their families back home that they are working in a shop or travel agency, the kind of job for which they had originally headed to the big city. For many of them, they feel they have little choice. There is a huge responsibility on their shoulders in that it is normal to send a large part of your wages home, often with the one working member of the family supporting their parents and all their siblings. Most children will be brought up by their grandparents, so the mother can work while she is young and then look after her grandchildren when the time comes. This keeps the family ties strong with up to four generations all living under one roof.

Twice, while in these bars, despite sitting relatively quietly and not requesting anything more than another cold beer, a line of young Thai girls, many with pupils so drug dilated they looked half blind, were presented before us. They wore matching outfits and numbers were pinned to the few clothes they were wearing. We were asked if we wanted to pick a number to take upstairs and 'play with'. Instantly sobered, and feeling slightly ashamed for being there in the first place, we would get up immediately and leave.

When the voting was over, we returned to the Khao San Road for our final night together in Bangkok. It would certainly be a night to remember; Darren would find out the hard way that Thai lady boys can make quite convincing women, especially when you're buying the drinks and I ended up breaking the nose of a drunken tourist who had joked that those who died in the tsunami should have been better swimmers – something I don't regret.

I'm not very good with goodbyes, and so perhaps a little selfishly, I left early the next morning before Darren had woken up. I knew he'd understand. I walked several miles to the outskirts of town and began hitching towards Ko Yai National Park. It took three lifts to get near the turnoff I needed and it was raining heavily, but I didn't mind as the drops were warm and made a refreshing change from being saturated in sweat. Having been dropped off by the side of the main road, I crossed over and walked into a petrol station, where I instantly fell in love with one of the petrol station assistants. She was called Pen, and when she saw me she came over with a beautiful smile and began to chat away to me – far too fast for me to understand anything she said – but perhaps feeling sorry for me, since I was soaked to the skin and struggling with a very heavy pack, she led me inside the little wooden staff hut and put the kettle on, before taking a towel and drying my hair. She gave me a cup of steaming Milo and we exchanged names while I tried to make sense of my now soggy map.

She kept pausing to laugh at the fact that neither of us understood each other before babbling on anyway. Once she understood where I was trying to go, she skipped off outside into the rain. I watched through the window as, with a spring in her step and between pumping gas, she got all her colleagues to ask cars for a lift for me. Maybe she was high on life, or maybe she was just high on all the fumes she was inhaling, but it was great to see someone who could be so content and happy operating a petrol pump in the rain, by the side of a filthy main road. I dreamed about asking if she wanted to come to see Mount Everest with me, but before I had a chance to daydream any further, she had found me a lift and I was back on the road again. This time I got as far as the next turnoff for the park, and from there, I just had another 5km to go. It was dark by then and raining so hard that I could hardly keep my eyes open. A man on a motorbike bike pulled over and offered me a lift to the entrance. I gratefully accepted, and when I got off, he turned around and headed back in the direction he'd come.

The guard in the security hut at the gate was engrossed in his newspaper, and I slipped through the entrance unnoticed, avoiding paying the 200 baht-a-day entrance fee. I walked down the road to a sign and found it was a further 14km to the park headquarters, and even further to the campsite. I walked far enough down the road so that I would be out of sight of the park entrance, pitched my tent and got some shuteye.

In the morning, I rose with the sun and hitched a lift in a truck full of wood to the campsite that was 25km inside the park. As I had all my own equipment and a fake student card, I was able to camp for just 10 baht a night. The campsite was practically empty, and I pitched my tent beside a lake surrounded by trees, mountains and a curious deer.

This is where I spent the next few days, relaxing, planning and daydreaming. I'm very happy in my own company and had by this time reached the conclusion that I like to travel alone. It started out as a necessity, since all my friends were either at college or too busy clubbing or playing Play Station to join me. Then I started to realize that travelling alone is actually easier – I'm not a fan of planning or reservations, and so any decisions I make that are good, bad, sensible or stupid, only affect me.

I also sewed up all the tears in my tent, made several weeks before when I was living on Khao Lak beach, and had drunkenly returned home one night and attempted to enter through entrances that didn't exist. Considering its poor condition, it's impressive that a few months later I actually sold it in Nepal to a shop selling camping supplies for twice the price I'd paid for it.

I had a general idea of where I wanted to go, but no real plan and only a world map designed for 10- and 11-year-old school kids listing little more than capital cities, as reference. I wasn't in any rush to get home, although my mum had told me on the phone the other day that I had to be back in London for my cousin's wedding in July, which at the time, seemed fairly doable.

I left the park in a relaxed state of mind, ready to begin the longest and toughest journey I had ever undertaken. It took just a day to hitchhike from the National Park to Nong Khai, the last town before the border to Laos. I travelled some distance with a Thai couple who had a daughter studying in London and they asked if I knew her and how she was. I said I'd not seen her around, but I had been away some time and that now I knew she was there, I would certainly keep my eyes open when I returned.

Before they dropped me off at a junction, they pulled over and the woman scurried off into a little shack of a shop and came back to the car with a big bag of food. She presented it to me, and said it was so I wouldn't get hungry on my journey back to England. It didn't quite last me until I got back home, but it did fill a hole that night. I found a cheap room in Nong Khai, if you could call it a room – the walls didn't touch the ceiling and I was kept awake half the night by a couple on the other side of the dividing wall doing a lot more than whispering sweet nothings.

I packed up early and began walking the 5km towards the border, where I bumped into a friend from Khao Lak, another freelance divemaster called Klaus who was from Germany. Since it was a border town filled with foreigners, it was less strange bumping in to him there, than the fact that I hadn't seen him since before the tsunami and had assumed that he was dead. We had breakfast together and then I carried on my way. At the border, I gave myself a few minutes to make sure I was a 100 per cent sure that this was the right thing for me to do, then I got stamped out of Thailand, blew the Thai flag a kiss, and began marching across the friendship bridge over the Mekong River. The Thai immigration guys came running after me and said I wasn't allowed to walk across the bridge, I must return and pay for a shuttle bus over the bridge. I argued for as long as I could, but you should never argue with a man with a gun.

Having paid a rip-off fare to travel a distance I'd already half completed on foot, I walked over to Laos Immigration where I politely asked the little woman behind the glass screen for a visa. I was told I'd have to give her $1 more than normal because it was a Saturday. I laughed and paid her the extra cash with no complaints, purely for her originality.

3

Mission Crocodile

Khao Lak to
Vientiane = 1,406km

As I entered Vientiane in the back of a pickup truck, I had to ask the driver if he was sure this was the right Vientiane since, for a capital city, it seemed quite small and very subdued. I couldn't see a single building over three storeys high, and it was simply too quiet. After he had assured me for the third time that I was in the right place, still not quite convinced, I jumped down from the truck and began walking. It was only when I turned a corner and found the Vietnamese Embassy, that I finally accepted that the driver was right. I walked around in the hot sun with my bag for the next three hours. There were no fast food franchises or brand name shops, only little family-owned businesses with handwritten signs in the windows. Shopkeepers sat on doorsteps staring out on to the street while others pushed food carts selling Pad Thai or hotdogs on sticks. There was a surprising amount of print and copy shops, practically one on every corner, and I passed a book shop, so crammed with books you couldn't see in the window. I had a feeling I was going to like it here, which was just as well, since I was going to be stuck in Vientiane far longer than I had planned while I waited for the Chinese Embassy to reopen after the Chinese New Year.

Eventually, I found the guesthouse area which consisted of fairly solid looking three-storey buildings, rather than the tin and bamboo shacks I'd seen everywhere else. For US$7 a night I checked in to a room just across the road from a monastery and from the shared balcony of the guesthouse I could watch the young monks sweeping the sandy dust of the courtyard in the mornings and gathering the fallen leaves at night. I showered and, not wanting to break with tradition, headed straight out to sample the local beer. There was only one available that I had not already consumed vast quantities of in Thailand and it was called Beerlao. After about my fourth, I decided that Beerlao was quite possibly the best lager I had ever tasted and headed back to my guesthouse ready to spread the word. Instead, I found an Englishman called Adam sitting on the balcony smoking a joint of opium. He was in his late thirties with a greying goatie and a red and purple cap on his head. It turned out he was an amateur magician and he impressed me with his sleight of hand tricks while we chatted for an hour or so before heading down to the Mekong River to find dinner together.

The banks of the Mekong were lined with clusters of plastic tables and chairs, set up beside roaring grills cooking a variety of seafood specialties. We wandered along looking at the stalls and their catch, proudly displayed on ice. There was an English-speaking waiter standing at each stall, attempting to entice customers to their particular makeshift eatery, but since they were all offering much the same, they weren't too eager to haggle over portion or price and in the end we chose where to eat purely on the basis that we preferred its seating layout. The moment we sat down and ordered a Beerlao and a "Lap", the national dish, we promptly began to be feasted upon by the mosquitoes. When the Lap arrived, it was so spicy I was convinced that my eyes were weeping blood, but I was so hungry I nevertheless finished it all.

Afterwards we made our way to a café bar where we got chatting to a group of travellers, and after a few more Beerlaos, moved on to a proper bar with a free pool table.

Here I met Matt, a seasoned traveller, who told me how he and a couple of friends had made it into Tibet the previous year. I pretty much zoned out from everyone else at this point and spent the rest of the evening quizzing him on Tibet and his experiences there. By the time the bar closed, and we all staggered off in different directions home to bed, my head was filled with images of the forbidden kingdom of Tibet, and I was so inspired and excited at the prospect of going myself, that I hardly slept a wink that night.

As soon as morning broke, and I thought a few shops might be open, I set out to find a bookshop where I might be able to buy a Chinese map or phrasebook, but instead found Matt in a roadside café learning to play backgammon. I sat down and joined him, and we spent the next couple of hours chatting over some surprisingly tasty French baguette. The bread in Laos was certainly far superior to anywhere else in Asia thanks to the heavy French influence there, a hangover from France's 50-year occupation. This was not the only western influence here either, as apparently the beer in Vientiane was also greatly improved by German Expats in the 1960s, who went as far as flying German brewers over to better train the locals. God bless German efficiency.

I got as much information out of Matt as possible, and asked about the best routes to enter Tibet – did he think the north or the east. He thought that the east would have been near impossible as there were so many checkpoints, but thought perhaps you could be smuggled in from the north. Cost was a big concern for me, and if I was going to try to bypass any expensive visas, I wanted to know what the consequences would be if I got caught. He said he thought that a fine and deportation would be more likely than being slung into a cell. Matt had found his way in from the west at the driest time of the year (I was planning on entering when it would be wet and snowing) and, for all my enthusiasm to follow in his footsteps, he told me it wasn't an experience he was willing to repeat – the Tibetans, he said, had not been very welcoming. But realizing I was as stubborn as a camel and was not going to be deterred, he took some napkins out of the dispenser on the table and drew me an assortment of maps.

With these precious sketches safely folded in my pocket, I left the café to hunt for cheaper accommodation, and found a bed for the night at the Sabadi guest house at a far more reasonable 4$ a night. There I heard there was live music that night at a bar a few blocks away, quite a rarity for Vientiane, and therefore not something to be missed.

That evening, first of all I set out to see if I could meet up with Matt again to glean more valuable information on Tibet, but, having forgotten to ask where he was staying, I instead bumped into two Scottish girls who I'd met the night before, and we decided to head to dinner together. Here we picked up three Aussie guys. So the six of us were soon sipping Beerlao in the front row of the music bar listening to a local band playing assortment of Rock classics such as *Stairway to Heaven* and *Hotel California*. They had a tired accuracy and a lack of enthusiasm that suggested they played the same setlist every time wherever they played. We shouted out requests for songs which the band had clearly never heard of and which they choose to simply ignore.

After a few beers I needed the loo, and as I made my way through a courtyard at the back to the toilets, I passed a tiny fish tank with five baby crocodiles inside. The tanks were around 2ft long by 1ft wide – only just long enough to accommodate each crocodile lengthways. Furious to see such cruelty, I stomped back inside and called my companions out to take a look. The manager quickly followed to see what the problem was and, assisted heavily by hand gestures, I explained that the tank was already far too small for the growing reptiles. He shrugged his shoulders. Apparently it didn't matter, when they got bigger he was going to sell them for their skin anyway. I was now even more furious, and long after we'd finished our drinks, and moved on to another bar, where we added a couple of giggly Swiss girls to our crew, I couldn't stop thinking about the cruel conditions in which those baby crocs were being kept.

After a cheap beer in a café, we roamed the streets looking for something different and somehow stumbled upon a party in a courtyard with a live band and karaoke. We were immediately welcomed inside, even though none of us knew whose party it was, and were plied with liquor-spiked chocolate and more alcohol. As we laughed and joked and got more and more drunk on whisky and beer, Mission Crocodile was born.

It took us a while to find our way back to the bar, which had now closed for the night. After a short debate on the possible repercussions of our plans, a couple of the Aussies and I climbed over the back wall and onto the toilet roof, then dropped down into the yard. How we were not heard I don't know.

We found the tank of baby crocodiles, which we had expressly come to free, looked at it, then at each other and burst out laughing. How we were actually going to get five crocodiles out of the tank and to safety was not part of the plan we had discussed. Drunkenly shushing each other, we searched around the yard and found an empty bin liner in which to put them. We then lifted the lid off the tank and spent a further few minutes arguing over who was going to actually reach inside to grab them. I ended up holding the bag, while one of the Aussies drew the short straw, grabbing each crocodile by the tail and depositing it's wriggling head into the sack. It was not an easy task, made more tricky by the fact that we only had moonlight to see by, also I was struggling to keep my balance, even with both feet firmly on the ground. We managed to take out four crocodiles, but had to leave the last one alone as he was loving his new-found space so much that he was standing on his hind legs and snapping enthusiastically at the Aussie's hands. So with our wriggling haul, we turned and made to leave, only to discover that we had no idea how to get back over the wall. After a few more minutes of panic accompanied by visions of imprisonment in Laos for theft and trespass, someone noticed the gate was unlocked and so we lifted the latch and walked straight out.

Outside, we proudly told our waiting companions of our successful rescue and patted each other proudly on the back, until we noticed the next flaw in our drunken plan. What do you do with four baby crocodiles? We decided the closest natural environment for the crocodiles would be the Mekong, and with an increasingly angry cargo, we just made it to the riverbank in time before the crocs had completely torn the bag to shreds. We emptied them out by the water's edge, and watched with satisfaction as they scurried off into the reeds that lined the bank. Looking back, I'm not sure whether we did the right thing or not, but I still reckon it's better that they had a slim chance of survival and a taste of freedom, rather than just a miserable existence in a tiny tank and a future as a handbag. As for the drunken criminality of the mission, well, all I can shame-facedly say is Brits abroad!

As I checked into the Sabadi Guesthouse the next morning, with a splitting headache and vague recollections of the night before, I met a Swiss–German guy called Simon. He was a few years older than me, 24, with blond hair and glasses and only a small amount of English, but somehow we managed to discover that both of us were intent on getting to Tibet. The only difference being that Simon had a detailed map of Tibet rather than a few sketches on some napkins. He told me how he'd been slightly put off by people's pessimism about the possibility of being able to get inside by land, and so I told him about Matt and that it was possible, and suggested we meet that evening at a free pool bar to discuss.

Later that morning I had another unsuccessful trip to the Chinese Embassy – apparently Chinese New Year didn't end for another two days. On my way back, I saw Adam the English magician on his way to sneak into the Plaza Hotel to use their pool. He told me that Matt was already there, and having not known how I was going to find him to arrange the meeting I'd promised Simon that evening, I felt fate was on my side. Adam waited while I ran up to my room and grabbed my swim shorts and I then spent the day lounging around the Plaza pool and resisting the urge to order drinks on someone else's room.

A little after 7pm Matt and I went down to the bar where Simon was already waiting. The conversation was a little limited due to Simon's lack of English, but we managed to get by and ended up going bowling until 2am. When Simon and I finally arrived back at the hostel we were not surprised to find that we were locked out. Borrowing the tarpaulin from a restaurant roof, we wandered down to the riverbank and curled up beneath it on some planks of wood. We slept terribly for about two hours before surrendering to the mosquitoes, and spent the rest of the night wandering around town, waiting for the sun to rise and the hostel to reopen its doors.

After a long sleep, I woke up feeling indecisive and sat on the balcony brooding over my options for Tibet. Everyone I spoke to was dubious that I'd ever make it in, and this negativity was seriously hampering my ability to make a plan. First they told me, there was the problem of the Chinese checkpoints which made entering Tibet undetected a pretty mean feat; there was the fact that I don't speak a word of Chinese which was another massive impassable hurdle; not to mention the high altitude sickness and exposure to the elements that came with travelling in the Himalayas. Oh, and I didn't have any suitable equipment for this type of expedition, the money or any intention of buying it. On the bright side, Simon was coming around to the idea of joining me, but he didn't want to leave for another month due to the wet and snowy weather conditions we would have to face there at that time of year. And then there was the problem of Nepal. The King had seized control and closed all the borders, meaning that my route out of Tibet, if I were to enter from the west, was currently blocked. With no decisions made, I went out for dinner, to a little café that had become my local over the last week. Here, over another meal of fresh baguettes with various fillings, I met an angry old hippy and, in return for hearing about his current beef with the world and its people, he gave me his opinion on my current troubles.

"Sounds like fun! Fuck what everyone else thinks, you should do it!" he said.

Surprised by finally being faced with a bit of enthusiasm, I drained my beer and said, "Yeah, fuck it, I will!" And so I was going to Tibet.

Early the next morning I was standing outside the gates of the Embassy at the front of a very long queue, silently inventing a fake route to Beijing. When I was finally admitted to see an official, I confidently told them the route I'd just made up, and then explained it was imperative they make an exception and grant me a two-month, rather than the normal, one-month visa because I needed more time than they normally allocated if I was to see all the stunning places that I had heard existed in their beautiful country and that I was so looking forward to spending time in the people's republic.

They submitted my application and told me that I'd hear whether it was successful or not in three days. I cycled back to the hostel eager to tell Simon my news, he immediately asked if he could borrow my rented bicycle, before racing down to the Embassy to try his luck too.

For the next three days we ate French bread and drank Beerlao at my favourite café, which Simon had named "The Secret Place", for reasons I never quite understood, since it was one in a line of many identical cafes. We spent the time reading and watching the world go by, this included a group of boys aged between 5 and 15 who we christened the "Vientiane Bicycle Gang", because all they seemed to do was cycle endlessly around town, with up to three of them per battered old push bike trying, and failing, to look menacing.

The night before we were due to pick up our visas and head north, we splashed out an extra couple of dollars each and moved to a guesthouse overlooking the river, before heading out to celebrate our last night in the town. The next morning, I woke up to someone banging on the door, and peeling my eyes open, winced at the pounding pain in my head. It was only as I rolled off the double bed, that I realized I had no idea where I was. The banging at the door was getting louder and more persistent and I now realized someone was yelling.

I looked down and saw that I was completely naked, but one glance around the room did not reveal any clothes. Picking up the rug from the floor and wrapping it around my waist, I cautiously opened the door to find an angry looking hostel manager accompanied by an older European couple, who, I imagine, were expecting to check into an empty room. I stood there speechless with no idea where I was or why, as the manager launched in to a full interrogation. Glancing over his shoulder for a clue as to my whereabouts, I was relieved to recognize the staircase behind him, confirming that I was at least in the right building, even if it was the wrong room. A crowd had slowly gathered and we eventually worked out that I was staying two floors down and so, still wrapped in a rug and closely followed by the hotelier, I began to search for my room.

I found Simon sitting on the bed looking very hung over and none the wiser about where I had been. Apparently, he'd just woken up lying face down on the concrete balcony just as confused as I was. This explained the neat parallel lines running down either side of his face. I clambered onto the bed, leaving Simon to deal with the irate manager who remained standing in the doorway fuming. Later, when I could finally think and speak at the same time, I eventually paid for the room I had ended up sleeping in and offered the manager a grovelling apology. Needless to say we weren't going anywhere that day, but after 24 hours of recovery, we successfully picked up our two-month visas for China.

On the way to the bus station, we stopped to wander around the local market, where stalls sold bottled scorpions and snakes preserved in herbs and spices, and sacks full of dried and fresh chillies. Simon took up the offer of a free chilli from one of the stall holders, but being from the Swiss Alps where spice is not exactly a local delicacy, he only chose a small one. Failing to impart the general wisdom that the smaller the chilli, the hotter it is, I chuckled away with the stall owner as Simon immediately turned red and scarpered off to find water, bumping his head on the low beams that held up the battered tarpaulin as he did so. We ended up arriving late to the bus stand and our bus was already packed, largely with goods rather than people, since it turned out this wasn't only a passenger bus. Even the roof was stacked double its height with all kinds of goods in sacks, cases and boxes being taken north for sale, all lashed down with a web of ropes under a giant tarpaulin. When we squeezed aboard I found we were travelling alongside some very precious cargo indeed – the whole floor and some seats were filled with crates of Beerlao. I thought this may at least mean the bus driver would take a little more care than normal along the bumpy and twisty roads, but was proven wrong. We did get seats, but with most of the legroom taken over by beer, we spent the next five hours to Vangveng with our knees against our chins. We were the lucky ones though, as some people who had turned up even later than us, were literally squeezed onto the bus and had to sit right on top of the bottle necks, which I thought, can't have been very pleasant every time we hit a bump or stopped abruptly.

We arrived in Vangveng late afternoon and, in accordance with my rules of the road, immediately went for a cold beer and took in our surroundings. I had been warned that Vangveng was a bit of a tourist trap, having heard it was Laos's answer to Bangkok's Khao San Road. Thankfully it was nowhere near that bad, but it wasn't for a lack of trying, only a lack of funds. There were still travel agents, money exchanges and countless restaurants filled with westerners eating western food, enjoying reruns of the sitcom *Friends* and catching up on the latest movie releases. Vangveng had become a popular stop-off point on the tourist trail thanks to the caves in the mountains, and the rivers that you could go "tubing down". This involved being driven several kilometres up river, and then being given a rubber tube (normally an inner tube from a tractor or truck) on which you would leisurely float back to your starting point. Another attraction was the huts along the river bank where you could buy a pre-rolled joint of opium or weed for around a dollar.

Having finished our beers, we walked away from the main town, where we found a room for $3 a night. Simon took the first shower, and as I sat on the balcony waiting my turn, I noticed a guy beckoning to me from a window a few buildings away. I'm of the opinion that travelling is all about talking to random strangers. Often, it's boring and awkward and you just end up waiting for them to ask you for some money for some reason, but it's also resulted in a lot of my most memorable experiences, making every accidental encounter with a conman or a drug dealer worth it. So, I got up wandered round to meet him outside the building. He was a short chap in his 20s, in a blue T-shirt and faded jeans, smoking some cheap tobacco. He led me through a restaurant, and then out of the back door, through the kitchen, then down a passageway to a little shack of a room. Before I had even stepped through the doorway the potent smell of bubbling opium smacked me in the face. There was another westerner sitting on the floor inside with his back against the wall. He greeted me with a goofy smile and a nod of the head before returning to his pipe.

My guide bent down and opened a drawer containing different bundles and wraps of drugs, and began offering me speed, ecstasy, opium and marijuana. I explained that I was crossing the border in a couple of days and didn't want to get caught with any drugs on me, what with the death penalty and all. He seemed happy with this excuse, and so we sat down on the only place available – a bed made from Coca-Cola crates tied together – and he began to ask me a little about how much things cost in Europe. The price of a packet of cigarettes, the hourly wage, a month's rent. He seemed fascinated by and quite envious of how we all seemed to be able to afford to travel for long periods of time and eat out in restaurants, when we were far younger than he was. He then led me back to the main road, shook my hand and wished me a safe trip.

Heading back to tell Simon about this little encounter, I soon realized I'd been in that little opium den a tad too long, as I now felt quite light on my feet. Entering our room, I flashed Simon the same goofy smile the pipe-smoking westerner had given me, and then spent 10 minutes trying to clear my head beneath the cold spray of the shower. Later, as the sun was setting, we climbed up on to the roof of the guesthouse and sat and drank beer into the night beneath a full moon that lit the mountains on the horizon. We had already begun to feel the difference in climate the further we headed north and that night Simon attempted to sleep up on the roof, but came down again in the early hours complaining it was too cold.

Early the next morning, we rented bicycles and set off to explore the caves. We dismounted at a wide but shallow river with a bamboo bridge, and pushed the bikes to a little hut about three quarters of the way across. A group of locals were playing cards seated on a grass mat, and informed us it was 4,000 kips for a foreigner to cross the bridge. Although 10,000 kips only equals $1, we were still angry at this unfair toll and pushed our bikes back to the other side. For if we paid every charge enforced by the random locals who expected us to pay purely because we were foreigners, we'd have run out of money very soon. Here we took off our T-shirts, emptied the contents of our pockets into them like a sack and placed them inside the baskets on the front of our bikes, before hoisting them on to our shoulders and starting to wade across to the other side. This seemed to amuse everyone watching from the banks and they began to shout encouragement as we wobbled our way across, nearly losing our balance a few times on the slippery rocks below the surface. At one point the water began to get quite high and threatened to soak the baskets and our cameras, the loss of which would have cost us far more than 4,000 kip, but thankfully, we made it without incident, and Simon took a bow to a couple of people on the other side who were offering up applause. Far more satisfying, however, was the look of annoyance on the faces of the men on the bridge, who did not find our actions amusing at all.

We cycled on and followed the hand-painted wooden signs to the caves, and when the trail became a dried-up riverbed we stopped and chained our bikes to the nearest tree and continued on foot. After a long walk, we came to a little shelter, from which a little man jumped suddenly and, delighted to see us, demanded 1,000 kip for the pleasure of continuing on our way. We ignored him and kept walking, but were pursued by his yells all the way up the trail, which led to a steep path up the mountainside and on into the cave entrance.

At the top, we climbed down a bamboo ladder in to the caves then waited for our eyes to adjust to the dark. It smelt damp down there, and as jagged shapes slowly began to come into focus, I saw that the walls were indeed moist. The cool temperature here was a refreshing change from the oppressive heat outside, and I took off my shirt and lay down on the cold rocks. We then spent about an hour making echo noises, before strolling back past our friend in the hut who was still demanding, "1,000 kip, 1,000 kip!" This continued to fall on deaf ears.

I stopped feeling quite so smug however, when we arrived back at our bikes and discovered that mine had a puncture. I was about to set off to return to town on foot when Simon gave me his bike and said he would jog and push the unusable bike. I told him he was crazy to even think about jogging in the midday sun, but he just smiled, and I thought, *Oh, he actually is crazy. Interesting.*

So gratefully taking his bike, I cycled on to a shack where I bought us two litres of water, and when he caught up with me 10 minutes later, he promptly collapsed in the shade and asked for his bike back. We stayed there for some time, accompanied by a couple of old women doing embroidery, who spent most of the time staring up at us and giggling at some private joke, while we watched young children dressed in rags running around outside the shack, harassing the cows and chasing dogs with sticks.

The restaurant we ate in that evening was showing *Seven Years in Tibet*, the film of the book I had read a couple of years before. I'd been especially fascinated by the process involved in discovering the manifestation of the Dali Lama – apparently it had taken three years after the death of the 13th Dalai Lama to find the reincarnation, which was done using a variety of secret tests, including the young Dalai Lama having to identify his predecessor's possessions. But if I'm entirely honest, this wasn't my first inspiration for wanting to visit Tibet, that had been the comic book *Tintin in Tibet*, which I'd read as a kid and left me desperate to see a yeti and monks who could levitate. The film itself wasn't much good. It missed out so much that the book mentioned, and Brad Pitt's attempt at an Austrian accent was pitiful. Simon barely understood any of it, so he didn't mind, but alongside a few beers, it was enough to give us the motivation we needed and we agreed that it was time to leave Vangveng.

By 11am the next day we were boarding the bus to Luang Prabang. We had read that the road we were to travel was the most dangerous road in South East Asia. We had assumed this meant in terms of accidents, but as we boarded the bus and saw two guys seated at the back, holding pump action shotguns, we realized that they meant more in the way of hold ups. We debated whether it was best to sit as close as possible to the guys with the guns, or as far away as possible. But since there was only one seat left which Simon and I had to share for the first few hours (a seat designed for your average Laotian, not two 6ft westerners) it became a moot point.

After three hours, the bus stopped and a load of people got off and we moved up to some seats at the front, and it wasn't long before we were drinking whisky and Beerlao with the driver's *friends* as we sped along the mountain roads. The scenery was so beautiful that as we wound our way around the mountain even the locals stared out the windows, mesmerised at the blankets of green tree canopies and farmland.

At our next stop there was a tourist coach already pulled over, and its passengers soon began taking pictures of themselves in front of our "authentic" bus, while I perched on the steps sipping a beer and chewing a stale pastry, taking pleasure in the knowledge that I was going to feature in the background of at least 10 holiday albums. The next four hours were nerve-racking. The bus weaved its way round the bends, its wheels inches from the edge of sheer drops. We passed the wreck of another bus on the way, but due to my slightly tipsy state, I assumed it had been vandalised rather than pulled up from the bottom of the cliff.

Arriving in Luang Prabang, we wandered over to the window of the bus station ticket office, and enquired when the first bus to the China border would be in the morning. We were told there wasn't one for a few days, but one was leaving tonight. When we asked at what time, he pointed at the bus we'd just got off. Waiting a few days wasn't really an option, as our one-month visas for Laos were due to run out before then. Simon's one day before mine. So with a shrug of the shoulders, we headed back to our bus and asked the driver to reattach our packs to the roof.

We had just enough time to buy some chicken and four baguettes, before returning to the seats we'd just gratefully vacated, where our old friends laughed and topped up our cups with more whisky. At first, we were thankful that there was a new driver – the old one had barely rested since Vientiane – but that was until we noticed that he'd been replaced by one of the guys with whom we'd been drinking whisky earlier in the day. I comforted myself with the thought that at least he'd been asleep for the past few hours.

We attempted to get some sleep ourselves, but only managed about an hour as the driver was singing, presumably in order to keep himself awake. We hurtled down the now straighter, but equally bumpy and pitch-black road, and at around 4am reached our final stop, which turned out to be a dusty T-junction. We were told there would be another bus to take us to the border in three hours' time. We hopped off and got our bags down from the roof, but unprepared for the cold in our shorts and T-shirts, were soon shivering. As soon as the bus pulled away, we were left in total darkness. We made our way to a shelter at the side of the road, where I whipped out my sleeping bag and drifted off to sleep, listening to Simon cursing in German because he had packed his sleeping bag at the very bottom of his back-pack and was now, in the darkness, trying to access it without dropping all his other possessions around him. From then on it was always secured to the outside of his bag.

Simon woke me a few hours later, to say that the bus had arrived. It was still freezing, and I was more than a little reluctant to get out of my cosy cocoon, but Simon, who hadn't slept well, had at least gone off on a mission in the dark to find us two last bottles of Beerlao. It must have been around this time that our catchphrase for the trip started – "Warrior!" which we always said to each other with two clenched fists raised shoulder height. We did this now, before clambering onto the minibus, where I got straight back into my sleeping bag and cracked open my last ice-cold Beerlao. As the bus set off towards the Chinese border, I must have looked like one very lost, homeless, alcoholic.

The road was either just being built or was in the middle of serious renovation. Elephants pulled logs beside the road, their front legs chained together meaning they could only take small steps at a time. This didn't, however, stop the mahout continually hitting their hind legs with a piece of bamboo, and yelling at them to move faster. When we reached the border, there was a small workers' village built on either side of the road, where cows wandered aimlessly, unaware of their bureaucratic location. The border post itself was a small Portakabin style building, and we had to call through the window to get the man's attention as he was watching TV at the back. He had stamped us out and we had begun walking, when we realized that our pockets were still full of kips, the local currency. Again we knocked on the window and asked if it might be possible to pop back into Laos for breakfast. Annoyed that we had disturbed his peace again, he agreed and motioned with his hand for us to go away. So, we enjoyed our last breakfast of Lao noodle soup back in the village and used up the rest of our change buying ourselves, and the local kids sweets, before shouldering our packs and setting back off through the 2km of no-man's-land between there and China.

4

China

Vientiane to Kunming -898km

It's a strange thing walking through land that belongs to no one, and to not officially be in any particular country, so of course conversation turned to "what if one of us went insane and killed the other? Would he be made accountable?" But this riveting discussion came to an abrupt end when we turned a bend in the road and the Chinese border loomed into view. It was intimidating to say the least. The path which led to it turned from a gravel track to a smooth, shiny, almost marble-like surface.

"That would have been good for skateboard," said Simon, shooting me a reproachful look. Having travelled with a skateboard for six months, I had persuaded him to post it back to Switzerland before we left Vientiane. By the look of the border ahead of us though, I'm pretty sure he'd have been shot for trying such a thing. There were at least 20 armed guards sitting around, with two standing to attention on either side of the road. As we approached, we were ordered to the immigration office, where our passports were carefully examined and we were questioned about where we were going, and why didn't I have an address for my made-up friend in Chengdu – only an email. The official, carefully typed in the address I gave her; iloveflapjacks@lying.com, and I tried not to grin. Then after a little more Communist confusion, they waved us through. A red line was painted on the asphalt, and the moment we crossed it and entered China we were set upon by English-speaking touts who held up calculators and offered us bad exchange rates. We had no option other than to use them, but we still tried to play one off against the other, managing to knock the rate down a long way, although undoubtedly still getting ripped off.

The next big town was an hour's minibus ride away, and our money touts turned out to be the drivers, so the whole process began again before we could finally get on our way. About half an hour in to our journey, we came to an abrupt halt as the four or five cars in front of us slammed on their brakes. There had been an accident. We jumped out and walked up the road. A 4x4 dumper truck was lying on its side, wheels still spinning, its cargo of gravel spilt across the road. It had collided with a small car, and we watched as an old woman and a screaming young child were hauled out of the car wreckage, both covered in blood. The womans' leg was visibly broken and they were both lifted into another truck and driven off. The driver of the crashed pickup had got off lightly with a cut to his hand and a bump to his head, but he knelt down at the side of the road and began to wretch and vomit. Having travelled extensively in Africa and India, car wrecks were a common sight, but I now realized that any squeamishness or horror

I had felt at witnessing injury and suffering, had also been stripped away since the aftermath of the tsunami.

We were stuck there for another hour, everyone standing around talking about what had happened. In that time, no police or ambulance had arrived, and it was left to the locals to sort out. Not a very reassuring first hour in China. We eventually made it to the next big town, Gejlu, and headed straight to a restaurant for lunch. We chose a table outside on the pavement, which was just as well, as this was the first time, I'd ever used chopsticks and it was not a pretty sight. Passers-by were stopping to show me how to use them without me asking which became annoying quite quickly – when you're hungry, you can do without a gathering audience standing around laughing at your table skills. I resorted to holding a chopstick in each hand and skewering the food with the pointy ends. Being an object of interest was something I would have to get used to in China, because as it turned out, I seemed to garner an audience almost everywhere I went. I soon discovered that restaurant owners would be so pleased that the westerners had chosen their restaurant to eat in, that they would insist on sitting us on display either in the window or outside.

After I had finished butchering my meal, we decided to head straight for the city of Kunming. The bus depot was confusing and the staff not very helpful. There is supposedly no class system in China, so we couldn't understand why there were different prices for the same bus. We went for the cheapest option and paid 200RMB (8RMB equalled $1US) for the 17-hour journey to Kunming.

All around the bus station were posters of horrific bus crashes with close-ups of decapitated heads. The captions were obviously all in Chinese, and so I couldn't quite work out what the purpose of these posters were. As passengers we weren't the ones who needed to be warned not to drive dangerously, so we decided perhaps it was to discourage people from travelling at all.

We boarded the bus and were immediately ordered off again to go and wash our feet under the outside tap at the side of the building. It was fair enough since we hadn't washed since leaving Vientiane and had been wearing flip-flops the whole time, meaning after 24 hours of bus travel and a night spent sleeping in the dirt, our feet were none too clean. We didn't have to worry about holding up the departure of the bus though, as the driver was already at the tap furiously washing his hair underneath the icy cold water. Once we'd finished scrubbing, we were a little disappointed to see that what we had thought was a golden tan was actually just dirt!

Back aboard the bus with our bright white feet, we were presented with a little red bag in which to place our flip-flops which we were then instructed to hang on the numbered peg matching our berth. This was easier said than done, since the difference between one Chinese number and the next seemed to be as little as a lack of a dash above a dot. We showed our tickets to other passengers who directed us to the very back of the bus where we found two bunks stretching the width of the vehicle. Simon chose the bottom bunk, while I was helped up to the top by the other five guys with whom I was apparently sharing. My designated spot was divided by two short metal bars, between which my shoulders were too wide to fit, meaning I had to roll my arms and shoulders forwards to slot myself in. To add to my discomfort, there was only about six inches between my head and the ceiling which had a fake wooden panel design, to really add to that trapped-in-a-coffin sensation. If ever there was a time to discover my tolerance for enclosed spaces, I thought, it was now.

It was a good four hours before the bus made a refreshment stop at a roadside café, and once my fellow passengers had helped unwedge me from my slot, I met Simon outside attempting to set the world record for the fastest smoked cigarette. "Never again," we both agreed with our shakes of our heads. After a quick but tasty dinner of rice and chicken soup, washed down by a sickly cherry soda, which the other passengers insisted on paying for, we returned to our coffin slots for the remainder of the 10 hour journey.

We finally arrived in Kunming, then walked the streets for three hours before finding anywhere to sleep for the night; all the hotels were reserved for the Chinese and there were only a handful of places in which foreigners (or 'aliens' as the Chinese liked to call us) could stay. For once I appreciated that a guidebook could have come in handy, as being without one here meant trying to find lodgings was like searching for the proverbial needle in the haystack. I assume the government did this so they could keep an eye on us more easily, and force us to stay in the more expensive hotels. We managed to beat the system though, and found a guesthouse for $5 a night. I don't think the family running the place knew about the rules for foreigners, and were overjoyed to have us stay, especially the teenage girl who, over the next few days, would continually climb the stairs up to our room on the eighth floor, on the pretence of bringing us Thermoses of boiling water and sachets of green tea. She would then stand in the doorway until we had drunk at least one cup each and watch the aliens going about our business – me usually reading books and Simon, a pretty good artist, sketching the day's events. She once took it upon herself to rummage through my bag while I watched, holding up anything she was curious or confused about, even trying on my dive mask and snorkel through fits of giggles.

Since we were being plied with it by our hosts several times a day, it didn't take long for us to join the Chinese obsession for green tea. The majority of Chinese people seemed to carry a small Thermos of it around with them everywhere they went.

Our lodgings were basic, but did have an en-suite squat toilet, which smelt so bad that we kept the door to the bathroom firmly shut and took to brushing our teeth out of the window to avoid any unnecessary time spent there. We also had a TV, which we thought was a real luxury, but later found to be standard in China. The channels consisted of CCTV one to nine, an appropriate name for the television stations because the world news it showed consisted purely of how great China was, while the only other news was of what was going wrong in America, the Chinese teenagers' idol.

There was no mention of the trouble in Nepal, one of their neighbouring countries, and the BBC and CNN websites were totally blocked online. Thankfully I was able to check my Hotmail account and get updated about the outside world by people at home. Twice while on the phone to my family in England the line went dead after certain keywords such as 'police', 'government' or 'borders' were spoken.

The window in our room looked straight across into the local school, a big ugly grey Soviet-style tower block, very similar in appearance to the guesthouse. The teacher's back was continually facing the window, and so we'd pull faces at the kids in class, hiding back behind the bedroom curtain as they giggled behind their hands and the teacher spun around to see what was distracting them. We were eventually caught and motioned an apology out the window.

Watching the children in their classes on the different floors each day, made me realize how lucky I was to go to school in England. Their classrooms were tiny and overcrowded, the only views from the windows were tall grey buildings, stained black at the bases from the continuous, ever-increasing pollution. They didn't seem to have any playtime, and even if they did, there was nowhere to play. Even Physical Education, the only break from the incessant lecturing and note-taking, consisted of pushing their desks and chairs against the wall, followed by a mind-numbingly boring hour of star jumps and running on the spot. It made me feel guilty about how badly I had behaved at school, and how little I'd appreciated the daily opportunities I had been given there.

One morning we awoke to snow, which prompted us to finally go shopping for warm clothing, realizing we could no longer get by in our shorts and flip-flops. I bought a jacket that despite it being an XXXXL in Chinese sizing, was still too small for me, but my best bet purchase by far was my first ever pair of thermal long johns which, later on in my journey, were probably the only thing standing between me and hypothermia.

I was also running low on toothpaste, so decided to go on a mini spending spree and stock up on that as well. I found a chemist in the city centre, and was pleased to spot the familiar red boxes of Colgate. It wasn't until I got closer that I realized it was no ordinary Colgate – there were a dozen different flavours to choose from and so I decided to forgo the usual mint, and bought three tubes – one honey flavour, another banana and the last strawberry. It took me two months to get through them and my conclusion was that mint is the only way to go – the banana one tasted so wrong it should simply be banned.

Kunming was very much like most big Asian cities – busy, overcrowded and impatient – but the people were generally friendly and I never felt threatened even in the more poverty-stricken areas. There were expensive res-taurants too, and posh shop fronts and fast food outlets, businessmen sitting in the street having their shoes shined. We'd generally eat from street stalls, but one night we decided to go to a restaurant for dinner, and it made a nice change to sit down at a table to eat. We were very hungry, and since most restaurants had no menus (although even if they did, we couldn't have read them) we attempted to order a very simple dish of chicken and rice. I say we, but I generally left the order-ing to Simon who had developed a very good repertoire of impressions and gestations over the last few days. I tried not to laugh as he clucked at the rather bemused looking waitress and flapped his arms, before she disap-peared off into the kitchen looking as if she had under-stood. Simon sat back down looking pleased with himself, and then I reminded him that he had forgotten to order the beer. But before he could say anything more, we were presented with our food; a huge bowl of boiled chicken feet and two plates of rice.

I tried a couple of the feet, but there was hardly any meat on them and they were also rather wrinkly and still had their claws in which rather took my appetite away. Instead I copied Simon, a vegetarian, who was just eating the rice. Unfortunately the hardly-touched chicken feet, turned out to be a local delicacy, and we ended up paying almost twice the price of our room for the meal.

Our next destination was a small town west of Kunming called Dali.

After a six and half hour bus ride we were let off in New Dali. It didn't look anything like we'd imagined, and we were grateful to find out that we actually wanted the Old Town, which was another half an hour away and was much more interesting with cobbled streets and buildings with the traditional curved roofs with upturned corners – even the rubbish bins had a traditional, old-fashioned look to them.

There was a light covering of snow on the ground when we arrived, and it felt like everything was a little too authentic. I was half expecting ninjas to jump out and start leaping from the rooftops and then for a director to call, "Cut"! As we carried on walking, I noticed that some of the shops had English writing on the windows, and inside they were selling branded ski gear at western prices. This was clearly a tourist town and as such, the town had been kept in pristine condition, like one giant theme park. We found a room that had that rare luxury of 24-hour hot water (although you had to climb up on the roof to switch it on), plus free internet.

It was -1 degree Celsius on our first evening in Dali, and since there was no central heating in our room, we spent the evening huddled around a fire with the two sisters who ran the place, who taught us the hand signals used in China for the numbers one to ten, which definitely made our time in China much easier from then on.

Also staying in the guesthouse was a man called Peifeng Xu, from Qingdao. A well-healed man in his 40s, he explained that he had come to Dali in search of his runaway 16-year-old daughter. He spoke better English than I did, and we chatted for hours. He told me how his wife had died the year before and how he had grown increasingly estranged from his daughter. Perhaps because I was only a few years older than her, he wanted my advice as to why she might have left and how he might find her. I told him that if she wanted to travel and answer her own questions, she was going to do it and resent anyone that stopped her. I said that perhaps it was best for her to get it out of her system. Before we said good night, he thanked me and gave me his business card – it turned out he was the Director of the Department of Foreign Trade in China.

The next morning, we woke to a heavy snowfall and I jumped out of bed like a child on Christmas Day. Coming from Switzerland, Simon was less enthusiastic to be dragged out to play in the snow. I soon discovered my boots weren't waterproof, and I wish I had done something about it there and then, as a few weeks later I would care very much. Despite the heavy snowfall, life in Dali carried on as normal, people darting from shelter to shelter as they made their way through the streets in the flurries. As we passed a man hacking away at a decapitated cow's head at the side of the road (he appeared to be attempting to remove its foot-long horns), a large chunk of snow slid off a rooftop and knocked Simon off his feet. I laughed so hard I nearly joined him on the floor. It snowed continuously for the next three days, and most of the roads in the region became impassable. We were snowed in.

We had planned to move on to a place called Lichen, and whenever we asked anyone about getting there, were just met with laughter, and we told that the road to get there would now be blocked for weeks. The only passable roads seemed to be back in the direction we'd come, and reluctant to backtrack we instead headed for a small town northeast of Dali. Referring to the map we had bought in Kunming, we thought we might be able to jump on the train that ran from Kunming to Chengdu at another nearby town, so copying down the name on a scrap of paper, headed for the bus station in the city centre.

It took a lot of pointing and hand signals, plus Simon's best impression of a train, but we soon found that we had guessed right, and jumped on a minibus that would take us to this small town whose name we still didn't know as the map was all in Chinese. The minibus remained stationary for another two hours, during which time we just sat there smiling at everyone who caught our eye, unsure of what was going on. When we were finally on our way, the journey which was meant to take just four hours, ended up taking eight, as two trucks had crashed and overturned on the icy roads. The scenery was stunning, but my enjoyment of it was spoilt by the fact that my legs were so squished into the seat in front of me that I ended up with cramps which I could do nothing to relieve.

When it came to road-building and train tracks, the Chinese seemed not to let anything get in the way, certainly not a small, inconveniently-placed mountain range. The road itself, therefore, was a work of art, cutting straight through the mountainsides using tunnels that went on for 10 minutes at a time, before emerging on to bridges raised high above the snowy fields and linking straight back into the next mountain tunnel. I couldn't help but wonder how many lives had been lost in building that road. Simon was impressed, but still claimed the tunnels were better in Switzerland.

We eventually arrived at our still unknown town, at 10pm. Luckily it appeared to have been built around the train station, making it pretty easy to find. We asked if there was a train to Chengdu and not only were we told there was a train, but it was due in 15 minutes. Slightly wrong-footed by this news (we had not expected there to be a train in the next 24 hours, let alone the next 24 minutes), we hesitated for a minute or two, but eventually shrugged our shoulders and bought our tickets. We just had time to grab a few well-deserved cold beers to drink on the train and a pot noodle, which at five times the size of the ones you buy in the UK had become part of our staple diet in China, once we'd figured out which colours were tasty and which were the revolting ones.

Before reaching the platform we were confronted by what appeared to be a fairly heavy security check. As it turned out, however, the metal detectors failed to go off, despite the fact we were both carrying knives in our pockets, and our backpacks went unchecked even though their contents must have come up on the x-ray machine looking like a small arms cache with the tent pegs and pen-knives.

The train was on time, but when we boarded, someone was sitting on my assigned seat and not keen to move. After such a long day, I wasn't in the mood for a discussion and simply threatened to punch him if he didn't shift. Despite constantly banging my head on doorways, getting caught up in streamers and ceiling decorations and generally sticking out like a sore thumb, being bigger than the average Asian did have its occasional advantages. Simon who was sitting on the opposite side of the carriage and who spent much of the journey entertaining some nearby kids with his psychedelic drawings, watched the whole incident with amusement, and from then on whenever we couldn't find a seat somewhere he'd joke, "Maybe you just hit someone and then we sit!" Finally, settled in my seat, I again discovered my shoulders didn't fit properly, and resigned myself to another uncomfortable onward journey.

I settled down with a copy of *Northern Lights*, which I'd treated myself to at a book shop in Dali. I'd finished it by morning and was more than a little frustrated to discover that as the only book I had bought, it was part of a series and 'to be continued… ' and I had no idea when I'd find another a bookshop selling English books.

It was an 18-hour train journey, but I only managed to get about four hours' sleep in that time, as despite coming down more than 1,000m in altitude, I was still wearing about seven layers of clothing and, unable to remove them, was baking hot and sweating buckets. The sun rose to reveal field after field of bright purple and yellow flowers. In the space of a month, I had gone from summer in Thailand to a winter climate in China, and now I was heading back into spring. No wonder my body was having a hard time keeping up – it didn't know whether to shiver or sweat!

Arriving in the fast-paced and polluted city of Chengdu, we were forced to walk more then 10km in search of accommodation that was not only within our budget but would even take us. Many of the budget guesthouses were above shops and businesses, and so at each one we trudged up two and three flights of stairs, only to be told they wouldn't take us. I suppose it wasn't that surprising, as up until this point I'd only encountered seven other foreigners in China, and five of them had been in Dali, so the guesthouses didn't exactly have much incentive to go rushing out to apply for an "Alien Permit".

We eventually found a room, thanks only to an English-speaking restaurant owner who took pity on us as we passed his window evidently on our last legs. He came outside and walked the streets with us until we found somewhere to stay. The place we ended up in was still being built, and we had to cover our heads and walk through a building site every time we went to our room, but this was compensated for by having the most incredible hot power shower!

A scandal back in the UK involving McDonald's and a few cases of food poisoning had actually made China's world news, and as a result McDonald's had cut their prices around the world to encourage customers back in. Never one to waste such an opportunity, I felt it was my duty to introduce Simon to the wonderful world of junk food (he'd only ever been to McDonald's once on a trip to Zurich). When we eventually found a McDonald's, not only were the prices slashed dramatically, but the portions were bigger than any McDonald's

I'd ever seen. A Big Mac really was a BIG MAC! Although it did seem a little unfair to me that the portions were so big in a country where the people were so small. Over the next two days I steadily worked my way through the entire menu, skipping only the desserts and Happy Meals. Then feeling utterly gutted and disillusioned by my UK McDonald's experience, we left Chengdu, several pounds heavier to head west in search of pandas.

5

Tibetan Pandas

Kunming to Chengdu = 1,334km

We had heard about a Panda Sanctuary that was about 80km away, but discovered that the bus that would take us just halfway, would take eight hours. An hour into the journey we understood why, when we came to the edge of a deep valley. To our left was a huge dam wall and to our right were the foundations for a bridge, which was slowly but surely being built across the valley.

We descended a steep winding road which took less than half an hour thanks to our driver's slightly unsettling confidence on the hairpin bends, and at the bottom we crossed a bridge over a trickle of a river and then started the tediously slow, two-hour climb back up the other side. We eventually reached the small town at which we were supposed to change buses, but all enquiries of where to find the connecting bus to Woolong – the nearest town to the sanctuary – were met with blank expressions. Simon resorted to sketching a panda in an attempt to communicate where we were trying to get to, but that simply resulted in a round of applause followed by looks of confusion. We eventually found the direction, when a young girl pointed to a gravel road and then held up three fingers. Unsure whether this meant three hours or three kilometres we set off on foot.

Four hours later, with nothing but one endless road in sight, we guessed the girl had meant three hours by car. Our route ran along the base of the valley, and below it ran a boulder-lined river of emerald green which we were required to crisscross several times using some fairly wobbly rope bridges on which I enjoyed swinging from side to side as we crossed, much to Simon's annoyance. We passed through many land-locked islands containing several settlements, and as we did so the inhabitants stopped whatever they were doing and called out to those still inside their houses, so that no one would miss the marvel of the foreigners wandering through their midst. The children shyly hid behind the adults' legs, then ran away giggling when we caught their eyes, the men made gestures to each other that suggested they couldn't believe how tall we were, and the women whispered in each others' ears until we were out of sight.

After another hour or so, the sun went down, and it was clear that we still had a long way to go. We stopped at a small village with just one shop. I grabbed a plastic litre bottle of what I thought was water for five cents, only to take a huge gulp and discover it was in fact nasty, cheap 50 per cent proof vodka. The shock made me instantly spit it all out over the shop floor, and after a lot of laughter from all who had witnessed this, I bought some actual water, plus a couple of bottles of local beer with the rather interesting name, Blue Semen.

We walked for two more hours until total darkness fell, and as the weight of our backpacks began to take their toll, we began stumbling and falling as we went. Then the rain started. At the first house we saw we decided to call it a night. The owner was a scrawny, shifty-looking chap, with scheming little eyes, and I instantly imagined he could see dollar signs floating above our heads. He fed us and then asked for an extortionate amount of money in return and with little choice but to pay we did so and then immediately went on our way.

Realizing his mistake, he came running after us with offers of a room for just a dollar a night. We were tired, it was pitch black and still pouring with rain, and as little as we wanted to give him more of our money it was an offer we couldn't decline. The room was about as basic as they come, cell-like and freezing cold. In fact, on closer inspection it looked like it actually had been used as a cell, as there was a glass spy hole in the door that looked inwards rather than out! Having checked that the only window in the room could actually be opened, we blocked the spy hole with a piece of chewing gum and braced the door with a chair, all the while joking about all the gory horror films of which this seemed so reminiscent. An hour or so later we heard disgruntled footsteps walking away from our door.

It was so cold that Simon decided to warm himself up by downing half the bottle of vodka I'd bought earlier. He was comatose within about five minutes, but a few hours later I woke to him projectile vomiting all over the room. Cosy and content in my sleeping bag I pretended I was asleep – helping to clean up puke in the middle of the night was not something I particularly fancied.

As the sun began to rise, we set off on our way once more, mainly to avoid seeing "Harzslar", as Simon had now named our overnight host, for reasons that were lost in translation. After a couple of hours or so a minibus came along. It wouldn't be quite accurate to say we "flagged it down", more stood in the middle of the road, arms folded, in total refusal to budge. With no idea how much further we had to travel, and this being the first vehicle we had seen in two days, this was not an opportunity that we were going to miss. The Toyota minibus contained six men who agreed to let us jump in. One of the men, dressed in an orange boiler suit and hardhat, spoke reasonable English, and explained that he and the other men worked for the company building the bridge. He explained that once it was completed they would explode the dam and flood the valley. I asked what was going to happen to the hidden villages we had passed through. He seemed surprised by my question or possibly by the fact that we knew of their existence, and simply said, "They must move: they are not good if they stay here." Apparently they had been simply told they must leave their villages behind with no offer of compensation or alternative housing, and I felt so sad for those people who would have to leave their homes, forced to merge with bigger, unfamiliar communities. It would take a huge amount of adjustment after living such secluded lives.

After another hour we were dropped at the entrance to the Panda Sanctuary, and as the only tourists there, had the pandas completely to ourselves and whiled away hours watching them go about their business. The sanctuary was built into the natural surroundings of the forest meaning that the pandas had lots of space in which to play, climb and wander. It was good to see them looking so content and at home in their enclosures, chewing on mouthful after mouthful of bamboo – particularly in a country with such a bad track record for human and animal rights. After watching them for some time, I got the impression they weren't the most intelligent creatures in the forest, but the way they sat and waddled about made them appear so human-like that I felt like I needed to start looking for zips and velcro hidden in their fur.

They were certainly not camera shy, and obligingly adopted typical panda poses for my album. They were quite clumsy, especially the babies who play fought like human children, pushing each other over repeatedly and grasping each other in headlocks. Then, when they were chasing each other about on the custom-built climbing frames, they would mistime their leaps and bounds in overexcitement and end up landing badly. After a yelp, they'd lie there stunned for a short time, before carrying on in the same clumsy fashion.

As it turned out, we had arrived on quite an auspicious day; the vets and keepers had just successfully artificially inseminated one of the pandas. It had been tried many times before but had always been unsuccessful, and due to the fact there were only about 1,600 pandas left in the world, letting nature take its course was not an option, especially since pandas don't reach sexual maturity until they are seven years old, and are then only on heat for three weeks of the year. Then if the female does fall pregnant, she will only produce two cubs, one of which she will normally leave to die. A year later I would open an issue of *National Geographic* to see pictures of this newborn panda.

As we were leaving, a well-groomed American couple who had clearly spent more time in the spa than on the road, turned up in a Mercedes minibus, complete with a smartly dressed driver wearing white gloves and a peaked hat. We got talking, and they told us that they had been chauffeured all the way from Chengdu, so instead of walking on, we had some lunch and waited to see how long they'd stay. As we suspected, it was only 40 minutes or so before they were getting ready to leave, and they agreed to give us a lift. It only took three and half hours to reach the place the bus had originally dropped us off a couple of days before, and when we said we'd leave them there, the Americans looked at us like we were mad and said they'd take us all the way back to Chengdu. I think Simon was keen, but I didn't want to backtrack, so we got out hoping we could continue from there.

In hindsight, backtracking might not have been such a bad idea, as four days later we were still miles from Lanzhou, the next major city, which we could have reached from Chengdu in just a day. Instead we left the village we'd been dropped at on foot, and walked a few kilometres to, what I suppose could be called a town, to try to find out about a bus heading north. Instead we ended up drinking spirits with a group of local men who were playing cards around a table in the middle of the street. We did ask them about a bus too, but I'm not sure they'd ever left that table, let alone the town.

As we played, a little girl pulled at her mum's hand and the two of them crossed the road to see us. In slow but comprehensible English, she asked us how we were, then introduced herself and asked our names. She then pulled her books out of her school satchel and showed us the texts from which she had been learning English. I spent the next 15 minutes repeating words with her until she'd got the pronunciation near perfect. Then, with the help of her mum, who until then had been standing in silence, beaming with pride at her little girl's ability to talk to these strange foreigners, we finally found out where and when we could get a bus north. I bought the little girl some sweets from a stall in thanks, and then, after being forced to down one more large shot of vodka by the card players, we marched on to find the bus stand.

When we arrived in the next city, we immediately began searching for a room for the night, only to accidentally walk straight into the police station. As soon as we realized our mistake we turned on our heels but it was too late – we were spotted and ordered to sit down. I knew I had nothing incriminating on me, my visa, as far as they knew was all in order, and I assumed they were just looking to entertain themselves with a bit of foreigner questioning. But before we had a chance to explain ourselves, we were ushered into the back of a police van. Fortunately, it was quite comfortable as police vans go.

Reassured by the fact we were being driven in the direction of Beijing for where I had my visa, I wasn't feeling overly worried, then the van soon stopped at a hotel, and we realized they were just making sure we only stayed at places with an alien permit. We shook our heads and mimed that it was too expensive for us, and so we got back in the van and moved on. After the fourth hotel they started to get a bit annoyed, and the final hotel we pulled into was clearly bigger and pricier than any of the others we had seen so far.

In the large marble-pillared reception area, two more police officers were waiting for us. One was the local Chief of Police, who told us in broken English that we must stay here. Their cheapest room was more than 320RMB ($40), and when we refused the police started to get angry, taking our visas and making phone calls. I figured they were just trying to spook us. The hotel manager then agreed to begin negotiating on price, and soon the room was down to 200RMB, apparently the lowest they would go. Again we refused, and said we'd sooner drink beer in a bar all night and sleep outside before we paid that. I began to pull my tent out of my backpack to show I was serious, and so the police who now consisted of seven officers arriving in three police cars, took over the negotiations in rapid Chinese. The room was then offered to us at just 80RMB ($10). We accepted.

As we were shown to our accommodation, we passed a sauna, bowling alley, chess, card and conference rooms. Our accommodation had a full en-suite bathroom and there were complimentary slippers which were far too small for my size 13 feet, but which I wore anyway. There was air conditioning, a television, a phone and a kettle with teabags and anything else you could possibly need for one comfortable night's stay. After a hot power shower, we went to brew a well-earned cup of green tea, only to find that the kettle was broken.

"This will NOT do!" I announced in mock indignation, and went straight down to reception in my boxer shorts and complimentary slippers to complain. On the way I noticed an unguarded maid's trolley and quickly rushed back to the room to tell Simon, who promptly came with a plastic bag and filled it with all the complimentary goodies he could squeeze in, including sewing kits, soap and teabags. Down at the reception they laughed, and said they would send a new one straight up – in fact, when it arrived, it was still in it's box.

The next morning we made the most of our luxury accommodation by taking excessively long showers in our complimentary shower caps and parading around in our crisp white complimentary bathrobes. When we finally strolled past reception an hour after check out, the manager just smiled and wished us a safe trip. They'd probably usually have tried to wangle a bit more cash out of us for our tardiness, but after last night's negotiations he probably realized it wouldn't work.

The bus journey that followed was one of my all-time favourites in China for its stark beauty. We travelled through some of the most desolate landscapes I'd ever seen, up and over 4,000m passes, passed herdsmen moving their yaks across the dry cracked earth and beautiful young women with dark red, wind-stained cheeks. They stared up at us through the bus windows from the side of the road, backed by nothing but vast plains, our eyes locking long enough to confirm we were both asking the same questions. The older generations reminded me of the photographs you see in the *National Geographic's* portrait section; the harsh climate and eternal winds had left the skin on their wise faces prematurely aged and badly weathered.

It took about six hours to reach the next small town. When we bought our tickets the driver had told us that he didn't have the right change but would give it to us at the end of our journey, however, he had now conveniently forgotten this agreement and seemed not to understand us at all. It was not a situation I was new to – in India bus drivers would often try to overcharge and so, while Simon continued to argue, I walked to the front of the bus and pretended to start noting down the vehicle's number plate before asking for the driver's name. Suddenly his amnesia vanished and with a scowl he begrudgingly paid us the money we were owed.

It wasn't much money but it went quite a way towards paying for the room in the guesthouse we stayed in that night.

We never worked out the name of the village we were in that night or ever found its location on any map but in the morning we were told by the wiry old man who owned the guesthouse, and its lumpy mattresses, that we had come too far and needed to go back to the last town to get the bus north. This seemed a bit crazy, as we'd only seen one road the whole journey and hadn't noticed any turnoffs at all, but, lacking the vocabulary to question this, we had no choice but to turn back. Simon suggested we take a taxi, but given there wasn't another bus until the morning I didn't see much point in wasting the money when we had time to walk. Anyway, it was only 7km.

It turned out to be 17km and took us four and a half hours, but despite some nasty ankle blisters, it was worth taking the slow route, as we passed through half a dozen villages where we began snowball fights with the local kids. We lost quite badly, as in the time it took us to make one snowball, we'd be pounded with 20 direct hits in the face. We therefore ended up fleeing most villages in a hail of expertly thrown icy missiles, but it was good fun. At one village we bought a huge chunk of dried yak meat (or biltong as they would call it in South Africa) and stopped for lunch on a nearby hillside. As we cut the strips of salty meat with our knives and washed them down with water, we watched the entire village pitch in to help erect a new house for a new neighbour.

When we reached the village from which we would take the bus, we found a café run by a young woman speaking fluent English, who laughed in disbelief when we told her from where we had walked. She introduced us to her friend Peter, who was also English and who worked for one of the adventure tour companies based in China. He explained that he was researching new places and new routes on which to bring tourists, but said that from what he has seen so far, it was going to be a while before this area hit the tourist trail.

At dinner that evening we bumped in to Peter again, as well as a German woman whom he quietly told us he'd already met, but who was "a little weird." It turned out we weren't the only ones waiting for the bus the next day, and most handily, Peter, who spoke fluent Chinese, had found out that the bus only went to a small village halfway to our destination. There was nothing of interest there and no connecting bus until the following day, but apparently this was done deliberately so that you were forced to eat and sleep in the village for a night.

Now that there were four of us, we decided to share a taxi from that village on, and so we all boarded the bus next morning before first light. It was packed high with rolls of foam and carpet which boxed me into a corner, meaning that all I could see was the ever-expanding horizon from out the window. The settlements we passed seemed to exist hundreds of years in the past; with buildings built from sand-coloured blocks that looked as if they had been cut from the earth and the residents were wrapped in colourless shawls and threadbare clothing. It was like something from a Bible movie – a world entirely untouched by the modern world.

I soon noticed, that every time we reached the top of a pass, the Tibetan passengers would throw little paper prayer flags (prayers written on brightly-coloured scraps of paper) out of the bus to pray for our safe journey back down the other side, and every time we reached a peak they would fly past my window like confetti. We arrived unscathed, and as we disembarked at the bus's final destination, we saw what Peter had meant about there not being much to see. The town itself consisted of one road and a dozen buildings surrounded in every direction by dusty plains stretching for miles. We had long since left the snow behind, although it remained cold and barren here. For some unknown reason though, this tiny strip of a village had a reputation for having great apples. Upon arrival, I assumed someone was getting confused with another town, because there were certainly no trees around or orchards in sight, yet sure enough right next to where the bus pulled over, there were a few stalls selling apples, and as it happened they were the finest apples I had ever tasted! Whether this was just because it was my first apple in months and my stomach was empty, I will never know, but at the time Simon and I both agreed that this strange little place in the heart of Central China, miles from any greenery, somehow produced the best apples the world had ever known.

We soon found a taxi willing to take us to Langmusi, much to the dismay of the guesthouse owner in town, who was missing out on four night's rent. The town of Langmusi was only 60km away, but it was going to take us four hours to get there since we had to go up and over another 4,000m pass. As we hurtled down the bumpy road, with four passengers plus our luggage, the taxi was more than a little cramped. When we crossed the pass, it was dust and rocky mountains as far as the eye could see, totally barren in every direction and not a good place to breakdown, I thought. The only other traffic was heavily overloaded trucks, which seemed to be carrying materials for building the road. This led to a bit of a Catch-22 situation, because our driver, being a typical male Chinese, was chain smoking inside the car, but any attempt to get some fresh air by opening the window, resulted in a faceful of red dust thrown up in the wake of the trucks.

Arriving in Langmusi, it was immediately apparent that this was a Tibetan town, most notably by the fact that most people were wearing traditional Tibetan coats. Lined with thick wool and stretching below the knees, they are often quite drab in colour, but always tied around the waist with a brightly-coloured sash. At first I remember thinking their sleeves, which were at least a third longer than the arm they concealed, were ridiculous, but I later learnt from watching and then purchasing my own Tibetan coat, that the sleeve length had multiple purposes. For a start, they acted as an extra belt, so if later in the day you got hot, you could remove half your coat, tie the arms tightly around your waist, and carry on with what you were doing while keep your bottom half of your body that is closest to the frozen ground, warm. The best reason for the extended sleeves though, as I later discovered, is their use as gloves. I had bought some professional mountaineering gloves to protect my hands from the freezing temperatures, which were all very well until I came into contact with something solid, as the cold would simply shoot straight through them to my hands and stay there. They were also impractical, as the thick insulation made it difficult to pick anything up, or even get my hand into my pocket, which meant I was continually taking them on and off. In the end I got so fed up with doing this that I decided to make like a local and use my Tibetan coat sleeves instead, and I never looked back. Now I had the full use of my hands in a moment, but could simply slide them back inside the cocoon of my sleeves to instantly warm them up.

After we had paid for the taxi and said our goodbyes to Peter, who already had his own free accommodation organized, we wandered down the road until we reached the Sana Hotel. There were only two places to stay in town, and this seemed the better deal as we were promised a heater in the room for three hours a night and hot water for two hours in the morning. For a $1.50, this sounded like a bargain. As it turned out, the heater made no difference to the temperature of the room at all, but I was able to hang my clothes around it at the very least, and therefore do my laundry for the first time since I'd left Laos a couple of weeks before – without any artificial heat anywhere else we'd stayed, it would have taken a week to dry any washing, and not having many clothes or the time to wait around, I'd had very little choice.

My leather boots, however, were still a problem, as they had been wet from the snow since Dali, and aside from the damp, sweaty smell they were now emanating, they were also beginning to take their toll on my feet, which were badly blistered and sore from the cold. I tried to buy some snow boots, but as is always the problem when you have size 13 feet, I couldn't find any that fitted. My current pair I had had custom-made in Africa a few years before, the soles made from old car tyres, but with just a 60-day Visa, I didn't have the time or money to do the same here, so instead took to wrapping my feet in plastic bags before putting my boots on, thereby swapping the misery of cold sores for sweat sores.

It soon became increasingly clear that the German woman with whom we had travelled to Langmusi was slightly insane. There had been something a bit odd about her when we'd first met, but after going out to dinner with her that first night, we came to the conclusion that she was most definitely crazy and should be avoided at all costs.

We had been to a local café a couple of doors down from our hotel which had been recommended to us for its yak burgers and chocolate cake by the only other foreigner in town, an Israeli whose name we never quite caught, and so Simon affectionately nicknamed Falafel.

Our new German friend, like Simon, was a vegetarian and instead of going to the place with burgers and chocolate cake made us traipse around town for an hour looking for somewhere vegetarian and "authentic". So instead we were sitting in a tiny, cold, but undoubtedly authentic restaurant, slurping luke-warm tofu and noodles, while the German woman talked at us about abstract things which seemed only to connect in her own head. Just then, our Falafel friend appeared in the doorway. "Why are you eating here? The place down the road is cheaper, warmer and has much better food," he said.

With that, the German woman began ranting furiously and loudly about not coming all the way to China for two weeks to eat chocolate cake and talk to other westerners. Her eyes were now darting irritably around the room, her chopsticks clutched so tightly in her hands that her knuckles had turned white. Simon and I slumped in our chairs, desperate for our now petrified friend not to think that we were actually with this crazy woman, and when she had quite finished, I got to my feet and said, "Well, we're not here for just two weeks. I've been travelling for eight months, and if I want to get some chocolate cake, I'm gonna."

We left with Falafel, and as I hurriedly explained to Simon what had just happened, the majority of which (aside from the part about chocolate cake) had been lost on him, we walked down the road to Leisha's Café, where we were greeted warmly by the biggest Tibetan I had ever seen. He didn't speak any English but had a huge smile, and I nicknamed him Lurch. His sister Leisha owned and ran the café, and it seemed he was in charge of security and cutting wood for the constantly burning fire at the centre of the room.

As in most places in China, the tea was free-flowing, but here, rather than green tea, it was yak butter tea. This was an acquired taste but one that I acquired surprisingly quickly considering it was thick and oily in texture, and a bit like drinking a cup of strong cheese. We soon found though that it was very effective for boosting your energy levels, and of course warming you up. We chatted genially over a slice of rich chocolate cake, and Falafel started to tell us all about the Tibetan sky burials common here and all over Tibet. Apparently, when a Tibetan dies and goes onto his next life, the monks are called and the following morning they ceremoniously take the body up into the mountains, along with a few of the deceased's former possessions such as photos and clothing, which are then burnt. In the mean time, the body is chopped into pieces as the monks chant, and prayer flags are hung on poles. They then return down the mountain, leaving the dismembered body to be taken by the vultures, which they believe to be "the couriers of life." It certainly made a western burial seem pretty tame, but then I figured this was probably easier than digging a 6ft grave through frozen ground. It was something we had to see.

Reluctantly waking early the following morning, we got dressed under the covers, a method we had developed in order to prevent having to expose any bare flesh to the freezing air in our room for any length of time, and left the guesthouse just as dawn was breaking over the snow capped peaks. We headed out of town using a shortcut through the grounds of a monastery, which led to a tall gateway with a brightly-coloured mural depicting the Buddhist circle of life on either side. Behind the monastery was a rough path leading up into the hills, and we knew we were on the right track when we saw clothing littering the surrounding slopes discarded after the burials. Despite the path only being a gentle climb, the thinner air exhausted us quickly, and I had to stop to catch my breath a few times. When we reached the top, we could see that sky burials had certainly taken place here, but were disappointed to find that nothing was happening today. Crowning the tops of the hill and tied together with poles and rope, hundreds of prayer flags fluttered in the wind. From a distance they looked like dozens of multicoloured washing lines all entwined, fighting to break loose as they flapped in the breeze.

On closer inspection we saw that each prayer flag had been tied on individually, and each one had a print of a picture or scripture on it. Many also had handwritten messages along the bottom. There were also lots of neatly stacked piles of rocks, but we never learnt their meaning or purpose. The ground was scorched in several places, and in the ashes was evidence of partially burnt clothing, some of it clearly the remains of monks' robes. We wandered further around the hilltops, and began to find random bits of bone, initially preferring to assume it was animal rather than human, but then Simon found a pile of unmistakeably human bones complete with skull. By now my feet were numb with cold, so I told Simon I was going to head back down and wandered back towards town via a different route. Approaching the outskirts, I heard lots of shouting and out-of-rhythm clapping coming from the grounds of a monastery. It reminded me of the sounds of playtime at school. As I got closer, I saw that all the monks were outside taking part in some kind of organized frenzy.

Not wanting to be seen, I quickly crossed over to the trees opposite and found a spot where I could sit hidden and watch. Some of the monks were wearing enormous curved yellow hats, and they appeared to be aggressively shouting and jeering at each other – not behaviour I thought particularly monk-like. They were grouped in pairs or threesomes, one monk among them sitting on the ground, still and composed, while the other monks shouted questions at them and slapped and pinched their hands. From what I could tell, the seated monk seemed to have to try to answer their questions quickly and calmly without reacting to the hostility. Two or three older and wiser looking monks strolled among them, listening to the interrogations, but never intervening or showing any sign of approval or disapproval.

Every so often the groups of monks would reverse roles, the interrogator becoming the interrogated. After a while, a monk appeared on the balcony of the monastery and struck a large gong three times. At this the monks fell silent for a moment, and then talking and laughing, began making their way back inside the monastery in a way that reminded me of kids chatting in corridors between class. The sun was shining brightly, but as the monks entered the monastery they were swallowed into total darkness, before two heavy doors swung shut behind them, and all was silent once more.

I sat there a while pondering what I had just witnessed, and feeling pretty privileged that I had. Before long a group of young boys spotted me and came over to make fun of my big sticking-out nose, even playfully trying to squash it into my face to look more like theirs; when I headed down to Leisha's for breakfast that morning, I was unusually aware of my very large nose. Inside, Simon was practically sitting with his feet on the fire in an attempt to warm up his frozen toes. I sat down beside him and did the same, and we enjoyed some tasty yak butter and honey on Tibetan bread, washed down by a dozen cups of complimentary yak butter tea.

As we ate, I told Simon and Leisha what I had just witnessed at the monastery and Leisha explained that it was the monks debating the scriptures. Tibetan Buddhists believe that everything must be questioned, and so the mayhem I had witnessed was the young monks attempting to learn how to answer any question without having to think too hard about it. Buddhists believe that if you have to think too hard, you're not thinking with your own mind, simply repeating what you have been told. The slapping of the hands was apparently because it is all very well being able to think clearly in a peaceful environment, but it's no good if you can't focus when it really counts.

By now, Peter, who was unexpectedly free after someone hadn't turned up for a meeting, had joined us as well, and we were all sitting around the fire, him vainly trying to teach us some Chinese, when his business contact burst through the door so suddenly that Lurch spilt his tea. The man looked very apologetic, and explained to Peter that he hadn't turned up that morning because he had been up all night riding around the hills on horseback, searching for a man who had stolen one of his sheep. Fortunately, he had found the sheep but not the man who had stolen it, although he said, he knew who it was and he was now on his way to the monastery to talk to the head lama about what punishment or action should be taken. With that he left as suddenly as he had arrived. Peter explained that as there were no police in Langmusi, punishments for breaking laws were determined by the monks – this seemed so alien to what I'd seen elsewhere, that I found myself questioning if I was really still in China. As we returned to our chatting about what we'd been up to, Leisha then told us that there had actually been a sky burial that morning, but we had got there too early.

Determined to witness a sky burial before we left, we returned to the same spot the next morning to see if we could catch a repeat performance, but had no luck that morning, or the one after that. During the day Simon and I split up to independently explore the area. I wandered around town finding discreet vantage points from which to people-watch, and walked in the hills where the vultures circled overhead, and women on horseback kept huge herds of yaks together with calls and well-aimed rock missiles. I was quite shocked at how hard they threw the rocks as the yaks were often at fairly close range, but I guess they have pretty thick coats to protect them. As time went on, I was pleased to find that I was getting less breathless on my daily climbs, meaning I was slowly become more acclimatised to the high altitude.

A couple of evenings after our first attempt at witnessing a sky burial, we met a couple from Beijing in Leisha's café. The woman was originally from Italy, but was married to a Chinese man and had lived in China for the past 12 years. I spoke to them of my plans, and they told me that they had travelled in Tibet the previous year, and so I enthusiastically quizzed them for as much information as they could remember. Unfortunately, it wasn't particularly helpful, as they turned out to be real pessimists. They proceeded to tell me how I was stupid to even think about it – that they had done it in their own four-wheel drive and nearly been killed in an accident. They had all the usual negative talk – how there was no public transport in Tibet, and so I'd need my own car and driver (foreigners were not allowed to drive in China, but that made little difference to me as I'd never learnt). Then they started going on about all the visas and permits I'd need for different districts, and how heavily guarded all the checkpoints were, plus I would have to pay for a government issued guide. And even if I did manage all of that, I had to remember that Tibetans didn't welcome outsiders, the towns were surrounded by territorial and vicious Tibetan dogs, and on top of all that I would probably die from altitude sickness or the cold unless I was properly equipped.

It was all stuff I'd heard before and it didn't really matter what they said. I'd already decided months ago that I was going to try no matter what, but they couldn't seem to get their heads around the fact that I wasn't asking for their approval, simply for a bit of practical advice. Giving it up as a bad job, I stopped talking to them about it and certainly didn't bother to tell them that I couldn't even afford any proper equipment or clothing, let alone pay for a dozen permits, a driver, a car and a guide. I already knew that I was a rather fool-hardy traveller, but I also had enough faith in my own common sense and abilities, that I would not become a statistic.

I ordered some more beers, and as I passed one to Simon I could tell from the look on his face that he'd understood enough of our conversation to be having second thoughts about my planned route. This was not the first time people had tried to dissuade us, but these two spreaders of negativity had really got to Simon this time. He didn't say anything as we finished our beers, but I knew it was coming.

6

Lambert and Garfield
Chengdu to Lanzhou = 962km

By 7am the following morning we were on the bus to Lanzhou, the next big city north. As it had been snowing heavily the night before it took over an hour just to get the bus started.

It was packed with Tibetans wrapped up in thick coats, mumbling mantras and running prayer beads through their fingers. We stopped at a handful of villages en route, where more Tibetans boarded, each pausing for a second to stare quizzically at the two foreigners crammed in at the back. The children were wrapped up so tightly I could only see their curious brown eyes staring out at me from between the layers.

As we sped along the icy roads, I felt very safe and entirely comfortable squashed in among the Tibetans, until we suddenly slowed to a stop on a bridge. A few passengers jumped off the bus and ran to the side to look over what remained of the railing. Those of us who opted to stay in the warm, fought for a view at the window to find out what all the fuss was about. Peering through the misty glass, I saw that a section of the bridge's railings had gone, and 10m below, lying on its roof in the shallow river with steam still rising from its engine, was a truck. It seemed highly unlikely anyone could have survived. The driver's cab had been crushed to a 10th of its original size, and was now submerged below the waterline.

We continued on our way in silence for the next two hours, the mood sombre, the beads in the Tibetans' hands running through their fingers at twice the speed, and the driver thankfully taking things a little more slowly. At the next big town some hours later, we had to change buses, and at the ticket office they demanded our insurance papers before they would sell us a ticket. I knew exactly what they were talking about since I had been forewarned about them doing this in certain parts of China, where bus and train travel was not possible without taking out personal insurance first. However, what they called insurance was in fact nothing of the sort. In the event of an accident, the insurance would not cover me, but would in fact only cover them and waive any liability on their part. If this insurance had been included in the ticket, I wouldn't have objected and would have happily put pen to paper, but to expect me to pay for it on top of the fare, was just plain cheeky!

I found the bus we wanted to board, and mainly using sign language managed to get the driver to agree to pick us up around the corner from the bus station, where we could pay him directly and avoid the insurance scam. We arrived in Lanzhou four hours later, having spent part of the time chatting to a policeman who seemed totally unaware of the rules concerning foreigners. We told him about the guesthouse rules, which he agreed seemed most unfair, and even offered for us to stay with him once we reached Lanzhou. As tempting as it was, we turned down the invitation in case it inadvertently got him into trouble.

In the bus depot we were told that all the guesthouses were on the other side of the city. Much to Simon's dismay, despite 10 hours of travel I still thought it would be nice to get to the other side of the city on foot. So we walked fully laden through the crowded streets for the next two hours, got hopelessly lost and ended up in the red-light district. By the time we found a room, Simon was no longer talking to me!

Performing simple tasks in a Communist country never failed to be an enormous hassle. At the Post Office the next day, all I wanted to do was send some CDs containing some digital photos back to the UK, but once I had filled out all the necessary forms and explained what these "suspicious" discs contained, it had taken a couple of hours. The discs even disappeared for a while, and I can only assume they actually went to the trouble of checking what was on them. Eventually they agreed to send them, even if it did take another three months for the discs to reach their destination.

That night, Simon finally told me he wasn't going to travel with me to Tibet. He had instead decided to go the shorter route and attempt to be smuggled in by bus from Golmud in the north, from where, after a day of hiding beneath a blanket in the back of a bus, he hoped to reach Lhasa.

I was sad to hear it, not only because for just a moment it made me doubt whether I was making the right decision, but also because we travelled well together, which was rare for me. I think because both of us were equally happy to do our own thing when we wanted and then to meet up for a couple of cold beers at the end of the day. There were no expectations of each other, never any pressure – we could sit in silence perfectly happily with no need to feel like we had to talk.

But I always knew I wasn't going to change my planned route. If I entered Tibet via Lhasa, it would be near impossible to travel much further beyond the city, since it is so heavily controlled by the Chinese government. Simon was unnecessarily apologetic, and seemed to feel he had let me down in some way. It took quite a few more beers for me to convince him that was not the case. After all, there were benefits to us travelling solo. For a start I reminded him, hitching is always easier alone, and one 6ft westerner would stick out far less than two! I promised him we would meet for beer in Lhasa when I got there, and he seemed consoled.

It took several attempts to buy my ticket to Urumgi from Lanzhou. I was feeling quite confident the first time I tried, standing in the long ticket queue beneath the enormous arched ceiling of the rather daunting Lanzhou Station. In Chinese, I had carefully written down on a piece of paper, the date, time and destination to which I wanted to travel. When my turn came, I approached the glass screen with the paper in my hand only to find a rather impatient ticket saleswoman, who briefly glanced at it before waving me away in annoyance. Assuming I'd made a mistake, I returned to my room and once more painstakingly copied the information back down on a new piece of paper. Half an hour later I returned to the ticket office, where the same woman refused to serve me despite my best expression of helplessness. With little choice but to carry on trying, I continued recopying the information over and again in various combinations, but each time I went back she still refused to serve me, until eventually I was approached by a friendly English-speaking business-man, who explained that the problem was that I hadn't written down which class I wanted to travel in. To my eternal gratitude, the man then queued up with me and bought the ticket on my behalf. Unfortunately, it had taken me so long to actually buy the fare that all was left was "standing class". That was, for the whole 35-hour journey to Urumgi. Luckily, I was not leaving for another two days, and so put the painful journey ahead to the back of my mind. I returned to the room and triumphantly waved my ticket at Simon, who was then able to learn from my mistake and buy his ticket in just one attempt.

We celebrated our success with a night on the town, although there weren't any real bars around. So we got some shop-bought beers and wandered the streets, stopping to enjoy them in various spots around the city – between the feet of the enormous statue of Chairman Mao, for example, where we found a large number of Chinese students doing the same thing, except they were drinking homebrew rather than local beer. Later in the evening we paused to watch a woman who was scream-ing and shouting in the middle of the busy main road. She looked in her late middle age, with a smooth face and wrinkled jaw line. The locals were stopping and staring and laughing at her, but when she saw us she crossed the road to talk. She was wearing a big baggy red jumper and grubby blue body warmer and when she stopped in front of us her mouth broke in to a gummy smile. She took out a sketch book which we saw was full of notes and pictures. We obligingly looked and tried to take an interest while she rambled on at us in rapid Chinese, breaking off only to occasionally point up at the sky. We were all laughing, us slightly awkwardly at the strangeness of the situation, and her because we clearly had no idea what was going on.

"Do you think she was insane?" I asked Simon, as we finally got away.

"No, I think she was a woman who knows too much," he replied seriously.

Unfortunately, we hadn't got far before we realized she was following us. In fact, she followed us all the way back in to our room, and no amount of gentle persuasion could get her to leave. In the end we were forced to trick her out into the hallway, and quickly bolt back inside and lock the door.

Now that we were splitting up, I needed to copy Simon's map of Tibet, as I realized that the sketches on the napkins Matt had drawn me, weren't really going to cut it. So, the whole of the next morning was spent trying to find a printing shop that could copy in A1. After an exhausting search I managed to get a black and white copy and then took Simon for his first ever Kentucky Fried Chicken in thanks. His vegetarian status now in tatters, we spent the remainder of the day wandering aimlessly, each lost in thought about our onward journeys.

The next day I was due to leave, but my train wasn't until late afternoon, so we spent our last morning together having a paper aeroplane-throwing competition out of our sixth floor window, until things got a little out of hand and we began setting them on fire before launching them down into the busy city below. When the time came to go our separate ways, we did a quick masculine goodbye, promised to stay in touch and then I boarded my train to Urumgi.

The city of Urumgi holds the record for being the furthest city from the sea anywhere in the world, so it was really quite a strange place for a diver to be headed, and the journey did not start well. For the first eight hours I had a very bad case of Delhi belly, and so in between standing and squatting, I couldn't stray far from the train toilet, which smelt like something had died in it, a long time ago. Thankfully, a Mongolian family, who were also on their way to Urumgi, took pity and adopted me, and I was able to share one seat with their three children, which we rotated between us every hour or so. I kept my mind off the aching in my legs and the movement of my bowels, by gazing out of the window at the scenery, which was slowly flattening out and becoming drier and more desolate.

Thankfully, we actually arrived five hours earlier than scheduled, and the Mongolian family had to convince me it was the right stop, since I was reluctant to give up the seat I had managed to grab at a stop an hour or so before. I joined them for lunch at a small local restaurant where they served a local dish of really thick pasta with meatballs. People came over from the other tables to be introduced to me and in the end I had quite an audience as I ate. I was pleased that my use of chopsticks had now improved somewhat since my arrival in China, and I didn't embarrass my new family. I wanted to pay for the meal but was firmly refused, and the father paid for everyone before we left in a taxi to find me a hotel. When we said goodbye, I rummaged around in my backpack for something I could give them to show my gratitude for all their kindness. All I could find was a packet of London postcards, and so I pulled one out and scribbled my email address on to the back. The mother then insisted that all her children give me a kiss goodbye, which was fine until I was reluctantly approached by the four-year-old who had snot bubbling from his nose but not wishing to offend, I braced myself as he smeared my cheek with slime. I wonder why mothers force their children to do these things when everyone else involved would prefer a quick wave or a high five.

After a well-earned nap, I set out to wander Urumgi, which turned out to be a very grey city. Perhaps it was just a bad day, but I got the impression that it was all about work and just surviving and not a lot else. Everyone looked depressed, and I came to the conclusion that it was probably because 99 per cent of these people had never heard waves break upon a shore.

I went to the government building and quickly checked with them that it was possible, in theory, to extend my visa in Kashgar. They confirmed this was the case, and before they could ask any more questions, I headed back to the train station which I'd only just arrived at a few hours before, and booked a one-way ticket on the first train out of Urumgi the next day. Although, as the train pulled away and I began my 20-hour plus journey to Kashgar, I did feel a bit guilty for only giving the city a day of my time. My allocated seat on the train left me with no space for my pack, so having complained to the guard that I couldn't spend the next twenty something hours with it on my lap, and that I was not willing to leave it anywhere out of my sight, I got moved up a class, into basic but spacious comfort with almost an entire carriage to myself.

The topography en route to Kashgar seemed unable to make up its mind; we skimmed the outskirts of the Gobi Desert, then on through valleys and under mountains through long dark tunnels. When I saw the state of the toilet onboard, I was relieved that my stomach was behaving itself once more, since the facilities were of the squat variety, and plastered all over the rim and surrounding floor with multicoloured dry and wet faeces. I ate very little over the journey in order to avoid any unnecessary toilet trips, and was consequently starving by the time I arrived in Kashgar. Unfortunately, Kashgar Station turned out to be miles outside of the city. The taxi drivers all warned me that it was a 10km walk but not trusting them, I began walking anyway. Just goes to show that sometimes you should give people the benefit of the doubt though, because it turned out they were telling the truth. This was one of those rare times it would have been a good idea to have a guidebook with me. And so started a few days of very bad luck.

I knew I wanted to stay at a hotel called Semen Binguan, and by the time I arrived, I was exhausted. Once the grand premises of the Russian embassy in Kashgar, it was now a cheap hotel with a reputation for being a good place to meet other travellers. It was not that I wanted company now Simon and I had parted ways, but more the fact that, with just a photocopied map and a few directions scribbled on to napkins by Matt back in Laos, I had no plan for entering Tibet, and was hoping to find some like-minded souls who did.

I stepped inside the enormous foyer and walked up to the reception desk, behind which the wall was filled with clocks meant to be showing the current time in numerous international cities, but all of which had stopped ticking a long time ago. I'd heard that the hotel had more than 500 rooms, and judging by the stir my arrival caused the two young girls at reception, I was guessing there was one spare. I took the cheapest room they had which at 10RMB was about the same price as three beers.

"How many people do you have staying at the moment," I asked, as I filled out the necessary paper-work.

She flicked the pages on her giant ledger and said, "Nine."

"Any foreigners?" I asked. She swivelled the book around on the desk so I could look for myself, and I saw that six guests were Chinese but the remaining two (she had included me in her count of nine) were two girls from Sweden. I took my key and followed the recep-tionist to my room with a spring in my step. Despite the fact that the Russians had clearly taken what they could with them, the place still reeked of wealth, and I found myself walking a little taller and lifting my chin in the air like some foreign dignitary, as I followed the recep-tionist down the red carpeted hallways and marble staircases with brass banisters. As I tried to remember the correct wing, floor and corridor I had to take to find my room, I realized that this wasn't going to be the last time I was going to have to be shown, since every hall, stairwell and door was identical. I don't think the girl would have minded, since on our way she showed me around the almost entirely deserted building enthusias-tically. The ex-ambassador's office was, of course, the most impressive room, and although pictures were clearly missing from the walls and a thick layer of dust hung in the air, some vestiges of its past grandeur remained, including a large old leather office chair and a beautiful oak desk. The receptionist waited patiently, as I sat in the chair, spun it round and put my feet up for a few moments wondering what covert conversations had taken place here years ago.

Once I'd settled in my slightly less impressive accommodation, I headed out to find a place Matt had recommended to me back in Laos, called John's Café. It had been there that Matt had met the guy he had travelled in to Tibet with, and likewise, I hoped to meet other travellers like myself who may be able to offer me vital information about crossing the border. Plus, it had been a while since I'd had a conversation in English, and I figured this might be the last chance for a good time to come. However when I found the café, the door was locked and there was a note saying it would be closed for the next few months. I peered through the window and saw that all the chairs and tables were stacked up against the wall and it looked like it had been closed for some time already.

Feeling a little depressed, I wandered around the city, searching for internet access, eventually finding a place offering equally slow service from the man in charge and the internet server. It was only when I logged on that I discovered it was a Monday. This was bad news since the one thing Kashgar is famous for is its Sunday Bazaar, a market where traders come from neighbouring countries to sell their goods. It had taken place every Sunday for countless generations running all the way back to the beginning of the ancient Silk Road, and if I wanted to see it, I would have to wait a whole week.

I continued to wander around the city in a bad mood until I passed a mother and toddler, the latter wearing

China's answer to saving money on nappies – a pair of trousers with no back which left the toddlers' bare bum exposed for all to see. The idea was that if they had to go, they could just squat down and relieve themselves all over the street. I reached for my camera to take a quick snap, only to discover it had stopped working. My first day in Kashgar had not gone well, so I bought some beer, headed back to my room and went to bed.

I woke up the next morning feeling positive, and headed straight for the camera shop in the hope that they might be able to fix the problem. They told me that they could, but they would have to send it to Beijing for repair, which could take up to six weeks. Going to Tibet without a camera was not an option, and neither was a six-week wait here, so I bit the bullet and shelled out on a brand-new camera – not the positive start to the day I'd been hoping for. In need of some cheering up, I set off in search of some junk food to lift my spirits and found a wannabe McDonald's in which I sat down and gorged myself. Here I met Lambert. Lambert (undoubtedly his "English" name, a thing which many Asians adopt when talking to foreigners due to our difficulty in pronouncing their real names correctly), was a young Han Chinese man in his 20s, with wet-look hair brushed in to a neat side parting. He wore a smart shirt and chinos – a look I suspect that was his casual but my formal – and he hovered around my table for several minutes before building up the confidence to come over and talk to me.

He introduced himself excitedly, and clearly wanted to talk to me to practice his English. He told me that he worked for the government, although unfortunately not a department that was of any use to me. I laughed as he tried to imitate the way I spoke, and I eventually told him not to, explaining I was hardly the right sort of person to give elocution lessons. He asked if he could take me out to dinner that evening, and since I as usual didn't have any plans, I agreed we'd meet at 7.30pm local time.

"Local Time" or "Beijing Time" was something that always had to be stated in China, as despite China being such a vast country, the government insisted that everyone should follow "Beijing time". Banks, hotels, schools, government offices, train stations, (but not bus stations) all followed this rule, while local shops and restaurants often ignored it, as did the locals, which made things doubly confusing. It was a rule particularly ignored in Kashgar where, according to the government, the sun would set at 1pm.

Given that Lambert was Han Chinese, which from what I could tell was the highest class in this classless country, and he worked for the government, I was pleased to see his watch was set to local time. Perhaps because in Kashgar at least, Han Chinese were in a minority, something which the government was keen to change. Here, most people were a mixture of races, and often rather scary and severe in appearance, with an unusual mix of Urder, Russian, Afghani, and Kazaki characteristics

Among the women at the time, leg warmers seemed to be the fashion of choice, largely worn with bare, unshaven, corned beef legs, which reminded me of Nora Batty in the sitcom, *The Last of the Summer Wine*.

Since I'd just bought a new camera, I now definitely could not afford any proper boots, even if I could get some in my size, so after I'd said goodbye to Lambert,

I headed to a department store to see what I could buy to improve the ones I had. I left with a dozen pairs of insoles, rubber glue, four pairs of football socks and 200 bin bags for waterproofing.

When I met Lambert that evening, it was immediately apparent I was underdressed. With only three changes of clothes I had opted for my genuinely (rather than designer) ripped jeans, and a not-so-recently-washed T-shirt. Lambert on the other hand, was wearing a three-piece suit and black leather shoes you could see your face in. As if this wasn't clue enough, as soon as we entered the restaurant I knew I wasn't in for a cheap eat, and unsurprisingly all eyes were upon me as we sat down. I hoped it was my white skin attracting the attention, but suspected it had more to do with my lack of respect of the dress code. Feeling pretty awkward already, I then discovered that my legs wouldn't fit under the table. So after various attempts at positioning myself, I opted for the splits, a position I was forced to maintain for the next three hours and ten courses.

Since I clearly had no idea what anything was, Lambert ordered everything, although many of the dishes that arrived at the table I recognized from the roadside stalls I frequented. I'd never learnt anything by name since I usually ordered simply by pointing, and in restaurants I had occasionally resorted to inviting myself into the kitchen to show them what I wanted to eat. Rather than annoying the chefs, most seemed delighted at my visits, and I was always sure to return after I'd finished eating to give them my "*Bellissimo*!" gesture.

In this restaurant, however, I instantly felt seriously out of place and uncomfortable. I don't think I would have minded so much if I had been alone, but I was worried about embarrassing Lambert, although when I realized he wasn't bothered at all, I slowly began to relax. He told me that he was going to enter an English-speaking competition and had brought with him the speech he intended to give. We went over it, and I was pleased to be able to make a few helpful suggestions and alterations, and tried not to laugh as he recited it to me in an unintentionally comedic over-the-top English accent. Next, he wanted to learn some London slang, and it took quite some time to persuade him that 'the dog's bollocks' was something good, and in the end I had such a great night that we agreed to meet the next as well.

The next day I was ready and waiting the moment the doors to the Visa Extension Office opened. I'd come up with the best story I could muster as to why I might possibly need my visa extended, but it turned out to be a waste of time since they only extended visas when there was less than 48 hours to go on them. This gave me just one month to reach Lhasa, the former capital of Tibet, and if there was any chance of this happening at all, my luck needed to turn around pretty fast.

I headed to the old part of Kashgar to look around. Many of the buildings here were crumbling and beyond repair, and I had no doubt this old and historic part of the town would eventually be swallowed up by the encroaching modern city. There were no Han Chinese, here only Kashgariens. The men mainly wore white domed hats, and sat around playing cards. I couldn't make any sense of the layout of the old town, and while exploring the network of narrow alleyways, got quite lost. After getting some directions, I headed back towards the modern side of the city, stopping on the way at an army surplus store, where I purchased a long, waterproof trench coat, complete with the iconic Chinese stars on each button.

Lambert must have guessed I was on a fairly tight budget, for when we met that evening and it was my turn to pay for dinner (he had kindly insisted on footing last night's bill), we went to his auntie's restaurant, where both our meals and beer cost a fraction of what Lambert had paid for the two of us the previous night. His auntie, who ran a small roadside restaurant, was just as genuine and friendly as Lambert, and I instantly felt welcome. After we'd eaten, we headed to the cinema which was showing *Garfield The Movie*. As we took our seats and waited for the film to begin, two young kids came rushing into the auditorium, each carrying two large film cans.

"What's going on?" I asked, and Lambert explained that to save money, the four cinemas in town all shared one film and that after it had finished running, the reel would be rapidly rewound, then the kids would collect the film canisters and cycle them across town to the next cinema due to be showing it. This seemed a lot of effort given that there were only 10 of us in the cinema, and the place had a maximum capacity of about 25. When the film started, Lambert felt the need to translate it all for me, and whispered every piece of badly-dubbed dialogue in my ear for the duration of the movie. This was kind of him, but fairly irritating – after all we were watching a cartoon cat, not Shakespeare. When we said goodbye that evening I explained to him that this was probably goodbye for good, since my visa situation meant I now had to leave the following day. He was gutted and told me how he'd even made plans for us for the weekend. Then as a sign of just how upset he was, he openly cursed his government, something that shocked me quite a lot, since among Chinese people like Lambert, this was only ever something that would have happened behind closed doors, if at all.

I was also annoyed about having to move on so soon, but more than anything because I was going to miss the famous Sunday Bazaar. As I said goodbye to Lambert and told him to let me know how he got on in his English speaking competition (he later emailed to say he came second), there were tears in his eyes. I went to bed that night vaguely worried that Lambert would be busy launching petrol bombs at the Immigration Office.

7

The Crossing

Lanzhou to Kargalik = 3,614km

It was a five-hour bus journey to Kargalik, from where I'd be able to take another bus to Tibet. Two teenage Muslim boys were seated next to me looking very smart in their matching blue tunics and white caps, compared to me in my ripped Levis and faded pullover. Resting between both their laps was a museum-piece of a boom box. They excitedly fiddled with the large dials and clicked buttons, frequently turning it towards me to ensure that I got a good look. I nodded and tried to look impressed, but was only grateful that they had yet to buy some batteries for it, because if they had managed to get this 1980s relic going before the end of the journey, I'm sure the five hours would have felt a lot longer.

They got off a few stops before me and were greeted by a huddle of friends, who all stared wide-eyed at what was clearly considered to be the latest music technology arriving in their village. As the bus began to pull away, they remembered me, and quickly pointed me out to everyone who began running alongside the window, pushing at each others' shoulders to gain a better glimpse of the marginally more interesting sight of a foreigner on the bus.

Kargalik was an unattractive little outpost and the last place I could be considered to be half legally visiting. I wanted to avoid as much unnecessary attention as possible while I was there, for while my visa allowed me to be in this small town, I would have a hard time explaining to any officials my reasons for being here when my visa claimed that I was on my way to Beijing, which was about as far away as it could possibly be, on the opposite side of the country.

I made my way down the steps of the bus with stiff knees, and instantly realized Kargalik was much bigger than I'd anticipated. I pulled out the napkin with the scrawl of a map which Mark had drawn of it for me, and wondered which of the 30 roads I could see and hear around me were one of the three on the map. I started searching for the red-light district, as Matt's notes said that this was not only where the bus went from, but also where the only cheap accommodation could be found. After nearly two hours of searching, I admitted defeat and checked into a room in the heart of town, not too far from where I'd originally alighted from the bus. I ate at my hotel, and then set off refreshed, and on the lookout for hookers!

I searched in vain for a further hour before deciding there was no point in being discreet anymore, and I started asking people if they knew where I could find the bus towards Tibet, using a few sentences I'd copied down from my phrasebook. But this just resulted in fits of giggles rather than any useful information until I came across a school where I was immediately mobbed by the kids who were hanging around its gates. Spotting an opportunity, I asked them for help, and rather than the frustrating giggles I had now come to expect, the children very firmly told me to stay where I was, before swarming back inside the school at a run. Glad of the rest, I sat on my bag and waited while some schoolgirls stood around staring at me. I assume from their gestures; they were commenting to each other about what a big nose I had. Presently, the scrum of school children returned, accompanied by a teacher in his mid-thirties who beckoned me over.

His English was good, and he introduced himself as Mr Tithandalumer, but said I could call him Mr T for short.

"Can we talk inside?" he said, looking around him slightly nervously. "If I am seen talking to you, it would not be good." I later learnt that this was because he was an Urder, an ethnic minority in this small corner of China, and if an Urder is seen talking to a foreigner they can get into serious trouble.

I followed him inside to his classroom. The children remained noisily huddled in the doorway and he asked them to wait outside, closing the door behind them. He then sat down and began to tell me about himself. He explained, that he had always wanted to educate himself about the world outside China, and to do this he first had to teach himself English. This was not an easy task for him, as unlike my old friend Lambert who was a Han Chinese, it was forbidden for Mr T's people to study many subjects at all, and it was made harder for them to access books and materials. He explained that the Urder's own written language was banned and they were forbidden from speaking it in public. While he was allowed a passport, he was forbidden to apply for one.

The schools for children of Urder origin were separate from those of the Chinese, and the funding for the Urder schools was next to nothing. He pointed out to me two ancient looking computers at the back of the room. "They are shared between 500 Urder students. Chinese students have one computer between two."

Once I'd heard his story, I offered my own story, and explained how I was trying to enter Tibet and wanted to know where the bus left for Ali, the first town inside the border. He shook his head gravely.

"There is no bus to Tibet," he said.

"There is," I said, "but because the border to Tibet is only open six days a month, it only leaves once a fortnight. I know because a friend of mine took it last year."

Mr T looked visibly shocked, and rather graciously, considering the short time I'd spent in his town and his company, he announced that together we would go in search of this mythical bus. He took me back to the front gates of the school and instructed me to walk further down the road and wait for him there. I waited on the corner of the block for a few minutes before I turned to the rhythmic sound of hooves and found Mr T upon a rickety old donkey cart with a young kid at the reins. I jumped on beside him and we bounced along a stretch of road that took us to the edge of town. Mr T seemed quite nervous to have me in his company, and I was very aware that he was taking note of everyone who saw us together. I realized then just how big a risk he was taking for me, and I felt such a mixture of guilt and humility at his act of selfless kindness.

I did not recognize the road on which we were travelling, which was just an old track which I did not think could lead to anywhere of significance – it was dusty and the gutters were filled with stinking piles of uncollected rubbish. Then I spotted a group of women who were a little underdressed for the cold climate, loitering outside a decaying building, and I guessed we had arrived in the red-light district. Mr T began subtly asking around, and soon someone pointed down the street, and our young driver took the donkey at a trot until we reached a gateway, through which we spotted a courtyard, and a bus.

The bus itself looked almost identical to every other bus in China, except that this bus had clearly been modified; its wheels were disproportionately large, and it was sitting on a raised suspension system. Mr T went and spoke to someone inside the building adjoining the courtyard and soon came back with a big smile on his face. The bus was leaving for Tibet the very next morning. I couldn't believe my luck! The Yin of my Yang was finally getting its act together!

I was so grateful to Mr T, for I would never have found the place in time without him taking such a risk to help me. I gave him my email address so that we could stay in touch. I owed him a real debt that I hoped one day to repay.

The wake-up call I'd requested from the front desk never came, but as a precaution I had slept with the window and curtains open, so just as dawn broke, I was woken by first light. I packed up and left my lodgings with plenty of time to spare, anxious to get back to the courtyard as quickly as possible. Mr T had shown me where to catch a bus that would take me back to the red-light district, and I arrived at the courtyard with

two hours to spare. It wasn't long before the staff
appeared and invited me inside their hut for tea. Inside
in the warm I sipped green tea and watched a Jean
Claude Van Dam movie with them. Soon a group of
Chinese guards in green uniforms joined us and my
heart began pounding when one of them asked where
I was heading. I told the truth as there was little else
I could do, but I don't think he could have been aware
that I wasn't allowed to be boarding the bus to Ali,
because the conversation soon turned to Manchester
United and David Beckham's latest haircut, one of the
few things to have made Chinas' world news. Even so,
I deflected further scrutiny of my itinerary by giving
each of them one of my London postcards, which I
don't think have ever been more gratefully received by
anyone before.

After I boarded the bus and waved goodbye to my
new friends, I found my bunk and was pleased to see
that I had been given the middle row bed which was
level with the ground and tucked away towards the
back. It was far too small of course and I was clearly
going to have to sleep in the lotus position for the entire
journey, but looking around I could see every other
berth on the bus would have been far worse and I
realized that someone in charge must have taken pity on
my size. As I, and the other 60 or so passengers on the
bus got comfortable, I became concerned that many of
the others had their own oxygen supply in the form of
inflatable plastic pillows fitted with a small valve which
appeared to control the oxygen flow via a hose that
clipped onto the nose. Not only that, but most people
had a crate of food and water for the journey ahead,
while all I had was a bag of boiled sweets, a pack of

biscuits, a fruit cake, 1 litre of water and two cartons of Honge cigarettes! Reassured by the fact that the people in the surrounding bunks seemed excited at having such an exotic travelling companion in me, I decided that they would hopefully help me out if I needed it, and I relaxed and settled down for a nap.

Upon waking, I found myself surrounded by breath-taking scenery – in the literal sense. We were winding our way up the first 5,000m pass, the road was narrow and the wheels of the bus seemed unnervingly close to the edge. I felt strangely fatigued for someone who had just woken up from a refreshing sleep, there was an annoying pulse pumping in my eyelid, and I was having trouble catching my breath. The air outside was evidently getting much cooler, and the jagged mountain-tops and precipitous drops to the valleys were slowly becoming obscured behind the steaming windows and ice gathering around the frames.

There was a checkpoint at the top of the pass and everyone else began getting off the bus and filing through the office. I pulled the blanket up over my head and pretended to have fallen into a deep sleep. This went unnoticed and the bus drove on throughout the day. In the evening when my tummy began to rumble, I was able to exchange cigarettes for oranges and sweet goat's milk.

We were stopped again during the night, and this time rather than getting everybody off the bus, the offi-cials got on and walked up and down the aisles, check-ing peoples' identity cards at random and shining their bright torch beams into others' faces. I pulled my hat down covering my hair and nearly suffocated myself burying my head into the pillow in an attempt to hide my nose which, over the last month or so, I had developed quite a complex about. I held my breath as the torch beam hovered above my closed eyes for a moment before moving on.

Over the next three days I sneaked through a further four checkpoints, although it could have been more because whenever we slowed to a halt, I hid myself and closed my eyes, never wanting to take the risk of seeing if it was for something else. On the second day I was forced to disembark from the bus and pass through a checkpoint with everyone else. I nervously approached the officer behind the computer, which from the sound of it was being run by a generator out the back. So far, I had watched him check every other passengers' paperwork thoroughly, and so hiding my nerves as best I could, I presented him with my passport and a big smile. He stared at the photo page in my passport with interest, but as I had hoped he could clearly neither speak or read any English. I started to speak to him conversationally stopping only to laugh nervously and smile, hoping he'd mistake my chattiness for someone who is perfectly entitled to be where he was. He continued to stare at the passport and so I reached over the desk and tapped at the large and official looking visa for Zimbabwe that I had from a trip a couple of years before. To save face, he stared at this for some time before going back to my photo page and holding it up against me. He did this a number of times before finally handing it back to me with a smile and waving me back towards the bus. As I walked away, the adrenalin pumping through my already wobbly oxygen-starved body, he suddenly shouted after me, "Hello!"

I swallowed a huge lump in my throat and turned. But he just grinned back at me, pleased that he had managed to remember some English before I had left. "Hello!" I said, in reply, before quickly darting back to my bunk where I was soon once more fast asleep.

I managed to pass a lot of time sleeping, probably due to the high altitude making me very drowsy and lightheaded. One of the other passengers, an older lady, gave me a vial of some clear liquid which I gathered from her gestures would help with the woozines. I had to saw the top off with my penknife to get it open and was more than a little suspicious of the contents, but on my neighbouring passengers' encouragement, I shrugged my shoulders, threw back my head and drained it. It must have helped, because when we later pulled over for a loo break (there were of course no facilities, everyone just relieved themselves by the side of the road), while I was still more than a little unsteady on my feet, I managed the task and re-boarded the bus without incident. This was impressive because a few of my fellow passengers failed to do so and actually fainted halfway through the process of urinating, collapsing backwards onto the ground with their trousers still undone. The driver and his helpers who were obviously used to this minor complication, simply walked over to the unconscious victim, picked them up by their arms and legs and carried them unceremoniously back to the bus where they were slung back into their respective bunks and revived with smelling salts. This was all very amusing to watch but also a little concerning. After that, I took to holding on as long as possible before going to the loo, and I wasn't the only one. I noticed that some of the women must have held themselves for the entire three-day journey, presumably because we never once pulled over anywhere with any shrubbery for cover, just rocky wide open spaces through which the wind whistled mournfully.

On the third morning we arrived in Ali. I was in Tibet. I could hardly believe I had actually made it, and it was such an incredible buzz I could have run around and shouted about it from the rooftops. Instead I stood beside the bus with a big smug grin on my face as I waited for the luggage to be unloaded. Then bag on my back, I resisted the urge to hunt down a bar, and instead went in search of a guesthouse. As I approached the glass doors of the first one I came to, I saw the desk clerk immediately reach for the telephone. Not thinking anything of it, I carried on through the doors and patiently waited for him to finish his brief call. I was shown to their cheapest room which was surprisingly large with a heater and a television, but the downside was that it was on the third floor meaning that after the exhausting climb up the stairs my head felt like it was going to explode. No sooner had I dumped my bag and laid down on the bed to wait for my eyesight to realign itself than there was a knock on the door. Thinking it was someone bringing me a flask of boiling water and tea bags as I had become accustomed to in China, I immediately got up and opened it only to come face to face with the police.

I was taken to the police station in the back of an unmarked car, and as I sat there staring out of the window through the metal grill, I realized that this was the second time I had found myself in a police transit in less than a month. I was taken into a room where they motioned for me to sit on a small wooden bench where I waited for five minutes or so, cursing the guesthouse owner because, looking around, I appeared to be in some kind of courtroom. About 10m away there was a single chair on a raised platform, which reminded me of a throne. A woman entered and said, "Good afternoon," before climbing up onto the platform and sitting down. It was still morning as far as I was aware, but rather than correcting her I agreed that it was indeed a fine afternoon this morning. No one else came in, and for the next half an hour she directed questions to me in good English, all of which revolved around finding out what exactly I was doing here in Ali. I answered each question cooperatively, careful to sound as innocent and ignorant as possible. I must have been saying something right, because after a while she apparently began to warm to me and got down from her perch, re-positioning another chair closer to me so we could talk on eye level. She told me I must pay a fine of approximately $100US and she would then issue me with a two-week permit for Ali, but that this was on the understanding that I travelled back the way I had come when my permit expired. Conveniently for her this was also when the next bus departed for China.

I nodded, but explained that if I paid the fine I wouldn't have the money to pay for my return ticket back across the border. This got the fine reduced to $60US, and I was apparently then free to go. Back outside with the newly issued permit in my hand I saw that the only English writing it had on it said in bold black print, 'Alien's Travel Permit'.

It was a long walk back to the guesthouse, and when I finally arrived I waved my permit at the receptionist who looked a little sheepish, but I forgave him his treachery when he later brought my long-awaited hot water and green tea up to my room and showed me that I could play Battleships on the TV. I soon got fed up with losing though, and set out to explore my new locale.

Ali was surrounded by sand dunes but it was not the fine sand you would find in a desert or on the beach, but more like the gravel you'd see on a building site. Beyond the dunes were a number of rocky mountains, and even further in the distance the white peaks of the Himalayan Chain were just visible on the horizon. I climbed to the top of the tallest sand dune and found dozens of yak and goat skulls. The larger yak skulls with the horns still jutting out from each side had been engraved with intricate writing, and alongside the skulls, prayer flags cracked in the icy wind which whipped up the sand in to my face so that I had to squint to look out across the city.

This was the third largest city in Tibet, yet it appeared to consist of only four roads and a partially frozen river which carried light blue melt-water from the mountains along the outskirts of the city. After inspecting the remains of a few sky burials, I took a walk through the town. Everyone seemed cautious of me, and a group of children actually ran back inside their houses when I turned the corner catching them by surprise. In the market, handicrafts were laid out on cloths, mainly jewellery, but also the handheld prayer wheels that I'd seen so many of the Tibetans carrying as they walked, continually rotating their wrists to make their prayers spin off into the wind and up into the heavens. I was still searching for a Tibetan coat, but could not make myself be understood enough to find out where to purchase one. Instead, I kept getting offered a variety of animal skins including one I suspected to be from the rare and elusive snow leopard.

By now, I was suffering pretty badly from the altitude and as I climbed into bed that night I was feeling extremely nauseous and my breathing was heavy. What little sleep I did get was riddled by some rather disturbing dreams that were just as vivid days later. Although my room had an electric heater, there was still no hot water available in the guesthouse, so I enjoyed another baby wipe wash before heading back out for another day of wandering. Walking down the main road I noticed that there seemed to be pool tables dotted along the pavements of every street. Pool, I soon came to realize, was the Tibetans favourite pastime, and as my travel continued I would discover pool tables outside the most obscure and unlikely locations.

It was that afternoon that I had my first experience of the highly territorial and vicious Tibetan dogs when three of them chased me down a sand dune on my way back to my guesthouse. I only escaped being mauled by scrabbling up on to a wall to safety. As I sat there gasping for breath, the three of them barking and growling and snapping at my heals, a little old lady came out from the shack opposite and began screeching and launching stones at them. After a couple of yelps they scarpered, and I climbed down feeling like a total wimp. I nodded an embarrassed thank you to the lady. She laughed, coughed up a ball of phlegm, and then disappeared back inside her house. Safely back in my room, I figured out how to change the mode on the games menu of the TV from 'moderate' to 'easy', and regained some of my lost dignity by winning a few games of Battleships. I then settled down for an early night in preparation for my flight from Ali, the next day.

8

Twenty-Four Hours
Kargalik to Ali = 1,067km

Knowing the guesthouse owner would report my departure to the police the moment I left, I tried to give myself a bit of a head start by sneaking out before first light. The manager was certainly a man committed to his job, for when I crept down the stairs he was sleeping soundly behind the front desk. I sneaked past him, took great care to close the glass door very gently behind me and hurried down the near-deserted streets with my pack. Just as dawn was breaking, I was heading down the only road east away from Ali.

I had been power walking for half an hour or more when my first lift came along in the form of a dumper truck. He didn't understand where I wanted to go, and I didn't know where he was going, but I climbed up into the seat of his cab nevertheless, offering him a pack of smokes as I did so. As we drove along the tarmac road that weaved through the beige terrain, I attempted conversation using the phrasebook I had bought in back in Bangkok. This wasn't the best idea as whenever I struggled to get my tongue around a word, which was fairly often, his eyes left the road to glance down at the book, and I had to keep reminding him to concentrate on what was up ahead. One saying I had been practicing on my own over the past month was the translation for "Long live the Dalai Lama".

When I said this to him, his eyes widened for a second, and then he smiled at me in a conspiratorial way to show that he appreciated my understanding of his somewhat underground Tibetan life. It was of course a phrase that was strictly forbidden from being spoken in China, and from then on I found that every time I said it to a Tibetan it seemed to instantly gain me a little more trust. I had to be careful to whom I chose to say it of course, for there were always those Tibetans who spied for the Chinese in exchange for an easier life.

Forty-five minutes into the journey the truck driver pulled off the road and pointed up at a track running down from the dunes from which an entourage of trucks identical to his were making a steady progression down to the road and turning back the way we had just come. Sadly, their trucks were laden with man-sized boulders, and ours was empty, and so I guessed this meant it was the end of the road for this particular lift.

I walked on, my feet quickly growing numb and the wind howling down from the icy mountain tops cutting straight through my so-called "Everest gloves" rendering my hands useless. After an hour I took shelter behind a boulder at the side of the road, which did little to protect me from the wind, but was slightly better than walking towards it. I squatted there for the next few hours switching my weight back and forth between the balls of my feet and willing a car to appear on the horizon. As I waited, shepherds appeared from the mountains on either side of the road, and slowly made their way across the dusty ground, chasing and calling at their herds of yaks and goats. When they reached the road, less than 20m away from where I squatted, they crossed and continued their journey across the dust before disappearing into the grooves of the mountains on the other side. None of them spotted me huddled there, nor thankfully did the first car to pass for hours which, as I went to stand up to flag it down, I only at the last moment realized was a police car.

Eventually another car appeared, and I desperately waved for it to stop. There were two men in the back and a woman in the front passenger seat wearing a slightly grubby white puffa jacket. As the two men shifted to make room for me, I gratefully squeezed in beside them. The man driving was old and weathered, the skin on his hands gripping the steering wheel were shiny and hairless and so lined with deep cracks and scars they resembled an aerial view of the Grand Canyon. His fingertips were a dark beetroot colour as if he had slowly worked on getting frostbite his entire life, but while he had managed to keep all his fingers, when he turned and flashed me a hearty grin, I saw that he'd not been so lucky with his teeth – only two remained, both in the front just like Bugs Bunny. The driver spoke a bit of English, which meant he was able to translate some of the questions being thrown at me from the other two men in the car. The woman in the passenger seat remained entirely uninterested in me for almost the entire journey, until via the driver, she asked if I was carrying any spot cream from the West. When I shook my head and said that no, Clearasil was not on my packing list of essentials, she looked disappointed before ignoring me again for the rest of the journey.

After about 45 minutes they indicated that they would be continuing their journey off road, and so once again I was left alone. As they drove away, I puzzled over how they knew where they were. The scenery hadn't changed for so long and there were no tracks the way they were going. I stood on the side of the road and watched the car slowly become a dot in the distance, then disappear over the horizon. As the noise from their engine faded to nothing, I was left in complete and utter silence. I gazed around and saw the remains of a dog. *Not the best of omens*, I thought, staring at its decomposing body for some time, wondering whether it had died of the cold or from starvation.

I lay down in the middle of the road, and using my pack as a pillow tucked into a bag of sultanas, but soon found that my lips were so cracked from the cold that they were bleeding. I wrapped my scarf around my face to protect my lips a little more which was great when I was stationary, but didn't really work when I was back on my feet, as it made it too hard to breathe.

I passed the time waiting for another lift, by taking artistic photos of the empty road stretching from horizon to horizon. It was so straight and seemingly never-ending that it would certainly have made the Roman's blush. I paced up and down collecting discarded glass bottles that I lined up as target practice for an artillery of varying sized rocks. Then, because the silence was driving me a little mad, I began to sing a compilation of songs, anything to save me from the stillness around me. I now understood how people left alone in the desert could be driven insane. Every half an hour or so I would see a car on the horizon, and squint at it, convinced I could see it heading towards me. I'd feel the hope and relief rise in my chest, only to realize after a while it was the same rock formation that I'd mistaken for a car half a dozen times before. The altitude was definitely beginning to play tricks on my mind, and so I started walking again. The wind was blowing towards me and stung every inch of exposed skin. I wrapped my head up as well as I could, and this teamed with the wind screaming in my ears, meant I didn't hear the car until it has already shot past me.

I ran after it waving my arms frantically, until it slowed suddenly a few hundred metres ahead and ground to a halt. As I began jogging towards it, I imagined those inside, debating whether they should pick up someone who was clearly a raving lunatic. But then the car slowly began to reverse towards me. It was an expensive white four-wheel drive and the family inside were Chinese and looked wealthy. I could tell they were slightly dubious about letting me inside, and I couldn't really blame them, but somehow I managed to persuade them and after a few moments hesitation they unlocked the doors and let me climb inside.

We drove on for around two hours, then as the tarmac road came to an end, we began following the dusty tracks of the vehicles that had gone before us, our progression significantly slowed. Some stretches of "road" were just a collection of potholes, and my arms began to cramp from clutching the handles above the windows to stop myself from being ejected from my seat in to the grandpa's lap beside me – I couldn't help but smile at the thought that in the West, the only use people really have for those handles is for hanging their dry-cleaning up.

There was not much talk in the car, but when we eventually pulled up at a building full of children, it was clear the family's destination was a boarding school. It was one of the first buildings I had seen since they had picked me up three hours before, and from the look of the place it seemed to me that attendance was more of a punishment than a privilege. Miles from anywhere, the only views were of dry and desolate landscape, and the building itself was a one-storey, rectangular block, simply built of local materials which made it camouflaged from a short distance away. When a boy appeared from the building, it was clear I'd lost my place in the car, and I was quickly kicked out and charged a 100RMB for the lift.

As the car turned around and headed back the way we came, I continued east on foot. There was no visible road in front of me now, only a line of telegraph poles dotted across the landscape. Figuring that this was my best bet for finding warmth and food, I followed the line of poles for four hours climbing up and down over the heavily trenched ground.

After a while a truck passed me headed in the opposite direction, laden with 20 or so Tibetan workers. The state of the road meant the truck passed slowly enough for me to signal to them for food or water, and I was passed down a bottle of orange-flavoured liquid so sweet I could feel my pupils dilate with each sip. I offered to pay for this donated sugar rush, but the workers wouldn't accept anything from me. I rested for 20 minutes or so, savouring each sip of my gift and slowly felt the circulation return to my back and shoulders. Having pushed through my pain barrier hours earlier, taking my bag off to sit down was a mistake, for my leg muscles instantly seized up, and my shoulders became tender to the touch. Looking ahead in the distance I could just make out what appeared to be a hut. It was probably still a kilometre or more away, but not trusting my own eyes anymore I trudged on, less than hopeful. Upon reaching it I not only discovered that it was real and not a hallucination, but that it was also vacant. It only had two walls that were fully intact and no roof, but it would give me shelter from the wind so it was all that I needed. Unsure of how long it would be until sunset and the pitch-black darkness and paranoia it would bring, I hurried around collecting anything I could burn which mainly seemed to be discarded clothing, something that appeared to be a common source of litter in Tibet. I found some bits of very dry almost fossilised wood and being the skillful bushman that I am, pulled out a can of lighter fluid, doused the lot and chucked on it a lit book of matches. As the fire roared, I squatted beside it and soon my hands were warm again, but my feet remained completely numb and lifeless. I opened the last of my food, a pack of salted nuts, but this was a stupid mistake considering my cracked and bleeding lips which now began to sting painfully.

I looked out across the eastern plains and noticed a large yellow building far away at the foot of some mountains. Thinking it was my mind playing tricks again and that it was just a different shade of rock, I stayed where I was and prepared for a night out in the open. Thinking there was still a chance a truck might come passed though, I delayed putting up my tent and simply sat on a pile of rubble from one of the shack's collapsed walls and looked back the way I had come, wondering how much trouble lay ahead.

When I first saw the truck approach, I did not move, but watched it grow larger through the holes in the walls, half convinced it was a hallucination. Also, if it was a real truck I reasoned, I didn't want the driver to see me too soon, in case he diverted his route to avoid having to pass me. The truck continued to approach though, and I waited until it was close enough for me to read the licence plate number, before jumping out of my shelter and standing in front of it. The driver had little option but to slam on the brakes engulfing me in a cloud of dust. When the truck stopped, the driver got down from his cab and acted as though I wasn't there at all, tweaking around under the bonnet as if to show me that he was stopping anyway for a quick bit of maintenance. *Fair enough*, I thought, and patiently waited until he'd finished. After a few moments he closed the bonnet, and turned to acknowledge my presence before pointing out that he couldn't give me a lift because the truck was already overloaded. There were already two people sharing the cab with him, and the back was piled up with cargo reaching heights greater than its sides. I could see his point. With a bit more convincing however, or perhaps more like pleading, he reluctantly agreed to take me. I was never sure if he just enjoyed watching me grovel or if he was really so reluctant to allow me on board.

After squashing my pack in between the ropes of his load, I squeezed into the cab alongside two women who were already sharing one seat between the two of them. My arrival made things extremely tight, particularly since I usually took up at least twice the space of one Chinese man. We pulled away and it wasn't long before we passed the building I had seen in the distance, which turned out to be relatively modern one with a yellow roof.

Another couple of hours passed before the light faded, and finally feeling warm inside the cab and for once not having the wind forcing my eyes shut, I was actually able to enjoy the remote scenery. When the darkness did come, all we could see was what the head-lights lit up directly in front of us. Every now and again I saw animals' eyes reflected in the beams before they darted for cover. The wheels crunched as they rolled over the thin coverings of ice layering the puddles, and when we reached a frozen river that was around 10m across, the driver only hesitated for a moment before putting his foot back on the pedal to plough through. We all fell silent as we crossed the ice. A few feet from the bank the truck suddenly lurched sideways and I fell against the door, as the ice gave way beneath us. Visions of being crushed beneath the weight of the other people in the cab as water rushed in through the windows flashed through my mind. I was just beginning to panic that I was about to drown as I felt the jolt of the truck wheels hit solid ground once more. Thankfully, the river was shallow and I found myself laughing with embar-rassment as I climbed off the driver's lap and back into my seat. He revved hard on the accelerator and we slowly climbed out and up the bank, and when we were finally on our way again, the driver turned and said something to me, which I assume was something along the lines of, "You big f**king girl!"

We stopped at a small village not far from the river, where everyone else went inside a restaurant and ate noodles. Even though I was giving up my first chance of a hot meal all day, I seemed to have lost my appetite, so

I stayed with the truck and more importantly my pack, staring up at the night sky. It was like nothing I had ever seen before. The moon was nearly full, so bright and clear, and the stars – well I thought I'd seen a starry night, but this was in an entirely different league. The Milky Way smeared the night sky like a smudge on a blank TV screen and the whole sky was tinged with pink. I didn't have to wait for a shooting star, there was a war going on up there – streaks frazzled across the blackness everywhere I looked. Astronomy had never been one of my strong points. I did have a telescope once but the cloud of pollution and the bright lights over London had prevented me from seeing anything, so I'd taken to using it to spy on my neighbours instead. Now as I looked up, the only constellation I recognized was Orion's Belt. I didn't need to know any more than that though; they were all right there. I could see them so clearly standing out from the other stars I could almost see the imaginary lines linking them. There were planets visible too, the rings looping them totally clear to the naked eye. When the driver and other passengers returned to the truck and we carried on our way, I sat back and wallowed in one of the most amazing natural highs I had ever known.

I knew I was acclimatizing to the altitude well when the driver was forced to wind down his window to let more oxygen inside to get his cigarette lighter working again. It must have been at least two in the morning when the truck stopped at my destination, the village of Darchen. The driver, in a hurry to get back to the warmth of his cab, pointed to a few faint glowing lights in the distance, then explained with hand gestures, that I couldn't walk straight towards the town because of all the streams and ditches, and instead I would have to walk around until I met the path. The light came from within the shadow of the mountains and the moon shone over the top of the range from behind. One mountain stood out much taller than the others almost as though it was guarded by the shorter ones. Capped with white, its four faces seemed almost hand-chiselled and I suddenly started craving a bar of Toblerone. Guessing that this had to be Mount Kailash, which at 6,656m was regarded by many as the holiest mountain in the world, I thanked the driver and began walking towards the light.

I tripped and fell a few times before I found the path, and I could already hear dogs barking as I walked through the gateway into Darchen. The buildings of the town were still a few hundred metres off, and I was now completely engulfed in shadows. Hearing the dogs around me, but not being able to see them, I decided it was probably best to wait until daylight before entering the town, so I pulled out my sleeping bag, and curled up by the gate.

After about 20 minutes of trying to sleep, I realized that no matter how heavy my eyes were I was never going to drift off since my upper body was shaking so violently from the cold. My sleeping bag, I should perhaps mention, was a tropical one with a -5C rating written on the inside tag. So arming myself with hand-fuls of rocks I started to creep towards the one visible light at the edge of town. I hadn't gone more than 30m before the first dog snapped at my feet, and before I knew it, I was surrounded. I couldn't see them properly in the dark and they were moving so fast and making so much noise that I couldn't work out where they were or how many of them there were. By now I had thrown all my stones and had failed to hear a single yelp. They had moved in so close I could feel their coats brushing against my legs, then I felt the first bite in the back of my calf. Abandoning any attempt to remain calm, I ran shouting and kicking the air, until I reached the light under which was a door. I banged on it frantically but there was no answer. I turned around to find most of the pack had gone, and only a few persistent dogs remained growling at me from a distance. I realized that the door I was banging on belonged to a shop, so I banged louder in the hope that someone would hear in one of the neighbouring buildings and come to offer some assistance. No one did, and I realized that now there were only two routes I could take – one was impassable thanks to all the ditches and streams that surrounded the town, and the other was back the way I had just come.

Using what little energy I had left, I gathered the stones lying around the doorway. My legs were numb below the knee by now and I'd not been able to feel my toes for at least 20 hours. I hadn't got far before the pack burst out from between the dark buildings, once again in full force. There were no warning snaps this time. I took bites to my ankles and calves, and as I fell to my knees felt teeth puncture my wrist. I called out for help while trying to fight back, lashing out with my fists but never making contact. I managed to get back on my feet and landed a few kicks to the ribs, but they were so quick and I was so tired. I stumbled on shouting for help and clambered up some huge stone steps onto a narrow foot bridge where the dogs couldn't reach me for the steps seemed too steep and uneven for them to continue their attacks with ease. Up on the bridge I had the advantage it seemed and they were no longer able to launch their fast in and out attacks from all sides and the attack finally came to an end. I checked myself over. I had bruising to my legs but only one bite had actually broken the skin, this was partly thanks to my ever-faithful thermal underwear. They had drawn blood on my wrist but it wasn't deep. Now mentally and physically on the verge of collapse, I once again pulled out my sleeping bag and was then able to sleep, dangerously peacefully, for an hour or so on the frozen bridge.

After the Tsunami

Chilling in a cave Laos

The Apple Brandy Day -River like mercury

On the bus that smuggled me into Tibet

Tibetan bearded monk....an unusual sight
worthy of a photo

Snow blinded with my bin liner feet

Saga where i phoned mum and saw a mirror
for the first time in weeks

Burnt, dehydrated and hungry but happy

Everest base camp

Between Everest Base Camp and Advanced
Camp looking towards the glacier

Taking a break at top of valley climb. Annnapurna

The kitchen in the cave

Showing some kids digital photos, possibly
for the first time

The boys that ambushed us with snowballs

The Tibetan prostrating

9

Mount Kailash

Ali to Darchen = 256km

As daylight broke the village sprang to life and I awoke to the bemused stares of two young brothers. Acting as though I often woke up on frozen bridges in foreign lands, I yawned and stretched exaggeratedly, only to feel a tearing sensation on the skin beneath my arms. I realized then that the sweat I'd accumulated from being in the warmth of the cab last night, had frozen. It was a strange sensation rather than a painful one, and I smiled to myself making the deep cracks in my lips reopen, and a warm rush of blood run down into my mouth. Both my legs had pins and needles, and so I steadied myself on the low wall of the bridge as I forced myself to my feet.

I'd been told there was only one guesthouse in Darchen with an Aliens' permit. Upon investigation, I guessed it was the biggest and most modern looking building I could see with two four-wheel drives parked outside. As enticing as a bit of home comfort was right then, I also knew that checking in there would inevitably lead to another meeting with officials, and so I searched around the village and found a family compound where they had a room reserved for pilgrims.

I gulped down noodles and yak butter tea with my feet virtually on top of the open fire, which was burning in the middle of the main room. My feet were still entirely numb from the cold, and it had been so long since my last hot meal that it took me a while to realize that my socks were on fire. I managed to put them out before any lasting damage was done, but the socks were beyond repair – although I did keep them as a souvenir.

Like all the buildings around, this one was built from a mud and dung type mixture, although you could not tell this from the inside, as wooden beams ran along the ceilings, and the walls were entirely covered with blue and white hangings, some adorned with the familiar Swastika and multi diamond pattern I'd noticed all over Tibet. All the furniture was well-kept and varnished, and the only thing that spoilt the room's authenticity, was a tacky and faded framed poster of the Statue of Liberty which hung in pride of place. The man of the house was out when I arrived, so I sat with two women; one I presumed was the mother of the four children who lay huddled sleeping on a single bed by the window; the other was far older, possibly the grandmother, and stared at me in a curious way, returning my smile with one of her own accompanied by an insane cackle. They were friendly and welcoming enough, but I couldn't help but look slightly disgusted when one of the women paused mid-sentence to wipe her nose along the fabric on the back of a chair, leaving a long glistening snail trail.

My room was back across the courtyard. It had four beds inside but I seemed to be the only guest. In the centre of the room was a huge furnace equipped with a full bucket of dried goats' poo which was used for fuel. There was one tiny window looking out on nothing but miles of barren landscape that ran all the way to the Himalayas on the horizon. The walls and ceiling were covered in blue, white and red plastic sheeting, which reminded me of a French meat market. At the end of the metal bed were three heavy-duty blankets, and after straining to pull my boots off my feet, I climbed fully-clothed under all of them, pulled my hat down over my eyes, and fell into a deep sleep that would last long in to the following day.

It was nearly 24 hours later that I came out of hibernation, to find I had frozen nose hair and my eyelashes were frozen to my face. I could feel my feet again though, which was a huge relief. I rubbed and checked the little button sized thermometer that was attached to my penknife case.

The needle was stuck on its lowest mark, minus 10 degrees centigrade. After another eye-watering moment defrosting my nostrils, I put a lighter to the inside of my boots to melt the layer of frost which had gathered on the insoles, then left to find the toilet, which was conveniently located next door. It was a roughly cut hole at the top of eight loose stone steps, with just a low wall to conceal your modesty. Below the hole was a pile of human faeces big enough to fill a wheelbarrow, and a few dogs were hanging around the base looking hungrily up at me. To their disappointment, all I needed was a good long wee, but unfortunately the walls were not tall enough to protect my modesty and I was aware as I turned my back away from the house that I may as well have been peeing off a podium for everyone to see. Spotting that the area around the hole was cracked and crumbling I spread my legs as wide as I could either side of it, in fear of falling through, however soft the landing would have been. Later, I was sitting by my solitary window staring out towards the Himalayas, when one of the women strolled past, walked about 50m from the house and began to squat. I stared at first, wondering what she was doing, until I noticed the puddle slowly developing around her ankles. *Ahhhh...* I thought, now that would have been much easier.

The next few days were spent preparing myself for the three to four-day trek around Mount Kailash, a clockwise circular pilgrimage around the base of the mountain which people come from all over the world to complete – the Tibetans call it a Kora. Some truly devout pilgrims do the entire circuit while prostrating themselves every few feet, but on balance I felt that just walking the 32 miles (52km) around it would be enough for me.

I finally managed to buy my long searched for Tibetan coat along with some cheap sunglasses to protect my eyes from the glare of the snow, at the stores within the village. I stocked up on tinned food and sugary sweets, and then spent time enjoying the village of Darchen, playing pool with the locals on the outdoor tables and lobbing snowballs at random targets.

As I wandered around, I noticed a number of decapitated dogs' heads littering the ground outside buildings. I didn't think much of it until I went to the restaurant that I had started to frequent at lunchtime. It never had a choice of menu, I just ate whatever was placed in front of me – as long as it was hot and it didn't come back up again, I didn't much care. I was halfway through a meal of thick pasta and mincemeat, when I noticed I was being stared at more than usual by the family who ran the restaurant. Even the teenage girl, who up until then had been irritating me by repeatedly playing the ring-tones on her retro mobile phone, now seemed to be awaiting my response to the dish. I gave my usual "Mmmm!" followed by a thumbs up, and this seemed to satisfy them all. It then dawned on me that this was almost definitely dog I was eating. It was tasty, if a little stringy I thought, but that may have just been the way it was cooked. I only hoped it was one of my attackers from the previous night.

When I wasn't enjoying a very cold bottle of Lhasa beer in the restaurant, or braving the low temperatures to sit around and people-watch, I was inside the family quarters where I was staying, watching them go about their daily lives. It was tough, but they always seemed to wear a smile. The two men of the house, a man in his 50s and an older man I presumed to be his father, chatted to me in Tibetan while continuously topping up my cup with more tea, seemingly unbothered by the fact I rarely knew what they were saying. Once when we ran out of water, I was sent with the grandmother to fetch some more. She armed me with a bent scrap of metal piping and instructed me to follow her. We headed out of the house and towards the foot of the hills. It was a slow journey, as Grandma had a badly hunched back which forced her to walk doubled over, as if in constant search of a contact lens.

At the bank of one of the semi-frozen streams, she pointed at me and then at the ice. I took this to mean, "Destroy!" and began smashing at the frozen surface with the metal pole, but this only resulted in us both getting covered in a load of slushy ice. She shook her head and hobbled over to me with a look of absolute disgust at my incompetence, then taking the pole from my hands began stabbing at the edges of the ice until she had made a fist sized hole. Then, under careful instruction this time, I used the hole to lever up the ice sheet until a thick slab broke off. My job was to then carry this block of ice which I estimated to weigh about 25kg, back to the house. By the time we got there walking at the grandmother's pace, my hands were a bluey-purple colour.

Inside, the ice was put onto a tray that was positioned and fastened above the fire and which at one end was curved into a funnel, this collected the melting water and fed it down into a large cooking pot that eventually boiled the water and from there this water was then collected and put into a dozen Thermos flasks to keep warm. Once all this was done, and we had sat back down again for more tea, Grandma explained to the others what had happened while we had been collecting the ice, and they all had a good laugh at my expense.

I hadn't actually dared to go for a number two at the long drop toilet yet, and waited until after dark to try. But as soon as I got into position, I heard movement below and realized it was the dogs. I tried to shoo them away from my podium, asking them for a bit of privacy and patience, but they clearly didn't speak English, so I did the deed and then listened to them all fight over the spoils. I wanted to leave the scene of the crime as quickly and quietly as possible, but this was too much to be hoped for, as just as I stood up to cover my bare white behind, one of the women came out to see what all the noise was about. I'm not sure who was more embarrassed.

On the morning of my departure, I emptied my pack of everything I didn't think I would need, and then spent

45 minutes strapping my feet up in bin liners and electrical tape. The whole family came out to wave me off, and I'm pretty sure Grandma was mumbling something along the lines of, "We won't see him again," as I waved them goodbye.

I set off in a westerly direction and then eventually picked up the trail where I stopped to have a nose around some piles of engraved rocks, all stacked neatly at the base of some prayer flags. As I did so, I spotted a group approaching who could only have been westerners. They were the first foreigners I had seen since leaving Simon, so eager to converse in English, I waited for them to catch up. When we finally became within hailing distance, it was clear they were stereotypical "Adventure Travellers", equipped in fluorescent North Face jackets, designer sun hats and trekking socks, with telescopic walking poles and two porters carrying their bags. They were a group of four, a strange mix of two young American women, a German man and a guy from Holland. I'm not entirely sure what they thought when they saw me standing there, feet wrapped in bin liners with no guide or porter to carry my bag. I'm assuming they thought I was a bit weird, but that was nothing new to me, and we chatted for a few minutes. They explained that they were on a government tour from Lhasa and had been driven straight from the former capital the day before. They had a local guide with them, but their driver, they told me, had decided to stay in Darchen until they returned – apparently, in addition to the permit to make the Kora around Mount Kailash, they had been forced to pay for permits for every region they had driven through. They were slightly bemused by the fact that I had no permits, no guide and no map. But my theory was that if people had been doing this for hundreds of years it couldn't be too hard to follow a trail and walk around the base of a mountain. Obviously, that wasn't quite how it worked, but while I was perhaps a little naïve and lacking in resources, this lot were most definitely the epitome of "all the gear and no idea". I left them to walk on ahead and said I'd see them for dinner at the monastery that night.

I passed a small pagoda as the trail turned north and into a valley gorge. The ground was loose rubble, with a semi-dried-up river running through its centre. The space in between the walls of the gorge was at least two football fields wide, and finding the best route across took time, as without a guide to navigate my route, I found that I could only walk 100m before I was penned in by slushy streams which forced me back again. Although this was frustrating, it made passing each section all the more rewarding. Finally, out of the gorge, I turned a corner and overtook the other travellers who had stopped for a rest. I tried not to look too pleased about this, and scolded myself for not pacing myself given that I had a further 20km to walk that day.

Not long after I passed them, I came to the edge of a frozen lake. I stopped, unsure whether to walk all the way around it or to cut across. Instead, I decided to wait for the group and, more importantly, their guide to catch up and show me the way. To save bracing myself against the icy wind while I waited, I lay down and curled up in the snow in the foetal position. As I waited, I started to think of all the experienced mountaineers who had lost their lives in these harsh conditions, yet I felt so safe and comfortable there in the snow that my eyes grew heavy and I felt like I could have drifted off for a few hours... By the time I realized what was happening, the group had long since passed, and were now just little black dots on the white canvas of the distance. I squinted as they disappeared out of sight, then casting around for their tracks and finding none, I took a deep breath and shouted "F**k it!" before stepping out on to the ice.

It held, and I nervously skated my way across to the other side. I rejoined the trail and passed a few abandoned shacks further along the way. Although they were not permanently occupied, people had clearly spent some time there as the floor was covered in empty tins of spam. It was easy to stick to the route for the rest of the day as, penned in by mountains, there were not many options other than forwards and back. A few times I glimpsed the group far ahead in the distance, but apart from that I saw no one else.

I came to another river far wider than the one I had crossed before – easily wider than the length of a football pitch. I looked at the ice that covered it and wondered if I should walk across. It looked as though I could walk for a little longer this side, but then would hit rock and be forced to walk along the river edges anyway. The other side of the river seemed the more promising, as it appeared to curve round more in the right direction. After a lot of indecision, I went for my second "F**k it!" of the day and once more stepped out onto the ice.

The surface of the river was different from the lake I'd crossed earlier. That had been totally flat, with a light covering of snow which enabled me to slide from one foot to the other all the way across, still leaving enough grip underfoot not to fall. The ice crust of the river was different; it was uneven and zigzagged with ridges. I imagined that from above it would look like a jigsaw puzzle. There were blocks of ice jutting out in places, and where the sun's rays reached down to touch it through the mountains, there was a 2cm layer of water submerging the ice. Unable to quickly skate across, I therefore had to resort to shuffling. I tried to even out my weight a few times by spreading my legs, but immediately slipped due to my bin liner layered boots.

Three quarters of my way across the ice began to creak and groan ominously beneath me. Then on my next step, white lines shot out from beneath my feet in every direction. I was paralysed with fear, unsure of what to do next. My heart in my throat, I held my position like a statue, and let hundreds of thoughts rush through my head. I didn't move from this spot for three or four minutes, then seeing no other option, I gently shifted my weight from one leg to the other, only to see the white lines spread like lightning around me and begin to join up. I knew in situations like this you were supposed to get down on all fours to spread your weight more evenly, but somewhat crazily I reasoned that I didn't want to get wet. Knowing I couldn't remain here like this much longer, I took another step, and felt the ice give way beneath me, and my body began to fall.

I stopped falling with a jolt, and looked down to see my foot had only sunk an inch below the surface of the ice before hitting something hard. Relieved, I shuffled like a penguin to the other side, my feet partly submerged and the remaining ice breaking up around me with each step. Once on solid ground again I let out a huge sigh of relief and looked up and thanked whatever guardians

I had for their ever-watchful eyes. I later found out that one of the porters who was tailing the Adventure Travellers, had in fact watched the whole incident from up ahead, and been in stitches as he watched me panic as the ice began to disintegrate around me. He explained that it had only been the ice that had formed from the previous night – the river below had been frozen solid for decades.

When I reached the monastery, I found it far smaller and less attractive than I had hoped it to be for the last 10,000 steps. I had been imagining high walls, big gates, turrets perhaps, but instead I found a two-storey wind battered concrete building, with a few decorative cloth banners hanging from its walls. Then when I considered that every brick and object it contained would have been carried there the way I had just travelled; I found the respect the place deserved. Climbing on to the roof of the monastery and accompanied by the continual whistling of the wind as it rushed through the valley, I took in my surroundings, and looked back at the route I had just come. I then went down into the communal fire room, where I found the Adventure Travellers tucking into giant bowls of noodles and talking excitedly about their day's trekking. They were not the only group of foreigners in the room, there was also a group of four Japanese trekkers, with their guides and porters. The monks, of whom there were around seven, sat silently on the other side of the room busy with their study, or boiling water for tea and food.

Over a much-needed cup of tea, I chatted to the group I had met first thing that morning. Both the American girls were feeling sick from the altitude and thinking about turning around the following morning as the following day's trek was supposed to be twice as challenging. I was quizzed on my coat by one of them. She couldn't understand why I would buy a coat like the locals when the designer brands were so cheap in China. "You're not seriously going to wear that in London?" she said.

Thankfully, it was all too much for the American girls; they went to bed early, and the next morning did indeed, quit the trek and return to Darchen. The Japanese, who had kept themselves to themselves all night, also retired early. This left the porters, the monks, the Dutchman, the German and me, all sitting around the fire in the centre of the room. Feeling perhaps a little less intimidated, or maybe just preferring the padded seats to the bench on which they had all been perching, the monks then came and sat by me, allowing me to watch them more closely. On what seemed to be hand-pressed paper, they were writing with ink quills and feathers, the likes of which I'd only ever seen in historical BBC TV programmes, or on school trips to palaces, where weird looking grown-ups in period dress spoke in funny voices and freaked me out.

The monks were writing scriptures, each line perfectly scribed with not a drop of ink wasted or smudged. I watched in fascination, aware that I was witnessing a nearly lost art form, being kept alive before my eyes. Tibetan writing is the most beautiful I have seen any-where in the world. It is written as one almost unbroken line, with lots of downward strokes. While most of the monks seemed to be in their mid-30s with just one older, in his 60s, there was one young monk of no more than 10 years old among them. He didn't seem to be busy doing anything, so I started showing him some tricks with a matchbox and a coin. He broke into a fit of giggles when he couldn't work out to where the coin was disappearing. Sadly, the other monks brought this to an almost immediate halt, after shooting him looks of disapproval. The child monk backed away from me a bit after that, clearly worried he might get into trouble. This seemed a bit unfair to me, but of course I didn't say anything and could only apologize for leading him astray. I felt sad for him though; he may have been a monk living in an adult world adhering to a strict code of conduct, but he was still a child, and every child deserves a childhood.

Leaving the monks to their duties, I began to talk to the Dutch guy, and for some reason began comparing phrasebooks. I was shocked by just how detailed and graphic his was, with some truly bizarre translations. One in particular was the translation for not only, "I would like to have sex," but, "I would like to have sex without contraception". I told him that surely by the time that topic of conversation came up with a Tibetan woman, you'd be beyond the necessity of a phrasebook!

I was amused, as when we fast approached our 20th cup of tea, the German and Dutch guys told me that they could tell when they first met me that day that I knew what I was doing and clearly had experience in trekking. I smiled and took the compliment, failing to enlighten them to the fact that my experience amounted to a whole week.

That night we all slept side-by-side and head-to-toe on the floor of a single room. I woke to the sound of the others packing up in the dark, their bright head torches flashing in my eyes as they prepared for the new day. *They're keen*, I thought, as I pulled my sleeping bag tighter around me and fell back to sleep.

When I finally arose it was only just light, but I later found out that it's best to start when the snowfall from the night before is still hard, because it only gets more difficult to walk as the snow gets softer. I collected my boots from the grill of the fire, and was pleased to feel that they were once more dry. After reapplying another layer of fresh bin liners and duct tape, I set off for day two.

The snow overnight had been heavy and each step was greeted with a loud crunch. At first, I was able to follow the footprints of my more well-informed friends ahead, but as I reached the more boulder-concentrated part of the trail, I began to lose them. Once I reached the top of the first pass, I took guilty pleasure in relieving myself in the snow, leaving a stain on the otherwise flawless surroundings. The first few hours were spent going up and down and over rocky, snow-covered terrain. Each time I looked up and around at the imposing mountains, I felt very small, and as if my progress was very poor. The snow quickly became deeper, and soon I was wading along with the snow up to my knees and my feet once more totally numb.

Every so often I would step straight into a hole blanketed by the snow, and find myself buried up to my armpits and spluttering up white powder. With the weight of the collapsing snow on top of my bag, this quickly lost its comedy value, as each time it would take me a minute or so to haul myself back out again, sometimes only to take another few steps before making a repeat performance. I realized that if I fell badly at any point and broke a leg, no one would come looking for me for a very long time and the reality that I could die where I fell was a very sobering thought.

A few times I was forced to stop and walk round in circles searching for footprints. This was usually when my compass and the landscape disagreed as to which way I should go. Then the snow began to fall once more, impairing my vision and making it nearly impossible to spot any old tracks. I'd been told last night, that today we'd encounter a 500m pass made up almost entirely of snow, but nothing could prepare me for actually seeing it. I wouldn't have even considered it passable had it not been for the scars left in the snow on the near-vertical slope by that morning's climbers, and would probably have continued on in the wrong direction and got lost. Perhaps my lie in had been a blessing after all. Even with the evidence staring me in the face, I checked around for more tracks, just to make sure they weren't just the tracks of a yeti.

When all I could find were the prints of a large dog, I sighed and started climbing. For every three steps I took, I slipped back down two. Large chunks of compacted snow would come free as I placed my foot down, taking my other leg out in the process and planting me head first into the snow. Each time I fell, I felt such relief from the weight being taken off my legs, that it was a challenge to pry my eyes back open again and force myself back onto my feet. The higher I climbed, the thinner the air became. For every five steps I took I had to stop for 20 seconds to catch my breath. As I began to feel more and more lightheaded, I knew I should stop for a rest, but having got used to the feeling, I pushed on until I was overcome with tunnel vision and fell to my knees and on to my side.

I released the straps on my pack and rolled on to my back gasping for oxygen, my sunglasses sliding off as

I did so, forcing me to squeeze my eyes shut against the blinding glare from the snow. I took a dozen or so long deep breaths, before feeling around to retrieve my glasses. When I was finally able to open my eyes again, I saw that my pack had slipped 10 or 15m back down the slope, a sight which brought me a crushing sense of devastation. I briefly considered leaving it there and continuing without the extra weight, but once I'd come to my senses, I realized I had to slide back down to get it. When I reached it, I felt like throwing a big tantrum and giving my pack a good kicking, but since I barely had the energy to lift it back up, I once more began the slow ascent. On I went for what seemed like forever, and each time I thought I had reached the top, it turned out to just be another edge. It took close to an hour and a half to make it to the top, which I finally knew I'd reached when I encountered engraved rocks and prayer flags. I began a little victory dance around them, went dizzy and tripped over one of the piled collections of rocks.

I'd hoped the way down the pass would be the same as the way up, only a little less steep, as I wanted to try descending with some commando style leaps. This wasn't to be the case. After a 20-minute walk across the top of the pass I came to the top of a lagoon. Above me in all its glory was the hidden side of Mount Kailash. Its crowned white peak shone proudly, and at that moment I could well believe there might be gods living up there. I paused for a moment and stared in wonder at the temple of nature that surrounded me, appreciating the fact that this was somewhere that no amount of money could bring you, only time and effort. In my exhilaration, I felt like the first person to ever see it. When I thought about how many pilgrims had made this journey of devotion, I felt even more humbled to be standing there, almost like I'd just been granted entry into a secret club. Religious or not, this was a place that deserved to be worshipped.

For the descent from the pass a trail weaved its way down to the ice floor, each turn a hairpin with a steep and unforgiving drop either side. I kept reminding myself to pay more attention to where I placed my feet on the narrow path, until I took one corner too quickly and slipped, sending half my legs over the edge, forcing me to claw along the snow on my belly to regain safe ground. I didn't have to remind myself to be careful after that.

Around 20m from the bottom, I spotted a patch running down to the base with no visible rocks. I couldn't resist. Dumping my pack on to the ground, I sat on top of it, gave myself a little push and began to toboggan down. Having misjudged quite how steep the run was, I picked up speed far quicker than I had expected, and I was too busy "Wooohooing!", to notice that the bottom of my hill in fact led to a vertical drop. I flew off the edge and came to an abrupt halt with a mouthful of snow and a ripped coat, my shouts of delight still echoing around the lagoon.

Getting a face full of snow made me realize just how badly burnt the underside of my chin already was. After two minutes of shaking snow out of warm places, I began crossing the solid ice of the lagoon floor. The light reflecting off its surface gleamed a salmon pink, and as I tried to look down through its opaque depths, I wondered what secrets lay hidden beneath me.

Sudden gusts of wind filtered through holes in the lagoon walls, and with the added width of my pack

I was nearly blown off my feet a couple of times. I only wished it had been coming from behind me, because I'm sure it would have allowed me to sail effortlessly across to the other side. It took a while to cross the expanse of ice, partly because I wasn't really sure where I was going. The exit hadn't been visible from where I'd crash-landed and didn't reveal itself until after I had crossed the ice completely. As I walked out of the lagoon, I found myself standing at the top of a valley, and half expected to hear a wall, slide closed behind me.

From there my options seemed to be limited to staying where I was, or descending. I chose the latter of course, and using a steep semi-frozen stream as my path, began to make my way down. After 45 minutes of bracing myself on the large boulders either side of the stream while walking on the rapidly melting snow that covered the trickling mineral water below, I made it down with no injuries, but soaking wet feet – my bin liner idea having failed hours earlier, leaving me with huge flapping shreds of plastic hanging from my legs like a ragged Morris Dancer.

Trusting my compass, I headed south at the base of the valley. A river ran through the middle and I decided to cross the river there, where it appeared to be completely frozen. I later realized it was a lucky decision to have made, as further up the valley around a corner, I saw that I would have needed to cross over anyway, where the river was 10 times the width and half thawed. Walking on, I saw a huge towering monastery built into the side of the valley ahead. There were at least six turrets rising from it; windows lined the walls and stone steps led around the perimeter of the building. A drawbridge, half up, dominated the centre and I could see the little red dots of the monks moving around the grounds and so, relaxing in the knowledge that I would reach the monastery before dark, I rested for a while. I sat down on a rock and scooped up mouthfuls of snow to quench my thirst (something I have since learnt is not a good idea, as your body wastes more energy warming the snow than you can absorb from the liquid). I held my cold hands to my scorched face, and watched as my sunglasses steamed up.

Continuing on towards the imposing monastery, peculiarly I noticed the wreck of a Volkswagen Beetle on the opposite side of the river, but thinking little of it I continued on at a lazy pace. Then, further up on my side of the river, I saw two first aid tents. I was sure I could see a cross on the roof of one of them and I was no more than 10m away before I realized that these tents were, in fact, just two round boulders and in no way even resembled what I had imagined. The closer I got to the monastery, the more its shape seemed to shift, until I realized I was just staring up at a plain rock face. There was no monastery, no Volkswagen Beetle. I now realized my oxygen-starved brain was hallucinating.

More annoyed that I had wasted time dawdling than the fact that I was mentally sick, I hurried on, and two hours later, just as the light was fading, I reached the real monastery. It was very basic in design and looked more like an army barracks than the mirage I'd seen, but it was real, and I was so glad to have reached it in time. When I entered, I was greeted with a friendly round of applause. The groups had been worrying about me and had been debating whether or not to send their guides back to look for me. Around the fire that night we shared our first aid kits, compared sores and blisters, and of course drank more tea.

The third day was relatively easy for it was a simple 15km over fairly level ground, so no one was off before dawn this time. Everyone still got a good hour's head start on me though. I was able to catch the Japanese up easily, as one of them had twisted an ankle. We walked back together and when we were about 2km away from Darchen, their driver appeared in their Land Cruiser, bringing gifts of Coca-Cola and Cadbury's milk chocolate, which they shared with me. Never did I think one small square of chocolate could taste so good. I returned to my lodgings with the family, who seemed pretty surprised that I'd returned – apparently they'd not been over confident in my abilities, and that night I met up with the rest of the travellers for dinner and enjoyed plate after plate of momos (a sort of dumpling), and lots and lots of Lhasa beers.

10

Civilization

Distance travelled from Khao Lak = 9,486km

Lying snug under my blankets the next morning, I had to decide whether to stay in Darchen another day and recover, or force myself up and on. My aching body begged me to stay and rest a while longer, but it was my mums' birthday in a few days' time, and I wanted to try to reach a phone. Ignoring the pleading of my limbs, I forced myself up and out of bed, packed up, waved goodbye to the family, and set off east once more.

About a kilometre outside Darchen, I came across an old man sitting in the dirt alongside a well-maintained motorbike. A goat was tethered across the back of it and he said that for 150RMB he would take me to the next village. After a lot of haggling, using a stick in the dirt, we agreed on 50RMB. He was certainly a skilled driver, as despite having my pack between his legs, me on the back and the goat squirming about behind me throwing the occasional hoof into my spine, he drove as if he were the only one aboard, bouncing out of the potholes and swerving deftly around random mounds of frozen soil without a care in the world.

As we approached the next village, I saw a huge crowd of people staring out across the land. I squinted in the same direction and at first thought it was just an approaching dust storm, but then the crowd started shouting and cheering as whatever it was moved closer and I saw what exactly was causing the cloud of dust. Ahead of it were around 30 Tibetans on horseback, all galloping at full speed. Their clothing was more colourful than normal, reminiscent of the jockeys at the Grand National, presumably for the same reason of making themselves identifiable to the gathered crowd, who were now jumping up and down in excitement. Soon they were galloping almost parallel to us, and even through the vibrations and revs coming from the motorbike, I could feel the pounding of the stallions' hooves vibrating through the dry ground. There seemed to be no chivalry among the riders as they rode tightly bunched together, deliberately cutting each other up with arms and legs flailing out to hinder their rivals' progress. I was so caught up in what I was witnessing, I barely noticed when my driver simply drove around the checkpoint in front of us, where the guards, were likewise too engrossed in the race to notice our detour or me at all. I laughed at this. A movie director would have needed a million takes to get the timing as precise as it had just been for me.

This seemed to be a race of stamina and tactics as much as speed, and the race skimmed the edge of the village and then continued across the plains towards a mountain range in the north. I watched them, until they disappeared into a distant yellow cloud. Once the dust settled, my driver dropped me off outside the house he was visiting and pointed me on my way.

Still a little nervous about being so close to a checkpoint, I walked to the outskirts of the village to sit and await my next ride, entertaining myself by watching packs of mini twisters spin their way across the dirt. I assumed this must be a fairly normal sight here, since everyone else carried on about their business without paying them any attention, but it was enough to keep me amused for the next few hours of waiting. I wondered what would happen if one actually hit the village, and how much power they really carried, but none did and before long an army truck arrived.

When I first saw it, I was not sure whether to hide from it or wave it down, but given that it was the first vehicle to pass in many hours, I took the chance. Inside, there were a couple of soldiers in green ill-fitting uniforms, who it turned out were happy to give me a lift as far as Hore, free of charge. I was excited, not only was Hore on the map, but it was somewhere I'd heard of because it was supposed to have a hot spring. My luck was clearly in, because sandwiched between the soldiers in the cab of the truck we were waved through two more checkpoints without even slowing down. It dawned on me then that everyone was so scared to be seen questioning the system, that no one really knew anything about the rules that did not directly affect them. Since the soldiers were not aware that the guards at the checkpoints would want to see my paperwork and stop my travel, they simply didn't mention me and we sailed on through.

Having found somewhere to stay in Hore, I discovered that there didn't appear to be a toilet anywhere on the premises, so straight after dumping my bag on the bed, I went off in search of a bush and then for a dip in the hot springs. The springs turned out to be some distance from the village, and when I arrived, I was surprised to find three Tibetan women there – two still submerged in the water, and the third totally naked and in the process of starting to get dressed. I stared at her for a few moments, unable to hide my surprise at the colour of the skin beneath where her clothes would usually be, for it was whiter than mine. It had never occurred to me before that those parts of their bodies not exposed to the elements on a daily basis, would be so pale. She was not at all embarrassed by my sudden appearance or my stares, and made no attempt to immediately cover up. Feeling extremely awkward, I pretended to be lost and briskly walked off in the opposite direction.

By sunrise the next morning I was already waiting by the side of the road, having left Hore in the dark not wanting to miss any cars that might be passing through. I sat there in the relentless wind, cold, hungry, blinded by the sand and bored out of my mind for the next eight hours.

Not a single car passed. I found myself thinking about how I had ended up there. At 19 years old, sat in the cold wind in this remote location and unsure where I was going both that day and in life, and where my determination to visit Tibet had even come from, where it had begun. I thought about the first time I had come across the whole "Free Tibet" movement.

I had been 13 at the time, and out exploring the streets of London with three school friends. Whether we were actually supposed to have been in school at the time or not, I can't remember, but I do know we had just spent hours at Piccadilly Circus pouring money into arcade machines, only to receive paper tokens which we could then exchange for stupid looking key rings and novelty lighters. We were just making our way to Trafalgar Square when we found ourselves blocked by barriers at the side of the pavement. Then from around the corner came a crowd of protesters marching and chanting, "Free Tibet, Free Tibet!" Some were holding up banners and others were flying the Tibetan flag above their heads. We had no idea what they were talking about, but they were heading in the direction we wanted to go, so we climbed over the barriers and joined in. Weaving our way through the mob, I was handed a flyer by a young woman who, looking back, I think must have been a student. She then proceeded to give me a quick but informative talk on what it was we were shouting about, and then on we went to Trafalgar Square. By the time we got there, my friends had lost interest already, but I ended up climbing up on the back of one of the giant lions there and listening with interest to the whole speech of the leader of the marches. The next morning on my early morning daily paper round, I was putting a copy of a national newspaper through a letterbox and I saw there on the front page were photos of the march and an article about it on their front page, and there I was sat atop the lion in the background.

I waited by the side of the road in Hore for most of the day, but hunger took me back to the town, and I stopped in the first place I came across so that I could return to the same spot the moment I'd finished eating. While awaiting my noodles and meat, I spotted a little hand mirror, and having not seen my reflection since leaving Kashgar, I picked it up, and immediately nearly dropped it again. The person staring back at me was not one I'd ever seen before. My hair was matted at the front and back from having a hat permanently on my head. My lips were swollen, bleeding and scabby, the whole of my face below my eyes was leathery, dark red and purple, wrinkles ran from my nose and mouth, and cracks lined my cheeks. I had aged 10 years in 10 days!

When the cook returned with some tea she saw me staring in disbelief at the mirror. Smiling, she beckoned me over to another room, where I found a full-length mirror. When she returned to the kitchen to check on some food, I braved the cold air of the room and removed my thermal vest for the first time in weeks. I had already noticed that my fingertips and toes had turned a dark red, but now I saw my chest in the centre was the colour of rhubarb and I was bruised all around the base of my ribs. I ate my meal in shock, amazed that I actually looked as much of a wreck as I felt, then returned to my spot on the road for another four hours without success before reluctantly settling back in to the same room in which I had started my day. By candlelight, I squeezed an entire tube of Savlon onto my face. There was no need to rub it in – my parched skin absorbed it all in seconds.

Once more I set off on foot before sunrise. To avoid walking directly into the wind, I spent the first two hours walking backwards, something that is far harder to maintain than I had imagined, but worth the trouble simply to not have my face in the wind for once.

After a few hours a car full of monks finally pulled over and took me some distance east. Maybe they had all taken a vow of silence, but I felt I had only been picked up because they felt a sense of duty and they didn't speak to each other or to me for the duration of the journey. My lift ended when they turned north towards the mountains, and I was glad to get out, preferring the pure silence of the planes than the awkward one in the car.

Saga was the next town marked on my map. I already knew something of the place as both groups I'd met around Mount Kailash had warned me the checkpoint on the road leading to Saga was heavily guarded and difficult to pass. They had all had their permits scrutinized and their bags thoroughly searched before being allowed through. Given that I was coming from the opposite direction, I reasoned I might be able to reach Saga itself before any checkpoint. Although the Japanese reckoned that if I was willing to make a large detour away from the road, it might be possible to walk right around it. I was optimistic, therefore, especially as I would be coming from the area they were supposed to be stopping me from entering anyway.

So when a three-car convoy of rich Chinese turned up and told me they were heading for Saga, I was excited. Each car contained just one driver which I thought strange. Given the general Tibetan hatred for the Chinese, I wondered if this was perhaps a matter of safety in numbers. Despite there being more then 15 seats spare between the three Land Cruisers, I was asked to pay, although being businessmen they were open to negotiation. I wasn't really in a position to argue, stood there alone in the wind and snow miles from anywhere, but I still managed to bring the price down a fair bit before we set off. I climbed into the front seat of one of the four-wheel drives, and as soon as I closed the door, the welcome warmth lulled me into a deep sleep.

I awoke to darkness and the feeling of the car slowing to a halt. "Are we in Saga already?" I asked, and was met with mocking laughter. Apparently, Saga was still a day's drive away and we were only in the next village – just another place that did not exist according to my map. Over dinner in a local restaurant, I couldn't actually understand what was being said, but it was clear that my travelling companions felt themselves superior to the locals. Their body language and the way they snapped orders at the hostess, made me feel embarrassed to be with them. It was no wonder that the Tibetans hated the Chinese, I thought, if they couldn't even show a little common courtesy when they passed through.

At the end of the meal, one of the drivers produced a bill of huge denomination that was probably more than the owner earned in a month. When she was unable to give change for it, he then proceeded to make an enormous fuss, and she ended up having to rush around to all her friends in the village to borrow money. When she finally handed him the change, I noticed that the obnoxious asshole actually had enough smaller bills in his wallet to have paid her with in the first place. Feeling more embarrassed than ever at the company I was keeping, I ignored the disapproving looks of the Chinese, and made a point of thanking her for her hospitality. We were stopping in the village for the night, and too lazy and tired to get the furnace going in the room I was staying in, I drifted off to sleep with my teeth chattering from the cold, only to wake a few hours later with a mouthful of blood having bitten through my lip.

We were back on the road by 5am. No doubt they would have left without me had I not refused to pay them until we reached Saga and already been up nursing my swollen lip. It was snowing heavily, which significantly slowed our progress. At one point we veered off route and pulled over in a nomad camp to get directions. The nomads' homes were dome-shaped tents, and from what I could see, had just one room, with at least three generations of family all living and sleeping in one space. It surprised me that there were so many children about given that there seemed to be so little privacy. But maybe that's just me being an English prude.

Even so, as I walked around the camp followed by an entourage of children holding their hands out to me for sweets or money, I found myself feeling envious of the simplicity of the nomads' lives. It seemed that they knew what was important in life, and had nothing to prove to anyone. I walked too close to the edge of a tent, and a dog leapt out from the porch making me shriek and jump. The kids behind me burst out laughing, as the dog, which thankfully was chained, strained to snap at me from the entrance. It was one ugly dog. It had no ears and looked to me like an enormous greyhound on steroids with a thick coat, and what I was sure looked like an extra row of teeth. I quickly returned to the warmth and safety of the car after that, and waited for us to be back on our way.

As we drove, we passed the remains of what must have once been grand monasteries, tall stone pillars marking the buildings stature of years gone by. Some were stained black with soot, a result of the Cultural Revolution during which over 6,000 monasteries, which was more than 95 per cent of them, were destroyed with most being burnt down by the Chinese. After passing the third ruin, I begged that we could stop. We did, and

I was able to climb around the ruins for half an hour or so while the drivers stayed in their cars, tapping their watches.

As I stood among the ruins, I imagined how it had once looked before the Chinese invaded. The isolated monks who had studied here would have been totally ignorant of the outside world. I imagined the long journeys people would have made on foot in order to make to contact with them, and to bring them food, supplies and messages.

Horses now grazed on the grass that grew up through the rubble, and I wondered how long before the land swallowed up every trace of this monastery. One day perhaps, Chinese tour buses would pass here down a paved road with no idea that their government had eradicated the Forbidden Kingdom, and all that Tibet once was. As for the passive monks whose blood had probably fallen where I now stood, their lives and existence would never be known to the Chinese with their censored education. But one thing I did know, I thought, as I reluctantly made my way back to the car, was that as long as there are Tibetans in the world reminding people of their plight, this will always be Tibet and never China.

We reached Saga mid-afternoon. There had been no checkpoints arriving in town from the west, which left me able to check into a two-storey guesthouse, possibly the only guesthouse in Saga. I walked in unaccompanied, flakes of dead skin hanging off my face and dry blood crusting my lips, and unsurprisingly was greeted with looks of disgust and suspicion. I was annoyed, because I had not managed to call my mum on her birthday. Nevertheless, after I'd checked in at the guest-house, I set off in search of the local telephone box which I'd been told was the only one for three-days' journey around. As it turned out, because of the time difference, I did actually manage to wish my mum happy birthday on her birthday – albeit at half 11 at night. Even so, she still had the cheek to accuse me of forgetting! We hadn't spoken for four months, although I had kept in fortnightly email contact so the family knew vaguely where I was. It was strange to hear such a familiar voice in such an alien setting. The line must have been tapped, because we got cut off several times, mainly whenever she asked about visas or checkpoints.

Back at the guesthouse, I wanted something quick and easy to eat so that I could spend the last of the daylight hours surveying the checkpoint and figuring out a way around it. Conveniently, the dusty English menu I was given had French Fries, which I ordered with enthusiasm. When they arrived, however, they were more like potato wedges, but they filled a hole. What really tickled me though, was that rather than tomato ketchup, I was given a huge bowl of tomato puree to dip them into. The chef came out to see what I thought. All his staff were standing around watching too, perhaps to see if he really was as capable of cooking the international cuisine of which he boasted. I therefore couldn't disappoint them, and so ate every single wedge smothered in the bitter puree, hardly gagging once.

Saga wasn't a huge town, and it didn't take me long to get a general view of the layout. I cautiously scoped it out, noting the checkpoint further down the road. To the left of it, a mountain base of steep rock ran along the road, and on the opposite side ran a river, beyond which lay a kilometre or more of sand dunes and streams, all penned in by a natural and impassable wall of stone. The sand dunes seemed like my best option for getting past this tactically positioned post. The only potential problem with this route was lying on the border of the town and the sand dunes at the foot of another rock face – a fully staffed army barracks.

Once again, before a new day had dawned, I had crept out of my guesthouse with adrenalin pumping. I scurried across the sand dunes in the dark, and not wanting to use my torch for fear of being caught, I mistook an iced-over stream for a dried-up one, and filled my boots with frozen water. By the time the sun had risen an hour or so later, the checkpoint was far behind me. Thinking I was in the clear and feeling pretty chuffed with myself, I reached a fast-flowing river the colour of a glacier. I began to follow it, and as I did so became increasingly alarmed, for not only was it heading back towards the checkpoint, but it was I realized, the very same river that ran along its barriers. I was trapped!

Deciding that there was no option but to cross the river, I began looking for where it was at its narrowest, and once I found it, began to cross. But a few feet from the water's edge, I quickly sank up to my knees into thick sandy mud, and with each attempt to free myself, sunk ever deeper. As the mud closed over my elbows, I was close to real panic, and just about managed to crawl and claw my way back on to dry land. Thoroughly pissed off, I trudged back towards Saga and the checkpoint.

I was sure I would be spotted now, as I could even make out the guards standing to attention. The army barracks seemed deserted though, so I looped back through town towards the checkpoint, trying hard to think up a story as I went that would explain why I was covered in mud so very early in the morning and why I was even there in the first place. As I approached the checkpoint, I wondered why no one was blowing whistles or shouting at me to halt, then realized the sun was shining directly into the guard's eyes, and that they could barely see the ends of their own noses, let alone a distant blob darting between the sand dunes. Abandoning any attempt at a cover story, I strolled up to the guards and said, "Morning!"

Unsure of what to do, the guards hastily ushered me into the building and on to a wooden bench, where I was instructed to wait, presumably for someone with authority to arrive. I offered around cigarettes, brandishing my now nearly perfected smile of innocence and ignorance, and soon had the guards on my side. When the big man finally arrived, he introduced himself politely, then loudly demanded my passport. He stared down at it intently, then without lifting his eyes held out his hand. "Permit".

My words failed me at this point and I just repeated, "I go to Lhasa". He stared at me, unsure if it was his English or mine that was the problem. He ordered a search of my pack. The guards had clearly been waiting for this and couldn't wait to get stuck in to the task.

Luckily, I'd anticipated this eventuality, and my pack was ready prepared for them with all my dirty laundry and possessions of just sentimental value at the top. When asked about a camera, I showed them a disposable kept in the top pocket, hoping that my digital camera would remain undetected rolled inside my sleeping bag. Strangely, the object that seemed to interest them most was my bowl made from a coconut in Malaysia. They wanted to keep it but I refused, managing to fob them off with a London postcard each instead.

I must have looked, among other things, hungry, and I was soon sitting in the staff quarters by the heater, enjoying a meal of ham, vegetables and egg-fried rice – the most substantial meal to touch my sides in a long time. With a full belly, I sat trying to hide my nerves waiting to find out what would happen next. The big man came over and announced I was leaving. I followed him outside unsure if this was a good thing or a bad thing. Out at the front, a minivan was waiting, containing six soldiers in green uniforms. They were to escort me to Shigatze, the second biggest city in Tibet, and my next destination on my itinerary anyway. So relieved, I departed the Saga checkpoint with no fine, still no permit and a full stomach.

My escorts were all fairly young and in high spirits, so I assumed they must have been on leave and were heading back to the city after weeks spent guarding some remote outpost. The driver of the minivan was appallingly bad. It didn't help that we were heavily overloaded, but when we hit a deep pothole at speed, I was propelled up from my seat and crashed my head hard into the ceiling, before landing back down with such force that the seat underneath me collapsed, crushing the foot of the man behind me. A few miles later, we had a puncture. It was a welcome break and we stopped for dinner in a small village, although when we left, I noticed no one paid. It was obvious from the way they all just got up and left without even a thank you to their hosts, that they were neither expecting or expected to.

As we drove on into the night, the driver's incompetence continued to shine through. He kept losing the road and getting lost and then stopping to get out of the van with his torch and disappearing for ten-minute intervals as he searched for it again. I knew we were approaching Shigatze when the road turned to tarmac. Then as we levelled out on the crest of a hill, I could see the brightly lit modern city ahead. It was now the early hours of the morning and the roads were empty.

I was dropped off at the entrance of a plush hotel and I made the pretence of going inside by starting to walk up the polished stone steps, then with one hand on the door, I waved to them as they turned the corner. As soon as they were out of sight, I about turned, crossed over the road, crawled under a hedge and slept where my head fell.

11

Lhasa

The next morning, I checked into a shared room, which smelt of old people. There were two other beds, one occupied by a man from India and the other a man from Israel. The Israeli had just successfully walked the entire length of the Great Wall of China, and now the pair of them planned to walk across Tibet together. Their departure had been delayed, however, because the Israeli was practically bedridden with tendonitis, and was only able to get about the room using a couple of sticks for support. Lying there among his crumpled sheets, all long hair and beard, all that was missing was Yoko Ono.

I was looking forward to my first shower since Ali, but on entering our shared bathroom it became apparent that the two of them had been there for a while, as it was doubling as a fridge. Bags of food hung from the shower rail and packs of noodles were stacked up beside the toilet. Along the edge of the bath lay a dozen or more half-used bars of complimentary soap.

Once I had used up all of the hot water and washed off my ingrained tan of dirt, I sat down with my new roommates and passed over all the information I had on the route I'd taken across Tibet, and described to them the luck I'd had at the Saga checkpoint. They had also heard of Saga's reputation for being tough to pass through, and weren't best pleased to hear that to walk around it would involve a very long detour indeed. I left them practicing their Tibetan on each other, and went to find a computer in a local internet café where most of the other computer terminals were occupied by teenagers engrossed in playing strategy video games. There I emailed Simon to tell him that I had arrived in Shigatze, and was only a day's travel from Lhasa.

Shigatze is home to the second largest monastery in Tibet, called the Tashilunpo monastery. It is here, along with 800 other monks, that the Panchen Lama officially resides. After the Dalai Lama, the Panchen Lama is the second highest Incarnation in Tibet. However, the one who is enthroned there is not the chosen Panchen Lama of the Dalai Lama and his advisers. In 1995 The Dalai Lama had recognized a six-year-old boy in Northern Tibet called Gedhun Choekyi Nyima as the reincarnation, but the Chinese promptly kidnapped him and his family and he has not been seen since. Instead, with the help of some pro-Chinese monks, the Chinese found their own reincarnation, a boy of around the same age by the name of Gyaincain Norbu and installed him at the Tashilunpo instead. He is rarely at his residence though; spends most of his time in Northern China and is not recognized or respected by most Tibetans.

I spent the rest of the day exploring the monastery. But for me, the highlight was not the monastery itself, but nosing around the smaller buildings that surrounded it where there were no tour parties, only monks learning astrology, medicine and history. I did, however, queue along with the Chinese tour parties to see the century-old 24m-high copper Buddha. Then, when prompted by an elderly monk, I also dropped a slice of butter into one of the lit bowls of floating candles fuelled by the fat from the butter around the chapel, for he explained to me that it would strengthen the light that would lead my soul to its next body.

After I'd had my fill, I left the monastery and walked along its sloping outskirts, where I found the ground littered with the now familiar piles of yak bones and paper trail of printed prayers. Higher up the slope, I saw a group of young Tibetan monks seated on the ground. They invited me to join them, and as I spent the next 40 minutes or so letting them practice their English on me, I noticed that despite the fact that they were all wearing matching red robes, they all wore individual footwear – two had white Reebok trainers, which were clearly their pride and joy.

Suddenly the shrill tone of a Nokia phone burst through the relative silence, and one of the monks leapt to his feet and hastily lifted his robes in search of the mobile phone that was in a black leather pouch, tied around his waist by a piece of string. When I saw this, it looked so out of place that I laughed so hard I nearly tumbled off the ledge on which I was sitting.

The next morning, I agreed to carry a video camera to Lhasa for the Indian, in exchange for him helping me to find the bus station and he bought my ticket for me in fluent Chinese. Eight hours in to the nine-hour journey, we left the dilapidated road we had been bumping along, and joined a dual carriageway, where to my amazement I found myself stuck in a traffic jam. A week before I'd waited days for a car to pass, now as I entered the "Forbidden City", as Lhasa is known, I couldn't move for them.

As we edged closer to Lhasa and passed under yet another billboard advertising China Telecom, I began to worry that all the romantic images I had in my head of the city were about to be tarnished forever. The last thing I wanted was to arrive and stumble across a KFC. I was under no illusion though that it would have been frozen in time and remain untouched, but I still wasn't quite prepared for what I found there. As we broke off the dual carriage way and into town, everyone on the bus seemed to be staring to the left in anticipation. I did the same, and caught my first glimpse of Potala Palace, the home of the Dalai Lama until 1950 when he was forced to flee over the 7,000m passes of the Himalayas into India to avoid capture by the Chinese. He has remained in exile there ever since. No amount of photographs or videos can prepare you for its magnificence. Built at the end of the 16th century and containing 1,000 rooms, its square turrets and glistening golden roofs rise 13 storeys and 120m above Lhasa.

When I got off the bus, I headed for the Pentoc Guesthouse where Simon had emailed to say he was staying. Sadly, having already been waiting for me in Lhasa for a fortnight, an hour before Simon had picked up my message to say I'd soon be arriving, he'd booked and paid for a seat in a four-wheel drive that was taking him to the Everest base camp and then on to the border of Nepal. He was leaving the next morning. The main reception desk of the Pentoc Guest House seemed to double as a bar, and when I arrived, I asked the man lounging behind it if there was a Simon staying there. He drew in a deep breath, stretched out his hand and said, "You must be Ben, pleased to meet you."

I took his hand, and he explained that Simon was out but had left his key for me. As I took the key, an Aussie came over and said, "Are you the Ben that's come from Ali?"

Slightly freaked out by my sudden loss of anonymity, and overwhelmed by the prospect of having to talk to people after so long alone, I made my excuses, went up to Simon's room and locked the door behind me. Simon arrived back 20 minutes later and, after a masculine greeting of a hand shake and a back slap each, we went back down to reception to order some beer and catch up on the last couple of weeks. But it seemed that Simon had built me up to be something of a living legend, and we were constantly interrupted by people coming over to talk to us and wanting to hear where I'd been and how I'd got there. This began to get annoying after a while, as all I wanted to do was talk to Simon, compare stories and photos and admire his latest psychedelic sketches from the past fortnight. Up until my arrival though, Simon had been the only one there to have entered Lhasa by road having been successfully smuggled in under blankets on a bus from the north. As a result, we seemed to be the only two foreigners in Lhasa that the government knew nothing about, which turned us into some sort of local celebrities among the other backpackers at the hostel.

Tired of fielding questions and my stomach beginning to growl, I suggested we go out somewhere to grab some dinner. We ended up at a fried chicken stall that Simon had clearly frequented the last fortnight, and as we tucked into the greasy chicken that dripped with oil, we laughed at how much weight I had lost and how much he seemed to have put on. We chatted about what we had seen on our separate routes and about the foundations for the new train line that he had passed on his way down.

We wandered over to the Jokhang Temple in Barkor Square, where we settled down with a couple of beers. It was dark by then, but outside the main doors of the temple a fire burnt in a container resembling a horse trough. It seemed that the fire never burnt out, as it was continually topped up with sheets of wax for fuel, by the pilgrims seated close by or by the caretakers of the temple – young monks whom, it seemed, had been given the honour of keeping this cherished light alive and insure the flames never ceased. We were not alone outside the temple. We were surrounded by pilgrims, some praying, some socialising and some just getting ready for a night's sleep on the hard ground. Laying out their thick blankets on the stone surface, worn smooth and shiny by the dedication of visiting pilgrims of centuries past. Some had the luxury of sleeping bags and even pillows but most just curled up under thick blankets and rested their heads on their sacks of possessions.

Having spent all their money travelling to Lhasa to pay homage at the temple, this is where they would make home for a night or two. The ground was cold but bearable next to the fire, and the air smelt of butter lamps and joss sticks. Above the murmur of pilgrims, was the constant clicking of prayer wheels.

It was my first night in Lhasa and Simon's last. We had reason to celebrate and didn't want the night to end. So, when the bottle store around the corner from Barkor Square closed its doors for the night, we moved on in search of more festivities and found ourselves in a Tibetan nightclub. It was certainly not like any nightclub

I had been to before. To start with there was no bar – table service only – but stranger than that was that after 15 minutes of watching the people on the dance floor bop along to some cheesy 90s pop, the lights came on, the music abruptly ended, and the dance floor emptied. Then some traditional Tibetan music began to play as a dozen dancers in traditional dress entered the dance floor and began a synchronized routine with bells and twirling cloths. They left as suddenly as they had appeared to a scattering of applause, then the disco lighting and pop was put back on and everyone resumed their spots on the dance floor for another half an hour or so, until the whole strange process began again.

When I woke the next morning, Simon had already left, leaving me to tidy up the empty beer bottles that littered the room. Wanting to avoid more questions from my "fans" downstairs, I checked out of the hostel and set off to deliver the broken video camera which I'd promised the Indian back in Shigatze I would deliver to a Scotsman called Calum who was staying at the Kirey Hotel. It turned out to be fairly cheap there, and so I checked in as well and asked the receptionist where I might find a guy called Calum and was given his room number. Calum's door was ajar, and when I received no response from knocking, I pushed it fully open to find him asleep in bed, a mop of hair covering his face. When I woke him, by almost shouting his name while stood at the foot of his bed, he was a little confused and knew nothing of the camera delivery, as he hadn't checked his emails in a while. Grateful nevertheless, we chatted briefly. He was a big Glaswegian with a ponytail and explained he was living in Lhasa, teaching English at an evening school to save up to continue his own adventure cycling from Singapore to Scotland. We agreed to meet later that evening for a beer and I went off to spend the day wandering around town.

That evening Calum took me to a small restaurant down a side alley which, funnily enough the Israeli and Indian I had met in Shigatze, had only shown him the month before. There I was served the best momos in town, and afterwards Calum introduced me to the only ex-pat bar in Lhasa, where I spent most evenings over my next 10 days in the city, getting to know a lot of the local foreigners, most of whom were studying Tibetan writing and language at the University. It was sitting at the bar here, that I was tipped off about a two-day meeting of congressional prayer happening in Lhasa which I was keen to see.

It took me a long time to find the correct temple, as it was hemmed in between many taller Chinese-built buildings. Inside the courtyard of the main building and all throughout the building, I was overwhelmed by the echoing voices of the 400 strong crowd of Tibetans all chanting in unison. At the top of five stone steps you entered a large room with a high ceiling and in there were housed the biggest prayer wheels I had seen yet. Massive golden wheels the size of small cars with Tibetan writings and symbols moulded into them. At the base of the wheels wooden handles stuck out like the end of rolling pins and with these in their hands, half a dozen people circulated around endlessly rotating the huge gold prayer wheel all the while mumbling prayers or mantras, and with their free hand many thumbed prayer beads on a never-ending loop.

Those seated outside in the courtyard, with their food and supplies tucked beside them on the ground, spun their own personal prayer wheels, their eyes staring ahead in deep concentration. Many of their wheels were elaborately decorated, and most of them were far bigger than those I had seen on any stalls. In fact, they were so big that they had to be grasped between the legs as well as the hands while being spun. I found a shaded spot in the corner, where I sat with my back resting against a pillar. The owner of the prayer wheel spinning closest to me, acknowledged my presence without breaking from his mantra. I noticed that the skin between his thumb and forefinger was as smooth and shiny as the wood of his prayer wheel. As I sat there in silence, trying to become invisible, others ran prayer beads through their fingers, all the while reciting the common Tibetan mantra, "Ha-mani-pen-ma-hom". When I later asked my Tibetan friends in the bar for the translation, I was told that it was impossible to translate into English because the languages were too different, but the closest they could come up with was, "Lotus Flower".

I sat there silently in the courtyard for the next few hours absorbing the atmosphere, breathing in the heavy scent of incense burning all round me and feeling quite at peace with the world.

I'd never been to, or ever wanted to go to a fancy dress party, but some students I'd met in the bar invited me along to one being held at the University, and since neither Calum nor I were required to dress up, I was happy to accept. Two of the students met us at the back gate and explained that the campus security was extremely strict and we weren't exactly allowed inside. In order to enter, therefore, we had to scale a wall, careful not to let our plastic bags full of beer, clink or break as we did so.

Finally, at the party, it was clear that everyone had put a lot of effort into their costumes. Jamie, one of the guys I knew from the bar, had me in hysterics with his. He was quite openly gay, however, due to the fact that homosexuality simply doesn't exist in the minds of Tibetans, it was kept a secret from our Tibetan friends, whom I assume must have just thought he was a bit effeminate. Jamie had therefore seized tonight's opportunity to truly camp himself up, opting for an alien outfit which consisted of a pair of tight silver hot-pants with gold stars painted around his crotch. The rest of his naked body was covered in glitter and on his head was a hair band with two gold balls on springs that bounced as he pranced about. Calum and I were not the only people not in fancy dress, but we did seem to be the only ones not dressed up, having a good time. I noticed a group of men sitting in the corner, not drinking or mingling with anyone else. I asked Jamie who they were and what was up with them and he explained that they were Christian missionaries, and were not really liked by anyone at the University. Apparently, people had tried to socialize with them, but their "holier than thou" attitude had put people off.

My past experience of missionaries hadn't been particularly positive. I was once stuck beside one on a 12-hour train journey in India, who managed to turn every conversation, no matter how off topic, back around to God and why his God in particular was so great. By the end of the journey I could hardly bear to spend another moment in his presence. Curious to see whether this lot might be different however, I went over to have a chat. I spent about 10 minutes attempting to raise a smile from them, while they sat there criticizing everyone else at the party for needing to "lower their inhibitions with alcohol" and saying how ridiculous they looked in their fancy dress. When they moved on to how the Tibetans' beliefs were totally absurd, I began to get annoyed, but resisted the urge to question their own religious fairy tales. Instead I simply asked why they had bothered to come if they weren't secretly desperate to join in? Nodding towards Jamie they said that they couldn't relax with such a blatant homosexual in the room, I told them not to worry, they were all far too boring to be his type anyway. After that I left them to it, feeling sorrier for the brain-washed idiots than anything else. The party continued well into the early hours when campus security arrived, confiscating the sound system and throwing us all out in a well-practiced manner.

The next day, I wandered about the city, deliberately losing myself among the crowds and meandering alleyways. I don't think I spoke to anyone all day, as slowly but surely, I left behind my hangover and slipped into daydream mode, imagining what Lhasa would have been like long before the Chinese had arrived. I began mentally extracting everything that the Chinese had introduced from the scenes before me and, after a while, I could see the old Lhasa hidden beneath the occupied city. I watched a cobbler as he hunched over a pair of old yak-hide boots, carefully and precisely restitching the worn ankle seam and then smearing it with a mix of fat and wax to waterproof it. I'd been sitting in the doorway opposite him for more than 20 minutes before he looked up and noticed me. When he realized that I had been watching him for some time, he gave me a huge proud grin and sat up sharply. I took a gamble in spoiling the moment and asked if I could take his picture, he was clearly flattered by the idea. I would even say he was blushing as I took his photo, but that was always something very hard to tell with the Tibetans, for they almost all had rosy cheeks from so much time exposed to the icy wind.

What I really wanted to imagine, was what it would have been like to have travelled for months across the Tibetan plateau, and then to look down for the first time and see Lhasa and the Potala Palace. And so, the next morning, I set off to climb around the peaks, which had once hidden Lhasa from the outside world. I spent two days up above Lhasa, looking down at the Potala Palace. From this vantage point, the palace was the only recognizable building, standing aloft from everything else. I couldn't hear the cars or see the tacky advertisements plastered across the city. All I could hear was the whistling of the wind in my ears, and the familiar flapping of prayer flags around me. Then I felt I could finally see the Forbidden City as it once had been. This was certainly one of the highlights of my whole journey and, as I looked down upon Lhasa, I thought of the flocks of pilgrims who had left their modest homes and tiny faraway villages a century before me, just to stand where I stood now. I had been to the top of the world's tallest buildings and touched things I wasn't supposed to in palaces around the world, but I found the Potala Palace more captivating than them all. I could not even begin to imagine what the pilgrims of the past would have thought looking down upon it for the first time, given that unlike me they would have had no experience of other grand palaces or distant lands. They would have found it just unbelievable; I imagine. I stared out across the city; at the river skirting it on one side, and at the neat blocks that created this little slice of urbanization in the foothills of the Himalayas, but my eyes always kept returning to the Potala Palace, that great symbol of what Tibet once was.

I decided not to pay to go inside the palace itself, for out of the 1,000 or so rooms ransacked by the Chinese, only a select few were available for viewing. While I was there, the roof from which the Dali Lama is rumoured to have viewed his subjects using a telescope, was also closed, so I was content to just complete the kora around it, while daydreaming about what might have happened the day the Dali Lama was forced to flee the city. I had heard that the Chinese attempted to trick him by inviting him to join them for a discussion, when their real motive was his capture. When word leaked out of their plan, the people of Lhasa came to the palace in their droves to protect him, enabling the young man, still in his teens, to escape and begin his gruelling journey to India.

By 5am the next morning I was on a bus to go to see the Sera Monastery. Built in 1419, it is one of the biggest surviving monasteries around the capital and sits just outside of Lhasa. The night before had been a heavy one involving 56 per cent Chinese vodka, and I ended up falling asleep on the shoulder of the monk seated next to me. When we arrived and I awoke to realize what I had done, I frantically apologized, since aside from being irritating, this was extremely disrespectful behaviour to fall asleep on a monk! The monk merely nodded solemnly and welcomed me to the Monastery in English, which I thought was pretty noble considering that if anyone ever falls asleep on my shoulder on the bus, they are met with a sharp elbow in the ribs.

After we got off, he showed me where I could begin the kora around the Monastery and its grounds. He then vanished into the maze of pathways between the closely bunched buildings, where once I had completed my kora and escaped an attack by a territorial goat, I later wandered unhindered. I came across a class being taught in one of the upstairs rooms. All the monks were sitting cross-legged on the floor, and the teacher sat among them perched on a stool. All wore long red robes neatly draped from their neckline to the ground. I slipped in at the back and sneaked a few candid photographs on my haunches. The way the monks were all sitting craning their necks up towards the teacher, while he read from an old tatty-looking book, one hand gesturing as he spoke, reminded me of story time at nursery school. Although I'm sure the stories being told here were somewhat more elaborate and detailed than those of the Hare and Tortoise variety, I doubted that the teachings differed so greatly in their lessons and morals.

I found my way up onto the flat rooftop and, as I sat admiring the view, a monk appeared carrying a kettle. He acknowledged my presence with a nod, before walking over and placing the kettle on a tripod contraption. I'd noticed this weird looking thing the moment

I'd arrived on the roof. It looked like some form of radar or satellite dish. At first I'd not really given it a second thought, but now as I looked around the other buildings, I noticed that there was one on every rooftop. After the monk had returned downstairs, I went over and stood looking at the device with confusion. Were they really boiling water like this? It seemed far too simple. The kettle sat on a circular holder in the centre of the contraption, while two concave pieces of metal directed the suns beam towards its base. I presumed that it must take ages to bring to the boil and so stuck my hand into the beam to test its efficiency. My hand was still sore a day later!

I had taken to doing a daily kora around the Jokhang temple, which started and finished in Barkor Square. It hadn't been a conscious decision but I seemed to have got into a routine. I enjoyed the opportunity to blend in a bit more while doing the kora as everyone was walking in the same direction and therefore no one was staring at me or even noticing me really, and so I was able to observe people before they observed me. As I finished my kora for that day, I was called over and offered a drink by a group of scruffy Chinese men sitting in the square. We began drinking Bijoe and chang, (not the branded beer of Thailand – chang in China is what they call any cheap local homebrew). A young Chinese couple came over, clearly intrigued by what my connection to these men could be. They were not the type of couple who would ordinarily have mixed with this class of people – they were too groomed, their shoes too clean and new – but my presence seemed to make it acceptable for us all to sit on the cold ground together. Both the man and his wife spoke some English, and obligingly attempted to translate the questions I had for my drinking buddies, although this was not easy as their dialect was apparently quite different. I learnt that these were labourers down from the north of China about to start work on the railway being built to connect Beijing to Lhasa. I knew a little bit about the work; it's construction would end Lhasa's isolation for good. It also defied all convention, reaching 5,000m in altitude through areas and terrain that any other nation would consider suicide to build upon. Many workers had indeed already died from the dangerous working conditions. When the Chinese first decided to build it, they had called on the Swiss, the nation most highly regarded for its railway building skills, a fact Simon had taken great pride in telling me on more than one occasion. After a careful examination of the intended route, the Swiss left, telling the Chinese it was far too dangerous to undertake. The Chinese began work anyway.

Through my translator, I was able to explain to the men that I had spent more than a year working as a labourer in London, which saw me even more welcomed into their group; a new space was created for me next to the man holding the bottle, who I guessed to be the foreman. Drinking games followed, and we were split in to two teams. The game, the rules of which I never quite understood, was a variation of paper, scissors, stone. I don't know if it was the winner who got to drink or the loser, but either way I ended up quite drunk. By the time someone had been sent off for the third time to refill the bottle of homebrew from a mystery source, quite a crowd had gathered around us. This, unfortunately also attracted the attention of the police, who came over wielding batons, dispersing the crowd and sending us all on our unsteady way.

I was one of the first outside the Jokhang Temple when it opened its doors for visitors the next morning. From the 7th-century rooftop I could see around 50 pilgrims below, prostrating themselves in front of the ancient temple. I knew that some of them would have taken years to reach this place, which was considered to be one of the holiest in Tibetan Buddhism. They would have prostrated themselves every few feet for hundreds of miles. It made my journey look like a walk in the park.

Now, as they went through the motions in front of the entrance with cardboard laid out beneath them to ease their repetitive sliding, stretching and standing movements, they had finally reached their goal, proving to themselves their faith and dedication to their religion. As I was leaving, an old man hobbled over to me and pushed a juniper branch in to my hand. I threw it into the kiln that smoked away outside the gate, a gesture that was believed to bring luck.

The next day I visited the Ganden Monastery, and on the way the driver slowed the bus to a halt as we passed two prostrating pilgrims on route to Lhasa. Considering the driver was of Chinese origin, I was pleased and surprised when he passed food and water down to them. Both of them had clearly come some distance, as each had a huge welt in the centre of their foreheads from having lain their heads on the ground so many thousands of times. Pieces of padded wood were strapped to their hands, elbows and knees and they wore long aprons, presumably as some protection against the rough ground, but holes had long since worn through the material that hung by their knees.

They looked tired but determined and grateful for this gesture of kindness.

The best part about the Ganden Monastery was our arrival, for it was so unexpected, I sat almost parallel to the driver at the front of the bus, gazing out through the large window as we wound our way through the peaks. We had been bouncing along for some time, when as we rose over a pass and the golden rooftops of the monastery suddenly caught my eye over the breast of the hill. Its location, tucked into the mountainside, was clearly chosen for its obscurity and seclusion. It was nearly entirely hidden from sight from the plains below, yet from the rooftop, anyone approaching would be sighted long before the monastery came into view. Camouflaged into the surroundings as it was, it seemed that only the knowledge of its location could bring you to it.

Inside one of the halls, I found a group of monks being taught how to play the Dung Chen. This is a Tibetan horn, around 10ft or more in length and sometimes telescopic. It is mainly used in ceremonies, and they are so enormous they often require a second person just to support its weight. I didn't stay for long, as judging by the sounds coming from the horn, these were clearly beginners under instruction. Inside another of the highly decorative halls were a number of larger-than-life multicoloured statues. Stuffed into their hands that were made of plaster and all over every surface, paper money had been left in offering. I wondered if anyone ever dared pocket any of the money, but when I looked at the statues' menacing faces and bright white bulging eyes, I decided that even the most dedicated of thieves would have thought twice about stealing from them.

That night I met Calum for a drink in the bar, and for the price of one beer I agreed to come along and help him teach an English lesson. Late the next afternoon, I met him in Barkor Square. He warned me in advance that he was banned from talking about religion or politics in his classes, and that if he was caught doing so, he would be sacked on the spot. Luckily, I had already chosen the subject I was going to be talking about, the one and only subject I knew well, geography.

The pupils were all in their late teens or early 20s, and as I arrived with Calum the prospect of having two foreigners teach them that afternoon caused quite a stir. I introduced myself, and was immediately asked why I spoke words differently from Calum. I explained that Calum was from Scotland and that they all spoke "funny" up there. I was from London in England and although I did not speak the Queen's English, it was better then Calum's. Rather than laughter, I was greeted with a sea of frowns, so apologized and explained that I was only joking – we both spoke proper English just with different pronunciation. More looks of confusion followed – it wasn't going quite as planned.

I decided to tell them a story from my travels, while Calum wrote the occasional bit of vocabulary that I had used on to the blackboard. Luckily this approach seemed to win the crowd over. So, I then started a little geography quiz, doling out a London postcard for each correct answer. I asked them to name the neighbouring countries bordering China. Of the 14 countries available to choose from, a class of over 20 students could only name Mongolia, India and Nepal. Moving on, I asked one of the students if money was no object, where they would go on holiday. I expected the predictable answer – the USA, but to my surprise she said that if she could go anywhere it would be Yunnan province, her neighbouring province at home. "Not America?" I asked. A few moments ticked by while she thought about this.

"Maybe, but first Yunnan province," she replied.

When I had finished talking and answering questions, I received a round of applause, and was asked by the students if I would be coming back the following day. Much to both Calum and my surprise, I told them that I could not, as I would be leaving in the morning for Nepal. I sat down, and as Calum began to explain the meaning of the long words I had used during my talk, I thought about what I had just said and realized that I would indeed, be moving on the next morning.

12

Everest

Darchen to Lhasa = 1,204km

That night everyone came down to the bar to wish me luck and the next morning I overslept and woke with such a bad hangover that it took me three attempts to pack my bag so that everything would fit. I missed my bus, but was told by people at the bus stop that it was running late and that if I hurried across town to the main bus station, I might catch it. I hailed a taxi and jumped inside.

"To the bus station, as fast as you can!" I said, as if I was in a movie. Unfortunately the driver just stared at me blankly, and we sat there with the engine idling for a few minutes while I pulled out my phrasebook to try to figure out what I needed to say.

Luckily, the bus was still at the station when I arrived, but the driver would not let me board because I didn't have a permit for outside of Lhasa. Sweating profusely as last night's alcohol seeped from every pore, I argued that I had already come from Shigatze without any problems and that my friends were waiting for me there with my permit. He did let me board in the end, but evidently didn't trust me, as I was made to sit right at the back of the bus virtually with the luggage.

The journey seemed to take far longer than before, although that may just have been the fact that every bump along the road was like having a sledgehammer struck against my already pounding head. Despite my fragile state, I still enjoyed the obligatory stops on the passes as the Tibetans scattered paper prayers and tied their flags. I arrived back in Shigatze about 7pm, and after a long walk checked into the same room I had stayed in before. I was pleased to see the Indian and the Israeli were still there, or at least their bags were, and when I finally caught up with them later, I was surprised to discover they were in fact departing for their walk in the early hours of the following morning, using my old ploy of leaving under the cover of darkness in order to not attract any unwanted attention. I decided to join them. So, with the Israeli on sticks, still not recovered from his tendonitis, together we walked out of Shigatze before sunrise. About 3km down the road, dawn was just beginning to break and I stopped at a petrol station hoping to catch a lift from there. The other two were carrying on, not on the tarmac road, but across the cracked earth instead. I wished them luck, and stood watching their slow progress, until the rhythmic tapping of the walking poles faded out of earshot.

It wasn't long before a truck driver offered me a lift for 100RMB (about £6.50), but I didn't mind paying, because he drove like a maniac, meaning I reached the turnoff for the Friendship Highway before lunchtime. I sat down on a low wall next to a stream for a couple of hours waiting for another form of transport to pass. There were houses scattered around, and the children who lived there came wandering over to see me. I gave them the last of my lollypops and pens, and they kept me amused while I waited, standing in a semi-circle around me, talking and giggling and pointing. Occasionally one of them would pluck up the courage to touch my hair, which having been under a hat for so long was pretty curly and matted, then they'd leap straight backwards, as if I was going to bite.

Finally, a bus began to approach, and as I stood in its path to flag it down, it nearly knocked me over. I leapt out of the way, and the bus carried on for a couple of hundred metres, before slamming on its brakes and beginning to reverse, presumably at the request of some of the other passengers. The bus was packed solid, so in order to squeeze me on board the doors were left open and I was allowed to sit on the metal steps. Perched with one foot braced on either side of the doorway and inhaling large mouthfuls of the dust skidding off the wheels, all the other passengers were very sympathetic and friendly, and offered me cigarettes and water on a regular basis. Unfortunately, I had to decline, since accepting would have meant letting go of the bars to which I was clinging for dear life.

I passed through two checkpoints unnoticed. With my Tibetan coat and hat pulled down to cover my hair, I simply turned my face away from the guards and managed to blend in. Just as daylight was fading, I was pleased to be told by my fellow travellers that I had arrived in the village of Tingri.

As I shouldered my pack and prepared to look for food and shelter in one of the dozen or so buildings that made up the village, a door opened behind me. I turned to see a little old lady standing there, her face half hidden in shadow. She beckoned me over, almost as if she had been expecting me, and I was led inside and instructed to sit down beside a fire. She then pottered off into the kitchen and I was left looking around at my new surroundings. I appeared to be inside a very homely little restaurant, with lots of old wooden furniture and nick-nacks on display. She soon returned with a pot of yak butter tea and, yet to utter a single word to me, sat down beside me and began to rub my hands to bring back the circulation. It had been a long day, and this small act of kindness made me realize that I was feeling a bit lonely. It was hard to keep having to move on, just as I had got to know people and made friends. But my spirits raised, I finished my yak butter tea, then went outside to catch a last glimpse of the sun setting over the Himalayas, which looked to me as though the giant mountains were sucking the sun down between them. The moment the last of the suns' light was extinguished, I felt an immediate drop in temperature and headed back to my chair by the fire, where the old lady served me a huge bowl of egg-fried rice and then showed me to a room across the courtyard where I could sleep for the night for a very reasonable price, thereby expelling any suspicions that I had, that her kindness was motivated by money. Unsurprisingly there was no heating in the room, and the door didn't quite fit the frame, so once again I returned to the warmth of the fire. Her restaurant seemed to be the eatery of choice for the locals as well, for it quickly filled up as the night progressed. She seemed to be the only host, serving everyone on her own. I sat quietly in front of the fire drinking beer, and every now and again she would come over just to check on me. I never made it back to my room that night; I drifted off on a bench by the fire, lulled in to a deep sleep by the peaceful chattering around me, and a sense of being safe, warm and welcome.

Non-Tibetan voices woke me the next morning, and from the looks on their faces I guessed I had either been snoring loudly or just farted. They turned out to belong to a group of rather unfriendly Frenchman who had stopped for breakfast on a tour from Lhasa to Everest base camp, which was also my next destination.

"Everest base camp? What a coincidence, that's where I'm heading next as well," I said brightly. Purposefully failing to take the bait, they asked if I had the correct permits to be here and I said no. Clearly disgusted by my answer, they finished their breakfasts and left after their Chinese guide rather smugly told me that I would need two more permits to reach the base camp from where I was.

This was not the best start to the day, but I was still feeling positive as I headed out of Tingri. I asked some locals which way it was to the Ronbuk Monastery, mainly because I couldn't remember the Tibetan name for Mount Everest and I knew that this was in the general direction. Unfortunately, they didn't know, or most likely didn't understand me, but not wanting to admit this smiled and nodded as they pointed to a dirt track and I set off in the wrong direction. I hitched a ride in the back of a scrap metal truck and as it trundled slowly through a valley passing from village to village, I became aware that I was heading east, when I should have been bearing south. I was enjoying passing through the villages too much to care though, for they were the first I had seen where not only did all the homes seem to match in size and appearance, but the layout of the houses seemed to have some sort of order, as if the they had been designed by an architect. Each home had a garden penned in by a stone wall, and when we stopped in front of one looking for any scrap to buy, a man came running out of one of the homes, keen to show me some ancient coins, possibly left over from before Tibet's invasion. There was no date or discernible writing on them, but they certainly looked like they had passed through the hands of half a dozen generations. I offered him some money for them, but he declined, hastily taking them back and putting them in his pocket. I think he just wanted confirmation that they were definitely worth keeping.

A couple of hours had now passed since I had boarded the truck, and we were still heading east, when the driver turned around at a village to head back the way he had come. I should have stayed in the back, but instead jumped out, wanting to see where the road led to – yet another one of my impulsive decisions I came to regret within five minutes of making. I walked on down the dirt track in the scorching sun for more than an hour, before I cut my losses and sat down on my pack to await a lift back the way I had come. I toyed with the idea of continuing east a number of times, curious to see where it would lead, but I managed to persuade myself to stay put – Everest was calling.

A truck eventually passed by and stopped for me. I climbed into the back using the off-road wheel as a step, and my sudden appearance scared a group of women already seated there, who huddled together and covered their faces with their headscarves. When we stopped for tea by the side of the road, I offered my hand to them as they battled to climb down from the truck with dignity. This earned me some brownie points, and they let me share their food, which consisted of some rather foul-tasting curd and some dense and chewy homemade bread. I even got a wave from them when I was dropped back at the main road from which I'd diverted my course many hours before.

Over the next two hours, a number of four-wheel drives sped past, ignoring my pleas for a lift. Preferring to sleep by the side of the road than to return, defeated, for another night in Tingri, I began walking south, when an army jeep appeared and pulled up beside me. Without much option, I climbed in beside a rather high-ranking officer judging by the thickness of his coat and number of gold rings adorning his fingers. He stared at me for a full minute without speaking, before he returned his eyes to the road and we set off. Around 30km later we came to a big checkpoint, complete with a razor wire-topped fence that stretched in both directions as far as the eye could see. The officer parked the jeep inside the barracks, and then handed me over to the guys in the main building.

A somewhat weak interrogation followed, but once they were satisfied I was just a confused, lost idiot, we all made friends and I enjoyed a hot dinner and a vast quantity of green tea with them. When night fell, and no more vehicles were passing through, a bed was made up for me in their barracks. But just after they had left me beside the bunk I had been allocated, they suddenly returned and began pointing at the aerial photographs and documents that were stuck to the walls, saying I was not to take pictures or even look at them. Of course, I was then intrigued and I had to give everything a good once-over when they had left. None of it meant anything to me though, so I lay my head down on the pillow and drifted off to sleep to the sound of hard-soled shoes making their way back and forth across tiled floors. I woke once in the night to find two guards struggling to share the single bed next to me. I realized then with some guilt that I had been given one of their beds to sleep in.

The next morning, I was given a breakfast of fried eggs and rice, and not long after, an American, accompanied by his driver and guide, arrived at the checkpoint. He had come from Lhasa and had hired the whole jeep for himself and so was happy to give me a lift to base camp. The guards were keen to get rid of me and pass the problem of an illegal foreigner onto someone else, so agreed to let me go ahead, despite having no permits. So, while the American was in the office having his passport and permits checked, I chucked my stuff in the back of the jeep and made myself comfortable.

As we pulled off through the gates, I waved to the guards hardly able to believe that once again, I was being let go, permit-less. The American was a nice guy in his 50s, but a stereotypical Yank – quite loud and brash with no hint of modesty. He spent the next couple of hours telling me his life story, going on about how much money he made living in the Big Apple, and how he only got 10 days holiday a year but because he hadn't taken any in seven years was able to go on this trip of a life time. Apparently, he had squeezed in eleven countries across four continents in just three months, spending close to $30,000 in the process. This was his one and only whirlwind tour of the world, and in just one week he was flying back to the States from Kathmandu and returning to work.

After hours of winding around monotonous passes, we reached the top of a plateau, and I glimpsed Everest for the very first time. I didn't need to be told which peak it was, for when the whole Himalayan range came into view, it towered above the others, a slight wisp of snow blowing east from its tip. Even the American was stunned into silence by the sight of it. We stopped the car, and the three of us got out, eyes transfixed on the highest point on the earth's surface. We were about 5,000m above sea level where we were standing and to look across at this giant, knowing that its summit was a further 3,500m above us, was simply mind blowing. *I wanna climb it*, I thought.

The Himalayas didn't really seem to fit among the dry, infertile lands that surrounded us. The mountain range seemed too clean and perfect to belong amidst all this red dust. At the entrance to Qomolonmga (Everest) National park, I reluctantly paid the 65RMB (£5) entrance fee, hoping that, along with the other £10 million the park makes annually from climbers, it would go towards the conservation of the park, rather than towards some bureaucrat's bar bill up in Beijing. Not far down the entrance road, we were forced to pull over and change cars, as from a certain point only government vehicles were allowed to pass. For this of course, you had to pay extra. As we sat in the compound waiting, my papers were questioned by the officials who manned it, and eventually refused to allow me inside a government car without the correct permits. After a heated debate, I grabbed my pack and said, "Fine! I'll walk."

I left the compound to yells that it was still 52km to base camp, but ignoring them, I marched on. I had been walking for about 15 minutes, trying to do the maths on how long it would take to walk 52km when I heard a car approach. Thinking I might be about to get into real trouble, I prepared for the worst, and was surprised when I saw my American inside. His guide had sweet-talked the National Park driver, and he had agreed to take me as far as the last turnoff for the Base Camp. From there he said, I would have to take my chances and walk in alone, but by consistently chatting to him along the way, and bribing him with cigarettes, he seem-ingly forgot about our arrangement and drove me all the way to the perimeter of the camp. There was no more bureaucracy here, and I was able to walk straight in to Base Camp and exercise my right to roam.

For those people not part of an official summit expedition who didn't have their own professional set up, there was only one place to get a bed for the night. In a large round tent, the size of a small apartment, that also doubled as the restaurant, and as I later witnessed, a place where many of the climbers from around the world met at night, to talk about the mountain and their plans for the summit. I ate lunch there with the American. The walls were made from layers of knitted yak hair it appeared and the smell of yak was initially overpowering but you soon got used to it and very soon it became the smell of comfort and security for me.

It was very cosy inside; a furnace burnt in the centre of the tent, and beds lined the walls, doubling as sofas during the day. The comfort was increased even more by the dozens of blankets stacked across each frame and I was most impressed when, after lunch, I was offered the option of cold beer by the friendly local running the enterprise.

That afternoon, I wandered around the little community of tent dwellers, feeling like I was at some kind of ice festival. A rather drunk Tibetan lifted his tent flap, made a noise like a dragon, and projected a ball of mucus onto the ground outside. When he noticed me trying not to cringe, he invited me in. I was greeted by a group of Sherpas drinking chang. Most of them spoke very good English as they had been guiding westerners up and down the mountain for years. They told me that they had all stood on the summit of Everest more than once, some without oxygen. One claimed he had looked down from the top of the world more than 10 times, and since this was not disputed by anyone else in the tent, I was inclined to believe him. Apparently, one in four people who attempt to climb Everest die doing so, and so I asked them why they did it. Pride seemed to play far more of a role than money. They did it because they could, when so many westerners for all their wealth, could not.

I felt honoured to be sitting there among these men, drinking cheap homebrew, and was especially pleased when one of them asked me why I travelled. I was able to give them the same reply they had given me about climbing Everest, similar to that of Edmund Hillary, (the first westerner to have summited Everest,) "Because I can," I said. This brought a murmur of appreciation from the group, which was by far the best response I'd ever had, having responded to this question in the same way so many times before. I've always been of the opinion that while I don't have the right to live anywhere, I should have the right to travel anywhere. We are all born on the same planet, and just because we put up fences shouldn't mean we don't all have the right to see the world in which we live.

I was a little tipsy when I left the Sherpas, but continued nosing around the base camp. I came across a group of Russians sitting inside their dome-shaped tents and introduced myself. Their expedition was a commercial one; they had each paid around $60,000 to take part. As a result, they were enjoying brand label food, and while we chatted, I indulged in my first Snickers chocolate bar and McVities digestive biscuits in a long time. One of the guys inside the tent sat by the doorway and kept a lookout for Chinese officials, who he said usually made their inspection rounds about then. They all found it highly amusing that I was floating around the base camp with no permits and with no real purpose. "I've heard about people like you," said one of the Russians, but in a friendly way.

Later as I once more watched the giant mountains smother the sun and black shadows start to slowly creep across the valley, I thought about the Russian's comment, *People like me*, and wondered what that meant.

It seemed that where I was staying, not only served food and provided accommodation, but also became the climbers' local bar in the evenings as well. Chatting to an American team I was told that most were waiting a week before continuing with their expedition out of respect for the South Korean team, which was currently up the mountain. They were attempting the retrieval of their friends' bodies, from an expedition the year before. This was apparently fairly unusual, as most bodies were left where they fell so as not to put any more lives at risk in bringing them back down. They told me how on the way to the summit, you have to pass, and even step over, the bodies of failed mountaineers long frozen to the mountain face. It was a sight they said that made you question your own sanity, because you realized that no matter how long you had trained for, or how much determination you had, the mother of all mountains could take you at any time.

Drinking with the expedition teams that night, I learnt a lot about climbing. They tolerated my pedestrian questions and were happy to explain all their climbers' lingo, which often left me totally lost. I heard a lot of horror stories about the mountain too, but they only left me more intrigued and wanting to climb it more. I was around $60,000 short to join an expedition, so I therefore decided to have a go on my own.

Even with a fire burning in the tent throughout the night, it was still freezing. I could not imagine the intense cold the climbers were feeling higher up on the mountain. I wanted to see the sunrise, and so I got up as soon as I heard the bells jingling around the necks of the yaks, as they set off past the tent for another day's arduous work. There was already a bunch of photographers, tripods at the ready patiently awaiting the sun. Some were jumping up and down on the spot to keep warm. The sun had in fact already risen, judging by the light blue sky above. But in the shadow of Everest and its smaller siblings, we were all still in the dark. When it did rise, it made every horrible second, on every cramped bus I had ever ridden inside, worth it, as I watched the light slowly penetrate the dark crevices of the mountain range, and stretch itself out and over the ridges. I thought it must be like watching hell turn into heaven, as the sun lit up the North Face of Everest.

Some climbers commented on how windy she looked up top. I couldn't see it though: I could just see a big fluffy mountain that was luring me, calling me to come closer.

There was no one watching as I hurried past the sign that warned me of a $250 fine if I was caught passing it without the necessary permits. I was not planning on getting caught though, so I didn't feel it applied to me. It wasn't hard to know which way to go to reach Camp 1, for there was a steady flow of yaks loaded up with barrels, bags and sacks full of supplies leading the way in single file. The yaks however, despite being so over-loaded, moved at a quicker pace than I did, and I regularly had to pull off the rough path to let them overtake. They were often unaccompanied by a herder, and simply trudged on, snorting their thanks to me as they passed. Even before the track began to gain altitude, it was hard work. I had to focus on each step as I climbed over the large boulders and loose stones that made up the track.

When it began to snake its way up a 600m pass, the gradient changed abruptly. By the time I reached the top, I was knackered and my lungs ached from repeatedly gulping down the air. I sat down on a boulder and looked down at the clear blue glacier that ran along the base of the mountain, the jagged ice jutting out in different directions, like sapphires the size of houses. It was unreal; I half expected to see a baby polar bear appear and crack open a bottle of Coca-Cola.

As I sluggishly made my way along the uneven track, I passed a group of climbers all wearing matching red team outfits and heading in the opposite direction. They told me to turn around, saying I'd be caught if I didn't. I ignored them and continued for another hour or so until I could see a corner of orange poking out and I was sure I could smell kerosene in the air. I hoped I was close to the next camp and picked up the pace a little, but just as I was nearing what I thought to be Advanced Base Camp, three Chinese guys, all in yellow North Face jackets, appeared on the track ahead. I smiled at them and attempted to walk past. No such luck. My dress and solitariness had this time given me away. They asked me what team I was with and to see my papers. I lied and said I was with the American team, but I had stupidly left my papers back at Base Camp. With a smile they said I would have to return and fetch them. I did not argue, as I was clearly not going to be able to talk my way out of this one, and I could do without the hefty fine. Content with having come further than most, I turned around.

Back at Base Camp that night, I looked forward to telling the climbers about my day's antics. However, when I entered the tent, after sun down, I received a small cheer. It seemed word travelled fast in this little community. Nursing a hangover in the morning, I departed Base Camp and headed 7km back the way I had come, to Ronbuk Monastery. I felt it was a must to visit this monastery, not because I was particularly bothered myself, but because as the world's highest monastery, I knew I would get too much grief from anyone who found out I had passed it by. So, I spent the morning looking around the Ronbuk Monastery. It was in fact only a few decades old, the original having been destroyed by Mao. The monks, used to foreigners, were almost too friendly and with their detailed commentary delivered in almost flawless English, I felt I was being given a tour around an art gallery rather than a monastery. As I left what was undoubtedly the smallest monastery I had visited in Tibet, under the watchful eyes of the monks I felt obliged into leaving a larger donation in the bowl than was normal – it seemed I was back in the world of Foreigner Tax.

It was too late by now to attempt to move on, so I crossed over the road to a thin strip of houses and the only guesthouse around. The houses were terraced, and looked like workers' quarters, except they were each only around the size of a stable. I peered through a broken window into the dormitory which was on offer at the guesthouse, and since it was clearly not the Hilton, I therefore expected to be charged no more than 15RMB for a bed. Inside the teahouse, I wolfed down a bowl of rice, and then enquired about the dorm.

"40RMB," said the landlady.

"Not a chance," I replied. But given she was the only option for a bed in these parts, she wouldn't budge. Over the next three hours, I sat drinking beer, attempting to drive the price down. After she taunted me by waving the key to the dorm in my face, I left, saying I would sleep outside before I allowed myself to be ripped off. A group of drivers who spoke some English and a couple of locals came after me, saying I should come back inside and that I could now stay for free. Confused, I followed them, but when they all began chipping in to pay for my room, I stopped them immediately, explaining I had the money, I just didn't want to pay an unreasonable amount.

Touched by their kindness, I thanked them and then left again in search of a sheltered place to sleep. Just as I was laying my space blanket down upon the ground beside a stone wall and a horse cart, the two locals came and found me again, and led me to the stable-sized houses I had seen earlier. We couldn't communicate, but I could see from their eyes that they were good people.

I entered through the tiny doorway; my back doubled over. There was no electricity and no windows inside: it was cramped and it had an overpowering stench of yak, but a fire was lit in the centre of the tiny room, a fresh brew of tea was boiling and it was warm. After tea and a few shared shots of some repulsive liquor, a bed was made up for me out of bundles of straw. Then with a toothless grin, one of the men handed me a yak hair blanket and left me alone to get some beauty sleep. The blanket was about as soft on my skin as wire wool and during the night I heard things scurrying around among the bales on which I was sleeping. I slept well though, and felt refreshed in the morning when the men returned, swinging open the door and blinding me with the brightness of a new day. As a thank you for their hospitality, I gave them a card and dice set encased in a little carved box. I had been saving it since Thailand for the right recipients, and they were certainly the ones. I also left them 20RMB, hoping word of this would reach the guesthouse owner, and annoy the hell out of her.

From here, I hitched a lift to near the entrance of Qomolongma (Everest) National Park. I hadn't been waiting long when a four-wheel drive came tearing along the dusty road containing a government driver, and Brook Alongi, the Expedition Leader for an American team called Ogawa Mountain Adventures who I had got to know at Base Camp. He explained that he had a family emergency and needed to fly back to the US. He was driving straight to the border, from there to jump on a flight from Kathmandu. "Room for a little one?" I asked with a grin.

My main goal had been to get to Tibet, and I'd been instructed by my mum that I had to be home by July to go to my cousin's wedding. It was now early May and I was still about 15,000km away so this was clearly not going to happen, but Nepal was the only real break in the Himalayan chain, and so it seemed a sensible next stop for me. As we made our way to the border, we stopped at the top of each pass so that we could admire the view, and the driver could smoke. Brook was able to name every peak in sight. This was mainly due to the fact that he had climbed 90 per cent of them. He had climbed all over the world and was keen to share his passion with me. He had reached the summit of the highest peak on six out of seven continents. I wasn't aware of it at the time, but I was travelling with one of the most respected climbers of his generation.

As we slowly descended, leaving the Tibetan plateau behind, the scenery and colour started to change and we began passing through forested areas. I felt energetic and could not stop talking. I presumed it was the prospect of crossing in to Nepal that was making me feel so excited and alive, but then Brook pointed out that my body was being flooded with oxygen again, which was making me feel wide awake. When my hands and feet began tingling, I realized I was probably overdosing on oxygen a bit.

Darkness began to fall and we realized we were not going to make it to the border before it shut. We carefully made our way along a ledge of a road, halfway up a valley with a deadly drop to our left and a steep wall of rock to our right. We came to where there had been an avalanche of snow which had blanketed the road. A 200m channel had been cut through the middle of it, leaving two walls of 6m high snow on either side. You could tell by the corners that this had been done recently as they were yet to melt into a smooth edge. If it hadn't been for the unforgiving drop a few feet to our left, it would have been easy to think that we were driving around the back of a film set.

We arrived at the border, and as we had suspected it had closed 20 minutes earlier, so we spent the night in Xangmu, the last town in Tibet. It was built entirely on the steep sloping valley, and I was glad when we took a room in a guesthouse at the bottom. Unsure of the quality of beer in Nepal, I made sure that night to drink a few Lhasa beers, and bought a couple extra to take with me to Kathmandu.

13

Freak Street

Lhasa to Kathmandu = 606km

In the queue at the immigration office I waited my turn to be stamped out of Tibet, unsure of what was going to happen given my conspicuous lack of permits. In fact, when I finally got to the front of the queue, the problem turned out to be the rather more unexpected issue of the officials deciding my passport was a fake.

I could understand why they would think this, given the state of my passport photo. A couple of years before I'd had my passport stolen while passing through Windhoek in Namibia, and in a hurry to leave the somewhat dull capital, I had only been able to obtain a black and white passport photo. Although the British Embassy had accepted this and issued me a new passport, my passport now looked like it belonged to some ghostly Victorian. Almost every immigration officer had commented on this since, but this was the first time anyone had seriously doubted its authenticity.

I was sent into the back office to talk to someone in plain clothes. Even though I wasn't worried about what they were going to do given that I was trying to leave the country and not enter it, I was anxious that if they took too long, I would lose my lift. The guy there wasn't stupid, and quizzed me quite hard as to the origins of my passport. I felt that he was assessing my body language as much as my replies. After I had given a detailed explanation and promised to get a new passport photo as soon as possible, he let me go, and in the confusion my missing permits were completely overlooked.

Climbing back in to the four-wheel drive, we pulled off into no-man's-land, and I commented upon the Chinese bullies manning the immigration gate. They clearly enjoyed their power to randomly deny people entry, and they were treating the Nepalese traders who were seeking to pass in to Tibet to sell their wares, with no respect at all, pushing them about and shouting unnecessarily. Brook told me it was always the same there. Sometimes they would let the traders in, sometimes not. It was a daily occupational hazard that the traders had to deal with.

We wound our way down a gorge and on into Nepal, and I was surprised to see just how many people there were living in no-man's-land, and once again wondered if laws applied here, or if its inhabitants could just do whatever they wanted? Littering certainly didn't seem to be a problem – every home was surrounded by unsightly piles of rubbish and household refuse. We crossed a bridge and changed from driving on the right-hand side of the road to the left. "We've just gained two hours and fifteen minutes," said Brook.

When we arrived in the Nepalese border town of Kodari, it seemed to be in a state of panic. The Maoists had apparently been causing trouble in the area that day. The Nepalese, all wearing traditional hats called dhaka topis which always remind me of tea cosies, seemed to be in heated debate, pushing and shoving each other around. The army was trying to get the situation under control but were not being particularly affective. I felt this could perhaps have something to do with their uniforms, which didn't exactly look particularly threatening or authoritative. I mean, with their peaked hats, starched shirts and cargo pants tucked into black ankle boots, they were trying their best to look military, but I think it was the camouflage design of the fabric, predominately grey and turquoise with the odd splatter of black, that was letting them down. That and the fact that their uniforms only seemed to come in extra large, which made them look more like a group of boys on a jolly paintballing weekend, rather than soldiers patrolling the country's busiest border.

I had never been to Nepal before, but had spent several months in India, which made the familiar smells of incense, curry and steaming cow shit seem quite welcoming. As I left the combined visa and immigration office, which consisted of just two desks, I couldn't help feeling a little disappointed that having paid $30US for a 60-day visa, that the visa in question resembled a rather amateurish-looking giant postage stamp. My younger brother could have knocked up something more official looking in five minutes on his PC.

At the border, a Nepalese official and his driver were waiting, and as we climbed inside the jeep, Brook was handed a huge stack of paperwork to fill out. The official ignored me completely, but proceeded to fire an endless barrage of questions at Brook, wanting to know why he had left his expedition early, and whether there was anything he could do to help him. Brook was certainly a well-liked and well-known person in Nepal. Whether that was because of his skill as a climber, or because he paid the country so much money to be there, I wasn't sure.

As we made our way towards Kathmandu, we passed several Maoist road blockades being dismantled. Brook explained that these were put up overnight around many of the roads surrounding the city to remind the people and its government that while Kathmandu remained under the control of the King, the rest of the country was Maoist territory, and that they were always watching and could strike anywhere, any time.

I knew that the Maoists had been fighting the government for Communist control since 1996, when they had declared "The People's War". Unofficially backed by the Chinese with money and arms, they had been growing stronger ever since. More than 15,000 had died in the fighting and unprovoked attacks over the years. More than 400 of these had been child soldiers who probably had no idea what they were fighting for, other than a bit of food and clothing. The borders had not been re-opened long before my arrival. After seizing control the King had closed the borders, dissolved his parliament, and cut off phone and internet connections, banning news reports in the process. Things had returned to relative normality a few weeks before, but the British government was still strongly advising against travel to Nepal, as were many European countries.

One month before I arrived, the Maoists had blown up a moving bus. The bus, unbeknown to the Maoists, had contained a Russian tour party. Most of those inside had been killed. To make sure the wrong buses were not accidentally ambushed again, therefore, the buses we now passed on the roads, had banners draped along their sides, labelling their contents; "SCHOOL CHILDREN", "TOURISTS ONLY". This seemed a bit unfair on the locals who mostly travelled by public transport, who may as well have had "TARGET" written along the side of their buses.

Passing through yet another armed checkpoint, I noticed that below a machine gun post among a pile of sandbags, some marijuana was sprouting through. While one of the guards checked the car for hidden passengers and examined our visas, I excitedly pointed this out to Brook, he laughed. "Open your eyes," he said.

As we got closer to Kathmandu, I saw what he meant. Marijuana was growing everywhere. It grew between the cracks in the pavement and swamped the empty lots next to businesses. It grew freely along the walls hand-painted with advertisements for Pepsi and whiskey. I had a feeling I was going to like Nepal, although I later learnt that it is the male plant that grows here in abundance, and while you can take the leaves and dry them, it's generally not the type that people smoke.

Driving through the narrow streets into the Thamel district, the main tourist area of Kathmandu, I was overwhelmed by the number of tourists, mainly backpackers, many dressed in the typical multicoloured loose-fitting clothes that so many "travellers" wear. According to Brook however, due to the recent trouble, the streets were practically empty of tourists in comparison to normal. We checked into the Yak Hotel; a place Brook assured me was the only place to stay if you were a climber. Sure enough the walls were lined with photographs of famous expeditions. Brook waited patiently until I spotted the one of him and a previous team hanging in pride of place near reception. The accommodation was clearly over my budget, but for my first night in Nepal, I thought I'd treat myself. As I stood under not only my first shower since Shigatze, but a hot one at that, I quickly felt it was worth every rupee.

The next morning, I thanked Brook for all his help, including the bars he had introduced me to the night before, then checked out of the hotel and headed across town to Freak Street. I didn't quite know why I was heading to a place called Freak Street. I just knew that someone, somewhere, had told me it was a cool place to stay. The Thamel area seemed to be just a collection of bars, guesthouses and shops all aimed at foreigners. It was clear I wasn't going to see much of the real Kathmandu hanging around there.

The city is one enormous maze of alleyways and squares, all bustling with life, so finding Freak Street took me forever. As I tried to find my way, I was surrounded by traders trying to push all manner of useless things upon me, beggars grabbing at my ankles for change, holy men or 'Babus', hassling me for money in exchange for a blessing and a Tika (a smear of yellow and red between the eyes). I often would get caught off guard by this and be smeared unexpectedly, then get hassled into paying for the unwanted privilege. I saw many tourists happily paying for this blessing though, obviously feeling they were immersing themselves in the culture, but personally, as a non-Hindu, it didn't appeal to me.

When I did find Freak Street in the heart of the old city, it was just what I was looking for. All the western conveniences of restaurants and internet access were there, but without the crowds. It was a street left over from the hippy era of the 60s. I checked into the Eden Hotel. While it lacked the facilities of the other guesthouses in Freak Street, such as clean rooms and running water, it was old and quaint, which gave me the feeling I had just entered the Twilight Zone every time I walked through the door. The place had clearly once been the Ritz of Freak Street: now, as the years had gone by, all that remained of its past glory were shiny stone floors, high ceilings and a lift. It was the small two-person lift with its sliding scissor-type gates that really sold it to me, even though it was of course a death trap; its broken mechanism meant that it didn't stop on my floor, only the one above it, but over the next two weeks, as I waited for my India and Pakistan visa to come through, I discovered that if I timed it right, I could quickly yank open one of the gates as I passed my stop bringing the lift to a bouncing halt, and from there open the other gate by levering apart the lock using my key ring.

That night I checked my emails, only to find I had just missed Simon. He had left that morning on the bus to Pokhara, after having already spent nearly two weeks in Kathmandu. The next few days were spent gorging myself on western chocolate bars and soft drinks. I discovered the Snowman Café which was just around the corner from where I was staying and which had been running since the heyday of hippy travellers. Inside it hadn't changed one bit, with its walls covered in murals depicting what I assumed must have been drug-induced visions. The reason the place had been going so long, however, was because of its mouth-wateringly tasty cakes. The proprietor was the son of the original owner who still cooked his father's original recipes 40 years on. After trying a slice of every cake on offer, all of which were displayed in the window, I decided the chocolate was the best, and quickly put back on the unhealthy amount of weight I had lost while crossing Tibet.

Simon joined me a couple of days after my arrival; having picked up my email in Pokhara which is a day's travel from Kathmandu, he had kindly backtracked to find me. He had previously stayed in Thamel for the duration of his last visit, so was more than happy to be introduced to Freak Street, and we soon fell in to a bit of a routine. Our day would begin with a visit to the Umbrella Man for breakfast, who was always situated in the same place on the corner of Basantapur Square, which adjoined the famous Durbar Square. Here, he squatted under a multicoloured umbrella cooking up omelettes and chai tea on a tiny pump action petrol cooker. Without fail, we would have two omelettes and two chais each and every morning. As time went on, the Umbrella Man seemed to grow fond of us, and our portion sizes doubled. Here we would sit and watch, as Kathmandu slowly awoke, and the traders laid out their goods of paintings and masks on blankets. In the mornings we would tick off all the tourist sights there were to see such as the monkey temples, palaces and shrines, although to be honest, none of these things really interested us and we only went because we felt we should.

Kathmandu is not a city in which you have to queue to see the sights, the whole city is one spectacular sight. It's a giant maze of squares, alleyways and narrow cobbled streets teaming with life; buildings are crammed into every nook and cranny – buildings built on top of buildings – with incense pouring from every window, and temples and shrines on every corner. It was so easy to get lost here, that when we finally started to get to know our way around after a few days, we felt pretty proud of ourselves. I'm not a big fan of cities, but I loved Kathmandu, and adjusted to the madness pretty quickly. Also, it felt good to be anonymous again after so long. The city was almost like one giant farmers' market, with traders just placing blankets on the ground from which to sell fruit and vegetables, shoes and cheap plastic Chinese toys. Cows, which as in all Hindu countries, were treated like royalty here, just wandered through the alleyways tossing their giant heads unhindered. Sometimes it would just be one or two cows, but a square might suddenly fill with a herd of 50 or 60 who would shit everywhere and then move on. It was crazy whichever direction you looked in, and was a relief to be able to dive into a doorway or shop just to take a breather from it all. It is also, I discovered, one of the only places in the world that you can get sun burn and frost bite in the same day. Situated between 3,500 and 4000m above sea level it's very cold in the shade but hot in the sun.

We got to know our favourite places to visit; an ice cream parlour and a place that sold the best chocolate cake. We found a good fruit seller, the guy who sold the best cold beers, and another who was paid to take your empty bottles back to the beer seller. Everyone seemed to be doing the things their ancestors had been doing for generations, except with a little bit more cheap Chinese plastic thrown in.

One of our favourite spots for people-watching was Maju Deval, a nine-stage ochre platform on which you could sit and look down at the Durbar Square below. Here we'd sit with a cold beer and watch Kathmandu life play out before us; the vegetable hawkers, fruit sellers, rickshaws and taxis, and flute sellers who wandered about playing tunes like the Pied Piper. It also seemed to be a popular meeting place for courting couples and young adults. Maju Deval was a triple-roofed 17th-century Shiva temple built by the king's mother in 1690. Considering who ordered its construction, we were quite surprised to find very erotic carvings all along the roof struts.

The city was a very different place at night. Totally silent and empty, but one night, we were sat on the top platform of the Maju Deval putting the world to rights with a couple of cold beers, when we encountered what we from then on called 'The invasion of the midnight cows'. Throughout the day there were no cows around the centre of Kathmandu, more due to a lack of space, than anything else. As we sat there that night in Durbar Square, cows began to appear from everywhere, mooing to their comrades that the coast was clear to invade the city and devour as much as possible before daylight. By the time a new day broke, they had disappeared as quickly as they had arrived, leaving only their droppings as evidence of their presence.

Opposite the Maju Deval is the Kumari Bahal (the house of the living goddess) and on another day we got to see its titular occupant. Inside this three-storey building, behind the intricately carved windows, lives the Kumari, a young girl who has been chosen to be a living goddess through a process not all that different from the selection of the Dalai Lama. Once chosen as the Kumari, she moves into the Kumari Bahal along with all her family, where she is worshipped daily, only really leaving the compound to perform half a dozen ceremonies and festivals each year. One of these festivals involves her being paraded around the city on an enormous chariot for three days. Another, is her annual blessing of the king. She is only a living goddess, however, until her first menstrual cycle, when she then returns to being a mere mortal. Unfortunately for her, it is considered very bad luck to marry an ex-Kumari, although I imagine this has more to do with the natural belief that an ex-goddess is likely to be quite high maintenance, rather than any superstition. You can go in and be blessed by her and make an offering, but you have to make a donation, so obviously we didn't, but we did head across to take a look from the outside. We passed between two stone lions that stood sentry at the front of the house, before entering the courtyard of the Kumari Bahal. We were told that as non-Hindus, and more importantly as for-eigners not willing to pay to worship her, that there was little chance we would get to see the Kumari. We were lucky though, as while we were looking up at the carved wooden balconies, she stuck her head over one of the mezzanines and quite literally looked down on us. She must have been about eight or nine years old, and was wearing a pink sari, with ear to nose jewellery and what I thought was a lot of makeup for such a young girl. She looked very bored, so I gave her a quick wave, before she once more ducked her head back out of sight.

Our evenings were generally spent in one of two places; the Thamel area, or the rooftop restaurant of the Eden hotel, which served no food or drink, but was six storeys above the hustle and bustle of the streets, which gave us a great view, as well as some solitude for writing, reading or sketching. Apart from an old Indian man who lived in the room next to Simon, and never gave up trying to sell him drugs, we tended to have the whole rooftop and hotel all to ourselves.

When we were in the Thamel area of town, we couldn't afford to drink in the bars, so we would sit on the steps of one of the many music shops, which sold pirate CDs and DVDs, and listened to the music blaring from the speakers by the doorway. We'd make occasional requests for them to change tracks, and took turns to go on beer runs to the nearest shop. We would often not eat dinner until after 9pm, because that was the time the bakeries would cut their prices to get rid of the day's leftovers. We'd step inside at one minute past the hour along with several other backpackers, at which point it was every man for himself, as we fought over the remaining chocolate croissants.

Our main task while staying in the city though, was attempting to obtain visas for Pakistan and India. While in London an Indian visa takes just a day, here it took a time-consuming 10 working days. Within an hour of receiving my Indian visa, I was straight across town to the gates to the Pakistan Embassy, where, after some rather over-the-top security procedures, I was allocated a time and date to return for my interview with the Pakistani Ambassador. I was slightly annoyed at this excessive bureaucracy, but not as much as Simon, as before a date could be set for his interview, he had to obtain a letter of introduction from his own embassy. Given that there was no Swiss Embassy in Kathmandu, this created more problems, as he had to get his letter via another embassy that was an ally of Switzerland. While I didn't have to shell out for this extra expense, we both ended up paying the same overall, because the cost of my visa was $30 more than Simons'.

The night before I was due to meet the Pakistani Ambassador, we dined on some form of deep-fried meat, courtesy of a wheeled street stall that passed us in an alleyway. This turned out to be a bad gamble, as it was my exploding stomach that woke me in the morning. Never have I been so grateful to be staying in such a tiny room, as in one fluid motion I was able to leap from my bed straight onto the toilet, where I remained for the next hour worrying that I was never going to make it to the Embassy in time. In an attempt to freshen up, I braved a shower – at this time in the morning it was still well below zero outside, meaning that the water was unbearably cold. In fact, when it first hit my body, I'm sure my heart stopped momentarily.

I then downed a handful of Imodium, donned the T-shirt that I had not only washed to impress the Ambassador, but had hung across the back of a chair to avoid creases, then hurried outside and jumped in the back of the first cycle rickshaw I came across, praying I could hold on for the toilet until I reached the Embassy. Arriving without incident, I was taken to an enormous waiting room. I thought at the time that the Imodium had kicked in, because I felt quite healthy and comfortable, as I looked around at the faded posters on the walls advertising the many sights to see in Pakistan, none of which I had ever heard of. This wasn't surprising though, since the only thing that I knew about Pakistan was that it was on my way home. For the next half an hour I rehearsed what I was going to say to the Ambassador, before eventually being called to his room. He sat behind a large wooden desk and twiddled the ends of his handlebar moustache as I entered. He shook my hand, gestured for me to sit down, and then poured us both a cup of tea. The questions he asked were not complicated. He wasn't trying to catch me out. If anything, he was setting me up for the opportunity to compliment him and his country. I thought I was doing a good job of this, when I became alarmingly aware of how tightly I was suddenly having to clench my buttocks. Then halfway through a comment about how much better Pakistan sounded than India, I jumped from my seat, barely managing to avoid spilling my tea all over the floor, and leapt for the door shouting, "TOILET!" before yanking it open and disappearing down the corridor. I returned a few minutes later the colour of beetroot, but he was very understanding, and after taking my passport, told me to return in two days to collect my visa. Then with a mouth quivering with repressed laughter, recommended a doctor I might like to call, before bidding me farewell.

Over the next few days, I managed to get arrested for drink driving and crashing a cycle rickshaw. We'd spent the night wandering the streets of the Thamel area. By this point, we were fairly well known to the locals here. The street kids no longer tried to beg money from us, and instead we entrusted them with our money to run errands for us such as the gathering of our food and beer. They would do this for a small fee of course, knowing that if they didn't steal the money this time, they would make more the next. The shop owners also now greeted us without trying to coax us inside to buy expensive souvenirs, while the rickshaw drivers had long ago given up offering us lifts since we always walked wherever we went, as we were never in a hurry.

On this particular night, however, one of the rickshaw drivers, possibly out of habit rather than hope, asked us if we needed a ride back to Freak Street. Now fairly merry, I suggested he let me cycle and he could sit in the back with Simon. This was of course under the agreement that we paid nothing. Highly amused, he agreed and climbed in the back seat with Simon, only pausing from his fit of giggles to shout to his friends that a foreigner was driving him. We set off, and I immediately had a new-found respect for the rickshaw drivers. The steering was incredibly heavy, and turning required quite some planning ahead. On top of that, you had to remember that the back was twice the width of the front. This made it quite a challenge. I soon picked up quite a bit of speed and began zooming recklessly past astonished locals who were staring in disbelief at the foreigner taking the Nepalese for a ride.

By now, Simon had cracked open more beer and was plying the driver with drink, who seemed to be having the time of his life! That was until I took a corner and he began yelling frantically from the back seat. I turned around to try to gauge what he was saying, but by the time I understood it was too late: I had entered a one-way road from the wrong end and was now hurtling towards a white taxi which had just appeared around the corner. The road was extremely narrow and there was no way I could stop in time. Everything seemed to slow down around me, even Simon's "SSSHHHIIZZZAA!!"

I swerved out of the way as best I could considering my reactions were slightly hindered by drink, and I managed to avoid a head-on collision only by ramming us sideways into the wall. We didn't miss the car entirely though, and the back wheels of the rickshaw ripped off his rear bumper. Screeching to a halt a further 10m down the road, I sheepishly climbed down and approached the taxi. The driver was not amused. After his initial outburst in full-flowing Nepalese, he reverted to English, demanding an absurd sum of $200 when all the repair work needed was a few new screws and a patch of paint over a two-inch scratch along the side.

I was willing to pay for the repair but not to be ripped off. By now a large crowd had gathered around me and it was beginning to turn nasty. Simon didn't really know what was going on, but was at my back instantly, warning off those who were grabbing at my arms. I was relieved when the police arrived to calm the situation down, but only until they began insisting that I pay the repair bill, which had subsequently gone up to $300.

It was starting to get a bit heated, and although the drink was keeping me from feeling too panicked, I was very aware that India was well known for it's vigilante justice, and I wondered if Nepal was the same. Fearing a mob lynching, but still refusing to pay such an extortionate sum, I willingly allowed myself to be arrested since I was unable to pay the compensation on the spot, which is what the police were now demanding. Simon wanted to come with me to the station, but I insisted he leave me and quickly head back to the safety of the hotel, while the rickshaw driver, clearly petrified at what was going to happen next, was also sent on his way, as I left the scene in the back of a police car.

At the station, I was handed over to the Chief, who led me past the cells filled with a number of depressed-looking chaps sitting on cold hard floors. He took me to a room where most of the officers were just standing around smoking, their guns dangling from their shoulder straps. He sat down at a desk, and I took the seat beside him. He picked up an orange and took a bite straight in to it, peal and all, and then began to tell me about his cousin who had left Nepal to join the British Army as a Ghurkha 17 years before. It had been five years since he had heard from him, he told me, and seemed to want me to tell him why this was ?When we eventually got down to why I was there, he agreed that indeed they had been asking far too much money. He reckoned the repairs should have come to no more than $15, maybe another $10 for the inconvenience, plus an apology. I ended up paying $35, and promised to leave the rickshaw driving to those who knew what they were doing. He was pretty lenient on me considering, which I think was partly because I was a westerner, and partly thanks to my age.

The next day, I was feeling a little bit guilty about my actions the previous night. Now sober, maybe I should have stopped worrying about being ripped off and just paid up then and there. Luckily Simon, who had been quite worried and scared at the time, was finding the whole thing a lot more amusing in the cold light of day than I was. In an attempt to rebalance my karma, therefore, the next evening I visited the Boudhanath Stupa, which was 7km outside of the city and the biggest Buddhist temple in the area. The Stupa reaches a grand 38m in height and on all four of its sides the Buddha's eyes are painted, staring down on all those who sit beneath his gaze. Lines of prayer flags were tied from the top to bottom of the Stupa, adding colour to its bright white base and glaringly gold point. During the daytime, the place is crowded with locals, tourists, Buddhists and Hindus. At night though, the enormous Stupa is home to only the committed Buddhists, who come to light candles, spin prayer wheels and make clockwise circles of the entire Stupa, earning themselves merit with each full rotation. I did almost 30 circuits that night, making sure to spin every prayer wheel I passed.

The next morning, we collected our visas for Pakistan and were finally ready to move on from Kathmandu. But not before we took in one last sight – the Narayanhity Palace. I was not so much interested in seeing the grand palace for its design and the wealth that it displayed – I wanted to go to get a visual of the place where the Royal Family massacre had taken place in 2001. It was there on the 1 June, that Crown Prince Dipendra had executed his parents, the King and Queen, along with several other members of the royal family, before turning the gun on -himself. This had all happened because of a *Romeo and Juliet*-style love story revolving around the class system and Clans of Nepalese society. When the Crown Prince had been denied permission to marry the one he loved due to her status, he had apparently left a royal gathering under the guise of drunkenness, before returning in full military fatigues and equipped with an assault rifle, firing on his family and everyone who got in his way. He didn't die himself immediately after turning the gun on himself, but instead lived for a further three days in a coma. Unbelievably, during this time, he was crowned King, and at first the massacre was described as an accident because, under the constitution and by tradition,

Dipendra as King, could not have been accused of mass murder or any other crime.

When Dipendra didn't recover and died without regaining consciousness, Gyanendra, his uncle, was crowned king. It was he who was ruling the kingdom (with some difficulty) during our time in Nepal. Many Nepalese refuse to believe that story, and think that Gyanendra and his son, Prince Paras, orchestrated the entire massacre themselves. Prince Paras had never had a good reputation among the people. He was known to act like a spoilt brat, driving around in fast cars and flashing the cash. Many find it too convenient that Gyanendra was unable to attend the royal gathering in the first place. They also argue that their beloved Prince Dipendra could never have performed these atrocities, their evidence being that he was left handed and he was shot in the right side of the head, although this ignores the fact that he was unsuccessful in killing himself, and this may well have been why.

After crossing this off my list of morbid curiosities, we boarded the bus to Pokhara. We had arrived too late to get a seat on the bus, which was the last one leaving that day, but to make sure every available fare was taken, it was acceptable to ride the entire eight-hour journey on its roof. Having never ridden such a long distance on the roof of a bus, I jumped at the chance. Sadly, I was not allowed to, as my foreigner status meant I was too precious a cargo to risk falling off. We were instead made to squeeze inside and stand for most of the journey, while those of less apparent importance, sat on the roof, stretching out their legs and enjoying the panoramic 360 degree views all the way to Pokhara.

14

Apple Brandy

Kathmandu to Pokhara = 262km

When we arrived at the lakeside in Pokhara, we were immediately set upon by a horde of touts pushing and shoving one another as they fought to beat the price of their rivals. They competitively shouted offers at us, inches from our faces, so close that we could smell the betel nut, which is a bit like chewing tobacco, on their breath.

I didn't know if this was a normal reception, but over the next few days it became clear that Pokhara's tourist trade had been badly hit by the country's recent troubles, and everyone was desperate for our trade. But after our arduous eight-hour journey, all we really cared about was a cold beer before we even began to think about our next move.

Unsurprisingly we got a good deal on the accommodation we checked into. We could undoubtedly have beaten the price down even further, but as the man was clearly desperate for our business, we felt too guilty to haggle. The owner had built the guesthouse in the low season the year before, and was now running at a complete loss, so we enjoyed our room, with its en-suite bathroom for the low season price of 150 rupees a night, which worked out just over £1.

With the whole guesthouse to ourselves, the best part about the accommodation, was the roof terrace, where we would sit and stare out across the lake and surrounding green hills dotted with fir trees and the odd stupa, and in the distance, the white peaks of the Himalayas. We had come to Pokhara to do some trekking and, not wanting to waste our time doing a quick three-day jaunt, we had decided to do the entire Annapurna Circuit, a trek we were told required 18 to 20 days. On the trail, which zigzagged through valleys and villages and forests, we would pass two of the biggest mountains in the country, second only to Everest, and that first night, as I looked out across at the distant mountain range, I wondered if I had bitten off more than I could chew.

We spent the next few days preparing for the trek, buying enough instant soups and tinned foods to be self-sufficient for at least one meal a day, hopeful that guesthouses and villages along our route would be able to supply the rest. We also traipsed around the whole of Pokhara in search of cheese for Simon, who swore he couldn't trek without it. We managed to find some, although we later discovered that village after village along the route, sold boulders of the stuff.

Once Simon had his cheese, and we'd got all the necessary permits to trek inside the Annapurna conservation area, we caught the bus from Pokhara into the mountains as far as the roads would take us. After five hours we reached the end of the line, and from where the bus dropped us, we began one of the most challenging walks of my life.

After only an hour of walking into the mountains, we had left behind the beeping of horns and the humming of engines. All we could hear was the gravel crunching beneath our feet. With only a few kilometres behind us I could see that Simon, who grew up in the mountains, was in his element, striding ahead with his walking stick, a souvenir he had picked up in the desert at the start of the Great Wall of China. As he powered on ahead, I realized that the two of us had very different styles of walking; while he saw each day as a chance to push himself harder and further and to march on without rest to the next destination as quickly as possible, I preferred to dawdle at a more casual pace, stopping occasionally to look at, touch or smell things. We therefore made no attempt to keep up with one another, and I would just keep walking until I came across wherever he had decided to stop, even if sometimes that was more than four hours after his arrival. He'd usually be sitting there with a cold beer grinning proudly and say something like, "You took a long time today."

Whenever he was a really long way ahead of me and reached a forking path or a trail that simply faded away, he would make his choice, either by investigation or instinct, and would then scratch into the ground or onto a nearby and visible rock face, an arrow with a smiley face for me to follow. The system worked well, apart from once or twice when I was too busy daydreaming to notice his messages or the path branching off, and I was left scratching my head outside some lonely goat herders' shack, wondering at which point I had gone wrong.

Although we completed much of the circuit alone, for the first few days we stuck together, and on that first afternoon we took great delight in our new surroundings. We passed caravans of mules laden with goods, ambling along and delivering supplies and mail to those living in the remote villages on the way. We were often passed by Sherpas, bent double and arms folded, carrying loads that more often than not appeared to outweigh their own bodyweight, yet their cargo was strapped to their backs by a single band stretched across their foreheads, which I can only imagine must have put a huge strain on their spines – they certainly all had crazy neck muscles. Their loads could range from anything from coiled piping, dozens of buckets, bags of sugar, sacks of rice and were so enormous and heavy the Sherpas were unable to lift them directly from the ground. Instead, when they needed a break, they would rest what they were carrying on a low wall, then help each other back on to their feet, before setting off once more for another few kilometres of climbing up and down the steep trails. Seeing these small men passing me carrying loads three times as heavy as my shoulder-strapped Bergen backpack, often gave me the boost I needed to continue, after having keeled over in the high altitude and struggling to catch my breath.

Even if we couldn't keep up with the Sherpas, we did manage to overtake a handful of tourists along the trail each day. This would make me feel less pathetic, as it seemed that every group we passed were having their bags carried by porters and being led by a guide. We always made a point of walking at least 3km further than the groups we passed each day, well Simon did anyway, and while this doesn't sound like an awful lot, when you consider that the whole day was spent climbing up and down steep hills, it was exhausting.

The constant ascending and descending was particularly disheartening for the first couple of days, as we knew we had to ascend from 414m, all the way up to 5,416m over the course of the trek.

That first day was particularly beautiful, as we walked along the river beside which we would travel for more than half the trek. We passed through green fields so bright that they bordered on fluorescent, dotted with farmers sowing their crops, driving buffalos with whips as they bounced up and down on the back of rickety old ploughs. We crossed the river frequently using rope bridges just like those out of *Indiana Jones*. With the raging water 30 odd metres below us, we took care to walk along the edges of the bridges, for some of the planks were cracked or missing entirely. I messed around on them at first by swinging the bridges from side to side and jumping up and down in the middle just to annoy Simon, then a little further up we saw the remains of where a bridge had collapsed completely, and I stopped. By about day four the bridges began to improve and had steel reinforcements along them and, as Simon took great pride in pointing out each and every time we saw a plaque confirming it, they were all Swiss built.

One problem we did encounter was finding places to stay, mainly because the villages were built a day's walk apart, and because of Simon's eagerness to cover more ground, we overshot the villages a few times and were forced to stop for the night in the middle of nowhere. This is what happened on the first night, but luckily we came across a cave just off the path, and thinking it might make a good place to camp, went over to investigate. It was clearly used as a shelter by mules, but the floor was sandy, and we were able to rake over most of their droppings. I constructed a foot-high wall out of the rocks lying around, while Simon collected water from the river.

As the light began to fade in the valley, we had just got comfy in our sleeping bags and were passing a bottle of warming vodka between us, when three men appeared and told us we should go with them to sleep elsewhere. They explained in broken English that the Maoists ruled that area at night, and it wasn't safe to stay after dark. They seemed genuine, but we were quite content in our little caveman existence, and told them that while we appreciated their concern, we would stay where we were. They sat with us for a while, and asked us why we would turn down the offer of a free bed in preference of a turd-covered floor. I explained that where we were from, we had the option to sleep in a bed almost every night, but never in a cave. This seemed to satisfy them, although they clearly thought we were weird. They left laughing, but not before warning us to stay quiet and not to make a fire.

That night, a huge electrical storm broke out overhead, but while the winds howled and bursts of lightning lit up the mountains and sky, there was no rain. In the flashes we could see that we were not the only ones spending the night in the cave, we were accompanied by dozens of bats that were flying in and out of its entrance on their nocturnal hunts. When the storm died down, I closed my eyes and slept soundly until Simon woke me and pointed at a procession of torchlights silently making their way along the river bank in single file. Unsure whether they were Maoists or not, we quietly settled back down in our sleeping bags, alert to every noise until we fell back asleep.

In the morning I had to dig out my scissors, for in the night I had rolled off my makeshift pillow, and now had mule crap encrusted in my hair. I could have washed it out of course, but the water was freezing and I wasn't brave enough. Once that was taken care of, we enjoyed a hearty meal of bread and vegetable soup for breakfast, courtesy of the new cooker I had bought in Kathmandu.

We walked on among the fields for no more than three hours, before we stopped and enjoyed a cold beer. The drink, though highly refreshing, left me slow and clumsy for the next few hours, and it became a very long gruelling day, not helped by the fact that most of it was spent climbing up hill, sometimes using well worn, uneven stone steps, but others up dirt tracks through forested areas. By the evening, I already had bruising across my collarbone and extremely sore hips, and I was very grateful to collapse into a bed that night.

After the first two days, the friction from my bag straps around my hips had already rubbed the skin away making the subsequent days an agonizing struggle. I took to smothering my skin in Vaseline and wrapping my sleeping sheet around my waist and under the buckles, just to ease the pressure. While this helped mildly with the discomfort, it meant the sores became wet with sweat all day, and began to rapidly widen. The bulk of the sheet also blocked the view of my feet, which I kept bare for large portions of the day since my walking boots were now also rubbing, and sometime before lunch on the third day, I lost my footing and slipped down some stone steps, cutting and twisting my toes badly in the process.

The scenery began to change quite drastically. The low-lying fields of the day before were replaced with rocky mountains, and the odd glimpse of the Himalayas ahead. The air also smelt different here, somewhat damper and more pure. The haze through which we had stared ahead before, seemed to be thinning as well, improving the views with each turn we made.

We stopped for the day to stay in a little wooden cabin that had been built to a high standard, with no gaps along the windows or below the door. But still that night, while I lay in bed reading a book by candle-light, a giant spider of at least four inches in diameter crawled across my bare chest and down underneath the table that separated our beds. We were understandably keen to find it and return it to its rightful environment, since although we were unsure if it was poisonous, we would rather not find out. We got up and crouched down to detect its hiding place. Simon checked under his bed, while I attempted to look under the table. As I did so, I suddenly looked up, thinking I could hear fire-works, and was just about to get up to go to the window when Simon began shouting in German and beating me over the head with his pillow. I began to fight him off, until I got the distinct whiff of singed hair and realized that I had managed to put my head in the candle and my head was ablaze. Fire out, we inspected my now frizzled bald spot, and laughed so hard that we completely forgot about the spider, and only had trouble sleeping because we couldn't stop giggling to ourselves as we lay in the dark.

It was with great relief that the next day's trekking was relatively flat and shaded, which gave my sores a chance to recover a little. Once again, the scenery changed, but the river was still with us, and we continued to crisscross it regularly. It now not only spanned a far greater width, but it was far below us, and a churning chalky colour. Thankfully I had lost the urge to jump up and down in the middle of the bridges entirely by now.

Over the next two days, we walked through forests of pine trees and would stop to cut open the pine cones to enjoy the fresh scent. Simon was like a child in a sweet shop, as it reminded him of summer in his village back home. He impressed me with his knowledge of the different trees and plants, and when I asked how he knew all this he seemed surprised and said, "I learnt it in school. Don't you in England?"

I shook my head. I could only remember once in infant school being taken out into the playground and being shown the different types of leaves, which we collected, covered in paint and then made prints with on a piece of paper. Simon frowned. "That's weird," he said, and I agreed.

Where the trail was not forested, we were often surrounded by banks of female marijuana plants, so we would stop to take photos of us grinning beneath them, shrouded by head height plants and giving the thumbs up. But the icing on the cake for Simon over those days, was when we were able to buy two enormous chunks of yak cheese, a very white and mature cheese which we had for breakfast, lunch and dinner for the next two days. We were now walking for an average of 10 hours a day, only really stopping for a quick snack and a lunch time beer, which was getting more and more expensive the further we travelled. Twice on the trek, I stopped to applaud a procession of mules carrying beer up into the mountains.

Arriving in Manang, after spending the previous night in a monastery, we decided to spend the next day resting and acclimatizing; we had now reached an altitude of 3,500m, but still had a further 2,000m in altitude to climb over the next two days. This was one reason to stay in Manang for a rest day, another was the excellent bakery there, not to mention the views which made all the uphill struggles and injuries worthwhile. The forests and pastures were now below us; the vegetation was sparse and the climate was damp and windy, but around us were the highest mountains in the Annapurna range. At 8,000m the mountain's summits were hidden above the clouds; monasteries sat tucked in their ledges, and running down between the bases of the peaks, a blue glacier glistened as it slowly melted and filled the lake far below with fresh water.

Our bodies reacted to the rest day by seizing up on us entirely, and so, apart from frequent trips back and forth to the bakery, we spent the day just taking in the views and relaxing on our balcony. We left the guest-house early in the morning, but then decided to wait another hour for the bakery to open. We also bought a miniature bottle of whisky each to drink upon reaching the Thorong La Pass, the highest point of the trek.

Within an hour of leaving Manang, Simon was a mile or more ahead of me. The morning was spent walking uphill through a valley where, through binoculars, I spotted an eagle returning to its nest with food for its young, and a herd of mountain goats making their way along a near-vertical mountainside. I walked gingerly along sloped ledges, as each step created a mini avalanche of loose stones. Along some parts, the wind blew with such velocity, the gusts catching my pack like a sail, that I feared being blown clean off the mountainside. Each time I felt one coming therefore, I crouched down and dug my fingers into the ground until it passed. In some places, avalanches from above blocked my way and left me no option but to climb over the displaced boulders that teetered along the very edge.

After eight hours of almost solid walking, I was relieved to reach the high camp at 4,500m. This was where most people spent the night after walking from Manang to prepare them for the crossing of the pass the following day. After having a good look around and not finding a single soul, I guessed Simon was still possessed of his need to cover ever more ground and had not stopped. I filled my water bottle, ate my last cheese roll from the bakery, and set off again. I then missed the correct trail and wasted half an hour walking down to a dead end, where I found myself penned in by the river's edge and a sheer cliff face. I retraced my steps, but still could not find an obvious trail. The only way seemed to be up and so I began a 20-minute climb up a steep bank. When I reached the top, I was greeted with a helipad marked out with stones, and leading down from it on the other side was a neat path, which would have made my ascent a mere walk in the park in comparison. Pleased that I was in the right place, but annoyed I had got there by an unnecessarily harder route, I stopped and looked back at the way I had come. I could see the faint white line of the path behind me, and tried to follow it with my eyes as it vanished and then reappeared within the folds of the valley, before turning and continuing on my way.

The air was thin and the path was a rough one which required concentration. As I pushed on, my legs felt like they were wading through water, and my joints like there was acid pumping through my veins. I heard a

shout and looked up to see Simon waving encouragement. When I finally reached him ready to collapse, he
tentatively broke the news that I had another 45 minutes
to walk to where we would be staying that night.
Although I hadn't said anything, he could tell I was in a
lot of pain from my sores, and he offered to carry my
bag for me. A long look passed between us, then Simon
simply turned and began to lead the way, while I followed behind cursing under my breath, but kind of
loving him for his craziness at the same time.

By now it was really cold, and since I had posted
my Tibetan coat home from Kathmandu, the cutting
wind was sending shooting pains through my fingers.
Everything was blanketed in snow, and I felt the familiar
feeling of slush seeping in through my boots. We walked
past icicles the size of cars hanging from snowdrifts that
had frozen solid to the folds of the mountains, and while
I caught my breath, I made Simon stop and stand still for
a moment to truly take in the solitude and silence,
broken only by the occasional snap of ice which would
echo around the mountains for minutes at a time.

Reaching the teahouse in which we were to stay, that
at 5,000m the two Nepalese owners claimed was the
highest in the world, we were greeted by two Israeli
men and a Swiss couple. They all thought we were mad
to have come all the way from Manang in one day.
I agreed with them, as I collapsed onto one of the camp
beds in the corner, but was proud to be travelling with
Simon, even if he did seem to want to make me suffer.
The two Nepalese guys who ran the place and had been
living up there for the past three months, seemed to be
living proof that prolonged exposure to high altitude
affected the brain. They really were like Laurel and

Hardy. They both wore woollen hats with little bobbles on top, which wobbled back and forth with every movement they made, and when later that evening I produced a tin of Spam from my pack, they became very excited and asked to buy it from me. I ended up selling them the whole tin for a 110 rupees, which was a tidy profit as I had bought it for just 60 in Pokhara. They were delighted, however, because since everything had to be carried to their guesthouse by mule, other items, such as bottles of beer, were far greater priority than tinned meat, and it was something they rarely got. Incredibly, the two Israelis had travelled up to 5,000m with no sleeping bags, and had just two blankets to sleep under for the night which they had borrowed from Laurel and Hardy. I felt sorry for them that night, as even with a woodburner glowing in our shared dormitory, and tightly wrapped in my sleeping bag with a space blanket beneath me on top of my Z-bed, the air was so cold that my teeth hurt. In the morning it was evident that the Israelis hadn't slept a wink: they departed for the pass while I was still waking up, and both looked quite sick. The Swiss had already left and Simon, not wanting to be beaten to the pass even if it was by his fellow countrymen, had also set off to claim his summit.

I hung around a while longer, and spent some time just looking down upon the sheet of white fluffy clouds below me, and then up at the mountains rising above, and felt quite insignificant. I overtook the Israelis not long after setting off – on their poor night's sleep, they could have been crawling on their hands and knees for all the progress they were making. I carried on for another half an hour before passing the Swiss who had stopped to rest – one of them was dry-retching and looking quite ill. Eventually, I met Simon at the pass. It was a momentous occasion, and he grinned as I approached.

"This is the highest we've been together," he said.

"And from here on in, the beer will only get cheaper!" I replied. We sat down among the prayer flags, our backs resting on the sign marking the summit, and clinked our now open bottles of whisky. We stayed until the bottles were finished, amusing ourselves by taking photos of each other in various Edmund Hillary poses, standing on the piles of rocks that marked the pass. By 8am, feeling on top of the world and a little tipsy, we had begun our descent, and within an hour we had descended by 800m. We passed the remains of an old settlement where we stopped for a breakfast of mush-room soup and bread. I obviously failed to screw the cap of my kerosene bottle back on properly before we left though, and that night found half my clothes were soaked in fuel.

As we continued down to Mutinath, a further 800m below, we saw two army helicopters storming out from in between the mountains. A few days later we learnt that there had been heavy fighting between the Maoists and the army in the villages we had passed through days before, and that both sides had sustained a huge loss of life.

After a quick rest and a bite to eat in Mutinath, we pressed on for another four hours until we rested for the night and checked into the Hilton Hotel. The only similarity between where we stayed and the other Hilton hotels, however, was the name.

The next day we walked for 12 and a half hours. For more than three hours that morning, we walked down the bed of what had once been a vast river, the whole time leaning forward into a gale. It was tough going, but we were quite excited as we knew we were fast approaching a village surrounded by orchards that supplied most of Nepal with apples. It had been a long time since I had eaten any fruit, especially some picked from a tree, and so I was drooling over the thought of hot apple pie when we came across the first few houses and Simon pointed out that the trees in the surrounding hills didn't seem to have a lot of leaves. Our suspicions were confirmed when we reached the first shop and were told it was the wrong time of year for apples. The only apple product available to buy was apple brandy, so we made do with a bottle of that each instead. It was good timing, as just around the corner, Annapurna One made its presence felt. At 8,091m, this was the highest mountain we were to see here, and although I'd seen Everest, I had been at 5,000m at the time, so the size of Annapurna One, from around 2,500m looked simply unearthly.

"Holy moly, that's a big friggin mountain," I said. Simon laughed. It was certainly worthy of the "cheers" we gave it, as we held our bottles up towards its peak, somewhere above the cloud line.

By the time we had washed our lunch down with a beer, we were under the influence of high spirits. We staggered down the trail and endlessly mucked around – it was amazing how the alcohol made our packs seem so weightless. Unsurprisingly, we got a little lost along the way and unable to find the bridge we needed to cross a gentle but icy river. We removed our boots and socks and waded across instead, splashing each other with the freezing water as we went.

After rejoining the path, it took us higher again, and we looked down across the gravelly expanse that stretched between the mountains, the silver of the river tributaries slithering across it like liquid mercury. A little later on, for the first time on the whole trek, I found myself in the lead, and a little worried, I back-tracked to see where Simon had gone. I found him standing gazing out across at the view and I frowned, unsure of what made it so outstanding compared to what we'd already seen that day. Then Simon told me to look again and pointed upwards. I followed his finger, but at first could still only see lines of white fluffy clouds. He didn't say anything, and just continued to point, while I squinted and looked harder. Then I saw that the white was not all clouds, but also snow on the mountainside. Looking back at Annapurna One from this distance, I could see how the locals believed that gods resided at the top of these mountains, for the peak seemed to end somewhere far above in the heavens, and only patches of the colossal mountain were visible through the camouflage of clouds. The discovery of that view, which I had nearly missed, was celebrated with a bottle of whisky at the next village we came to. By the time we stopped walking that day, dark had long fallen. Most people had already bolted their doors for the night, and it took us quite some time to find a bed in a guesthouse, although we finally did.

The next morning, the decision as to whether we should rest for a day or move on was taken out of our hands, for our bodies had gone on strike. The simple task of walking down the corridor to the toilet required a great deal of effort. Every limb felt 10 times heavier than normal and ached with every movement, and we remained bedridden all morning. From the window by my bed I could see the one and only road that ran through the village. A tractor pulling a trailer loaded with locals came bouncing along the dirt road, and we yelled, "Namaste!" out of the window at them and waved, and they cheered and returned our greetings.

Later that afternoon, the Swiss couple we had last seen at the Thorong La Pass arrived, looking stricken. This time it was Simon's turn to translate to me what was wrong. We learnt from them that the tractor and the trailer we had seen pass by hours earlier, had over-turned while making a shallow river crossing, trapping and pinning many of the people below the surface. Over a dozen people had drowned in what was no more than two feet of water, we went down to the riverbank to see if there was anything we could do, and found the bodies were now laid out in a line along the river bank, await-ing collection by the family members, who were slowly being informed. Those who had escaped stood around in shock; some were wrapped in blankets still shivering from the cold of the icy water in which they had been immersed. Unfortunately, I'd seen the expression in their eyes before; that look of uncomprehending loss and overwhelming guilt of still being alive. In my mind, I was immediately back in Khao Lak with the survivors of the tsunami and I didn't want to be there, I didn't want to be reminded of all of that, I didn't want to think about all that again. I had just reached a point where I was not thinking about it every day and was feeling at peace and then I was cast in a second back to the scenes of the tsunami. It was a shock how quickly it all came rushing back. I spent the rest of the day in a very sombre mood, and the next morning we set off early for

Tatopani. Simon went on ahead and reached the village after six hours of power walking. I set off at my usual pace, and around midday the sun was becoming unbearably hot and I had already savoured the last dregs in my water bottle. Amongst the shade of the trees, I noticed a large solitary boulder. I climbed up on it, lay down and rested my eyes, only waking hours later when the scorching sun had begun to cool.

When I reached Tatopani, many, many hours after Simon, I found him sitting at a table by the roadside, accompanied by a number of empty beer bottles and with soaking wet hair. He said he had been worried about me and had been considering going back to look for me. I asked how many beers ago that was and why was he dripping wet? It turned out that there was a hot spring close by, but apparently it wasn't very hot and had just left Simon feeling sticky as the water was not clean. Seeing as it had already been nearly two weeks since my last shower, I figured I might as well hold out for a few more days.

In the morning, I used up the last of our rations making us a foul breakfast of yak cheese and noodles. As we set off battling to keep the strange concoction in our stomachs, Simon was cursing my culinary skills. As it was hot again, I had reverted back to my flip-flops instead of my boots, and walked a number of kilometres barefoot. We spent most of the morning looking over our shoulders, unwilling to leave behind the view of the mountains, and it was while doing so that I had a nasty fall. I smashed my head into the ground with quite some force, jarring my wrist badly as I attempted to brace myself with the weight of my pack behind me. The main injury though was once again to my feet, which were torn to shreds as I attempted to stop myself sliding down the gravel slope. After cleaning them the best I could, I limped on. Then, less than an hour later, I was once again not paying attention to the path ahead of me when I felt the squelchy warmth encasing my foot as I stepped in a large pile of fresh mule crap. All my open wounds were now filled with faeces. Once Simon had recovered from laughing, and I had finished screaming obscenities, we again scrubbed my foot with the last of our water, and removed what dirt we could. That night I soaked my feet in a bowl of Betadine and scrubbed the wounds with an old toothbrush which hurt like hell! Luckily, that day was to be the last day of walking, for we had arrived in the village of Beni, from where we could catch a bus back to Pokhara. Beni was no more than a large village really, but after so long in gentle laid-back surroundings, to us it seemed like a bustling metropolis.

The bus back to Pokhara took far longer than we had expected, due to countless checkpoints along the way. All the recent fighting meant the area was in a state of high security, and we were forced to continually disembark from the bus, file through the checkpoints, passports in hand and then re-board further down the road. *Take me back to the mountains!* I thought.

Later that afternoon we arrived back at the guest-house at which we had previously stayed in Pokhara, and the owner, who had been looking after some of our things for us, was pleased but surprised to see us, as we had been gone just 16 days, rather than the 18 to 20 we had been told to allow for. After a gloriously hot shower, we celebrated the success of the trek up on the rooftop with seven large bottles of beer each, and slept well that night.

The next morning, I woke feeling excited. It was the 27 May, my 20th birthday, and I was no long a teenager. While Simon remained snoring, I crept up on to the rooftop and watched as the sun rose across the lake. When he woke, Simon went out to get us breakfast and returned with a true birthday meal for me; muesli with yogurt and a banana milkshake. He'd even managed to get hold of a little yellow napkin, quite a rarity in Nepal!

Throughout the day, we rounded up every foreigner we spotted around town, and invited them to my birthday party, which was to be held at a place we had picked at random without even going inside. Considering that I knew no one there but Simon that night, it was a very impressive turnout. The drinks were flowing, and toasts were still being slurred well into the early hours. The owner of the bar, who was feeling very grateful for the sudden rush of business, gave me many a drink on the house, and sometime before sunrise, Simon and I decided to move on to India the next morning.

15

Maharaja McMeal

Annapurna Circuit = 248km

By morning, all our good intentions for leaving that day had gone out the window, having woken not only a lot later than planned, but also feeling slightly under the weather. Without raising our heads from the pillows, we agreed that another rest day was in order; after all, we'd been walking for a very long time. So, we had breakfast, lunch and dinner at the café we had adopted during our time there, despite knowing the food always gave us Delhi belly. We ate their tasty baguettes and slurped their milkshakes pretending they had nothing to do with our frequent trips to the bathroom in between. Then late that night we packed up our stuff and went to bed ready for our departure to India.

The bus we needed to take to the last town before the Indian border had no glass or plastic in the windows, and after seven hours in transit, we arrived very dusty and weary and with a good idea how all the livestock we had passed along the way felt. It was a further 5km walk to the actual border, and when we got there we were told that while the border was still open, the moneychangers were closed for the day which effectively meant that there was no point in us crossing over, as we'd have no money for the bus on the Indian side.

We checked into the only room we could find. It was by far one of the worst kept and filthiest rooms that I had ever paid to sleep in. As we opened the door, cockroaches scuttled into the dark corners of the room, dead insects lay scattered across the floor, the walls were a sticky nicotine-stained yellow, and in the corner the roots from a plant outside the building stretched out across the ceiling. We had an en-suite, but the shower was no more than a hole in the wall above a floor so stained that it was impossible to tell its original colour, while the hole for the toilet was out of bounds since it was already occupied by several other species. Simon went for a shower – I had decided that it was a waste of time as I doubted any water would come through the rusted old pipes. Then I heard the sound of water hitting the floor.

"How is it?" I shouted, but before Simon could reply, there was an almighty crash from inside.

"You alright?" There was silence, then I heard laughter. He was still laughing when he emerged from the bathroom a few minutes later, and indicated that I should take a look. I stuck my head around the door. Inside, the entire sink and a handful of pipes lay in a broken pile on the floor.

"All I did was put my foot up on the edge of the sink to wash between my toes, and everything collapsed around me!"

We didn't get much sleep that night. One of the two beds in the room was so disgustingly stained it should have been quarantined, so we were forced to share the remaining single. Aside from this, we were woken numerous times by bugs crawling over our faces; the sensation of having cockroach legs scamper across my lips is one I wish I could forget. We very much doubted that the owners of the guesthouse would have known whether or not the bathroom was a pile of pipes before we rented the room, but we took no chances and left at daybreak to flee across the border.

The Indian immigration office took a ridiculous amount of time to get through; Indians just seem to love paperwork, and as we left, they kindly informed us that we had just gained a further 15 minutes on the time line. I had spent a few months in India before, but had never really warmed to the people who seemed to view me as a walking wallet. While I had become used to this in other countries, in India I had failed to find a single person who just wanted to chat and didn't have a sick mother or crippled brother they needed financial help with.

In fact, my last trip had ended extremely strangely with me getting caught up in some weird jewellery smuggling scheme, which essentially saw me being forced to post some precious stones to the UK for a "local businessman" whose crew then held me hostage for three days until I agreed to pay them £1,000 insurance. When I say "hostage" it was in some pretty comfortable 5-star accommodation with hospitality thrown in, but even so I quickly realized I'd got myself into a bit of a mess, and after a lot of protest, anger and furniture destruction on my part, I finally agreed to pay them the sum, willing to do anything to get out of the mess I was in. Money received; they then flew me home to England with a gift of some jewellery as a gesture to show that I'd get my £1,000 back after I had recovered the precious stones I had posted to England for them. I assumed this jewellery to be worthless, particularly since the contact that was meant to be waiting for me at the airport to return my money and then collect the precious stones with me never appeared, but when I finally decided to go to the police and confess all, it turned out that the jewellery was worth more than the £1,000 I had paid the crooks, and although I was probably guilty of Indian tax evasion, in the police's eyes I was free to go as long as I promised to never do anything of the sort again. I managed to sell the jewellery on for £1,000 a few months later, which meant I was back exactly where I started moneywise, but totally at a loss as to how exactly I had been scammed.

Anyway, this time I promised myself I would give the Indian people a second chance despite how strangely my previous visit had ended. I also decided not to tell Simon about any of it, partly because I wanted him to make up his own mind, and partly because it was a very long story which would take forever to explain to someone who only had a partial grasp of what I was saying.

Across the border, and not far off sea level, the climate had grown increasingly hot and, as our bus departed for the city of Varanasi, there was an intense stench coming from all the rubbish and cow crap at the sides of the roads which, without any breeze, just lingered in the air. Varanasi, formerly called Benaras, is considered by Hindus to be the holiest city in India. It sits on the banks of the River Ganges, the most sacred of all rivers to Hindus. Many head there when they feel that their time in this life is almost over. This is so that once they have passed on to their next lives, their bodies can be burnt on the ghats or steps, that line the banks, and their remains thrown and swept into the river. Despite this, the ghats are still the heart of the city, and everything revolves around them, and people wash their clothes and themselves in the holy river, as burnt remains float past. I had been aiming to go there on my last jaunt around India, but had never got that far. As we waited for the bus to Varanasi, I remember reading what Mark Twain had said about it being one of the oldest living cities in the world. "Benaras is older than history, older than tradition, older even than legend, and looks twice as old as all of them put together."

The bus was practically empty. There was only the driver and three men standing at the back. Simon had run out of money when we left Pokhara and couldn't get any more funds until we reached a bank in Varanasi, so I had to pay our fares. One of the men who had been lurking at the rear of the bus, came over to us under the pretence of being the bus conductor. I enquired as to the fare, and he said it was 290 rupees each. I was sure that was too much and said so. He calmly explained that the reason for the high price was due to it being an Express Local bus. I'd never heard of an Express Local bus before, but the driver was aware of what was going on and did not say anything, so I paid up.

The bus continued for another few minutes before the man came over again, and said we must pay 150 rupees each for our luggage. I knew for sure this time that this was not true, and told him we were not paying any more, especially since our bags were hardly taking up any extra space. At this, he flipped and suddenly the other two men were at his side as he leant over me shouting that unless we paid, he would throw us off the bus. Next, he began insulting my mother using a muddle of English obscenities, before he grabbed hold of my arm and demanded I fight him. I stood up, and Simon, unsure of what was going on said, "Just pay and complain at the other end!" Seeing some sense in this, I begrudgingly handed over more money.

A few stops further on, the three men jumped off the bus and disappeared into the crowd, taking with them any chance of us getting our money back. I shot an accusatory look at the driver, who sheepishly turned away as I realized that it had been the driver's cowardice that had allowed us to be ripped off. At that very stop, the true conductor boarded the bus, and the driver redeemed himself slightly by telling him not to charge us our fare. This was not, however, the fresh start I had been hoping for in India.

It took nine hours to reach Varanasi, during which time the bus slowly filled until it was packed. The journey was not made any quicker by the fact that seven of those hours were spent with a naked toddler seated on his mother's lap beside me, squealing loudly and pinching my arm. The mother, who was well aware of her child's constant assaults on me, however, did nothing to stop her, and just beamed with pride, while I glowered in irritation.

On arrival in Varanasi, we found a cheap place just five minutes from the ghats of the River Ganges, which was perfect, because it afforded us all the atmospheric benefits of being close to the holy river, while avoiding the downsides of extreme proximity; the early morning cries of religion, the mosquitoes, and worst of all, the smell. It had been a staggering 47 degrees centigrade in Varanasi for that past week, and our small room was head-spinningly hot, even with the ceiling fan pumping full speed. At night, the walls seemed to radiate the day's heat, making it impossible to sleep, so we took to sleeping on the tiled balcony that adjoined our room instead, but even then, found ourselves virtually panting in the suffocating temperatures.

We were keen to spend one full day, from dawn until dusk, around the ghats, and so the next morning we were up before the sun and watched from the rooftop of an old building as it rose across the city. We listened as Varanasi came to life around us with ugly early morning noises, bangs and crashes; the ritual snorting sounds of men clearing their throats out of the nearest window, the hooting of horns which would slowly build to a continuous hum and metal shutters rattling open as shops began their day's trading. The sun was a deep fiery red and formed a perfect circle, giving us the rare chance to stare directly at it through the haze as the light stretched out across the surrounding rooftops. As visibility slowly improved, we saw we were not alone in watching this early morning spectacle; on rooftops as far as we could see, many others stood watching the new day unfold.

We decided to go our separate ways that morning, and as I walked alone along the ghats of the River Ganges, I watched the day begin in Varanasi as it had done so for centuries. The Chai Wallas, or tea vendors, were boiling up their first brews of the day, getting ready to supply the needy with a morning shot of a spicy, sugary tea beside the water's edge. Women stood waist-deep in the water, nattering as they pounded their washing against the ancient stone steps, the brown river water glistening as they wrung it from their laundry, and their children playing in the shallows, splashing friends and passers-by. Young and old were washing their bodies in the river, while others stood waist-deep with the palms of their hands pressed together against their chests as they muttered prayers, then ducking below the surface for a few seconds at a time. Squatting higher up on the steps were the holy men, Sadhus, who were preparing their first hashish pipes or "Chillums" of the day, while all along the ghats, people, cows, dogs and water buffalo lay sleeping, ignoring the building heat that would soon send them into the shade.

Near the area of the ghats where the bodies were cremated, an older man dressed fairly smartly in a short-sleeved shirt, approached me and asked if I would be interested in a guide. Normally I would have turned down such an offer, but as this was a sensitive place to be, I didn't want to accidentally offend someone through my ignorance and so I accepted. He explained that he worked for the hospices that surrounded the area of the ghats which were filled with people waiting for the ends of their lives – many Indians believe that to die beside the River Ganges will bring instant enlightenment.

The sacred river begins far north in the Himalayan cave of Amarnath and flows down to India's southern tip, Kanyakumari. Apparently, some arrived at the hospices far too early and would wait there to die for up to three years. He asked if I wanted to go and view some of the dying people, I declined and just put a couple of hundred rupees in the donation box outside the hospice instead. This satisfied him, and the tour resumed at the cremation ghat.

Here, men with scales awaited their next customer surrounded by piles of wood. My guide explained that they weigh the body, and then they work out how much wood you need to buy to burn it. We watched from a distance as a corpse, wrapped in a shroud, was dunked and doused in the River Ganges before being placed on the pyre. The pyre, built using the exact amount of wood needed to incinerate the body, was then ignited using a torch taken from the Eternal Fire which was burning at the top of the steps, and which the Sadhus ensured never went out. For a donation, they would bless the flames on each torch that was lit from it. I asked if any Hindu could be cremated on the ghats or if there were exceptions. My guide explained there were five exceptions; children, pregnant women, Sadhus, lepers and, most bizarrely I thought, people who had died from a snake bite. Instead, these bodies were rolled into the river from a boat, after being weighted down. When my guide noticed me watching a large pile of human hair blowing about under an archway, he pointed out two barbers sitting in the shade, and explained that it was customary for close family members to shave their heads after a loved one had died, as a sign of respect and so others would know that they were grieving. We watched as the ash from the remains of a funeral pyre was swept down towards the water's edge. The man with the broom, possibly a relative of the deceased, seemed to be sweeping into the wind, and much of the ash was blowing back into his own face. I noticed a cluster of children at the base of the ghats and fearing I already knew the answer, asked what they were doing, for they were rummaging through the piles of ash with their bare hands. "Scavenging for jewellery or gold teeth," he replied, confirming my suspicions.

Later that afternoon, I returned to our room to find Simon sitting on the balcony with a pair of scissors in his hand and surrounded by clumps of hair. He ran his spare hand over his scalp and said, "How does it look?"

"Might have been better to have done it in front of a mirror," I offered.

"Remember how I looked after I set my head on fire in Nepal with that candle?"

"Yeah... " Simon frowned.

"Well it looks like you stuck your head in an oven." Later that day, Simon went out and had his head completely shaved. To add to the look, he returned wearing some super loose and very white robes. In the space of an afternoon, I had gone from travelling with an eccentric Swiss guy, to a Messiah, and when he took to wrapping a black scarf around his neck at all times, I joked that he looked as though he was about to walk on water.

We spent the next few days hanging around the ghats, people-watching and drinking tea. It sounds a bit odd, considering its use as a burial site, but it was also a meeting place full of families, people fishing, and actually a nice environment to be in, as long as there was a breeze to keep the smell of the river at bay. We rented out a small rowboat and drifted slowly along the water, finally able to relax and watch the life on the banks of the River Ganges, out of reach of the beggars, Sadhus and street sellers, who on dry land were constantly baying for our money. We let our legs trail behind us in the river as we went, which in hindsight was probably ill advised, as it meant that the water seeped inside our open mosquito bites putting us at risk of infection – not only were the city's sewers emptied into the river along with human body parts, but it was also well known that the dumping of heavy metals by factories upstream had given the river other harmful qualities. This did not, however, stop the hundreds of families frolicking in the water around us.

Our evenings were spent in the rooftop restaurant of our guesthouse, and while the owners of the place irritated us by constantly trying to persuade us to go with them to their brother's tailor shop, they came in very handy for the 36 hours when for the second time on my trip, alcohol was banned due to an election, and they supplied us with black market beer. Every evening we heard the Muslim call to prayer broadcast over speakers in the distance, and watched as those unable to make it to the mosque would appear on the surrounding rooftops to face Mecca and pray.

We spent a day away from the ghats in the old city, which was a tight mesh of alleys and crowded houses. Here we were passed by a wedding procession announced by trumpets. The groom appeared elaborately dressed riding a white horse, followed on foot by his relatives in formal costume, banging drums and cheering, while the teenagers among the entourage, swigged from shared bottles of beer. We seemed to be the only ones to stop and take notice of this – elaborate wedding processions appeared to be an everyday occurrence in Varanasi. Later that same day we were nearly run down by a group of wailing men as they jogged down towards the ghats, the body of an old man wrapped in a bed sheet, hoisted above them. Varanasi was certainly an active city, full of life and death.

Having stayed three or four nights in the city, our next stop was Agra, the home of the world-famous mausoleum, the Taj Mahal. We left on the overnight train hoping to reach the Taj Mahal in time to see the sunrise, but the train was delayed by three hours. To add to our disappointment, when it finally got moving we found that not only did the fans above our designated bunks not work, but we were also unable to benefit from the air from the windows below us, given that we were both on the third bed up from the floor. And so, began a long sweaty sleepless night. As the sun rose, we sat in the open doorway of the train, our legs dangling below us, and Simon continually mopping his head since his new haircut meant sweat kept running into his eyes.

We passed through the shanty towns which bordered the tracks where people survived on next to nothing each day; yet there was an unmistakeable air of pride about the residents we saw. Walking among the con-joined shacks, we saw school kids, their white shirts as clean as any in a washing detergent advert. The men, in ripped and weathered clothes, all had neatly cut hair and groomed moustaches. Plants hung on wire from the rooftops, while women swept the dirt from outside their doorways. These people were not ashamed of what they didn't have, they were proud of what they did have – which was clearly self-respect and a sense of community.

The only thing slightly spoiling our view, were the people lining the tracks and dotting the passing fields enjoying their first bowel movement of the day. Some even managed to give us a wave as they balanced on their haunches. Even smartly dressed businessmen were taking part in this early morning ritual. "I wouldn't want to shake his hand in a business meeting," I said, nodding towards one who was just getting to his feet, adjusting his tie and retrieving his brief case.

For 10 rupees, we left our packs in the station's luggage room, and power-walked our way to the entrance of the Taj Mahal, where we paid the $20 entrance fee – Indians were allowed in free. My first impression of the Taj, was that it was not worthy of a place in the listings as a Wonder of the World and I was feeling a bit underwhelmed to be honest. But by the time I left that night, I realized how wrong I was. One major difference between the Taj Mahal and other architectural masterpieces, is that the Taj is not a building built for religion but for love; the Indian poet Rabindranath Tagore once described it as "a teardrop on the cheek of time".

It was ordered to be built by Shah Jahan in 1632, to enshrine the body of his favourite wife who died shortly after giving birth to her 14th child. It took 25 years to build, and a work force of over 20,000 men. It was decorated with turquoise, crystal and mother of pearl, imported from around the world, and the glaring white marble, which is the main building material in the Taj Mahal's structure, was brought from Jodhpur, a city west of Delhi.

For the first few hours we were relatively alone inside its grounds, and were able to tick the boxes of all the cliché photos while it was quiet, as well as slightly more imaginative shots including one with Simon sprawled out across the marble steps looking uncon-scious with a blurry backdrop of the building behind. We split up for a few hours and found our own favou-rite viewpoints. No shoes were allowed around the tomb itself and these had to be removed before climbing up the steps onto the platform on which the tomb sits. I regretted not heeding the warnings I'd heard about bringing some socks, as you could have fried an egg on the marble flooring, and I was forced to teeter around on the sides of my feet, quickly tiptoeing to shaded spots when the burn grew too great.

I spent much of the day sitting around staring in silence at what I was coming to realize was a man-made marvel, but half the time was being approached by families and groups of Indians on holiday wanting their picture taken with me. Often the Taj Mahal would not even feature in their photos, as momentarily I as a white man, was apparently the more impressive sight. They wrapped their arms around me and posed alongside me as though we'd been separated at birth, then once we had all said, "Cheese!" they would simply say thank you with a wobble of their heads, and wander off, never to speak to me again. I could just imagine them back at home, flicking through their holiday snaps with relatives saying, '"And this is our English friend..."

The tour groups began to arrive around midday, and for a while it was pandemonium. I felt embarrassed for my nation when I had to listen to a couple of English women complaining about the indignity of having to remove their shoes, and another complaining about the ban on smoking within the grounds. Tour groups dressed in uniform yellow, pink or red T-shirts were herded around, told where to take the best photos, and constantly reminded of their time schedule, before being led back to their designated tour buses. Hardly any spent more than 45 minutes there before moving on to their next sight of the day. It seemed such a waste to me, to spend such a little amount of time somewhere so monumental. It was clear to me; this was a place that required a few hours of adoration at the very least.

I came to realize that what you really needed to do was watch how the sun moved around the building during the course of the day, slowly changing the colour of the marble, shifting the shadows, and moving the reflections around its unbroken symmetrical curves.

At lunchtime, I met Simon back outside the entrance. Across the road was a small restaurant, and we sat on the balcony with cold beer, looking out over the trees at the Taj, so as not to miss any of its light-changing moments. After a bowl of egg-fried rice and a couple of 8 per cent Kingfishers, we spent 20 minutes persuading the guards at the side gate to let us back in on our single entry tickets. Back inside, we lay down on the manicured grass of the gardens and watched the sun set over the Taj Mahal, creating the picture postcard images I had grown up seeing in the windows of travel agents. Seeing it with my own eyes, I realized no picture could ever do it justice.

As the Taj slowly became a silhouette against a striped background of purples and reds, we played hide and seek with the guards around the gardens as they attempted to usher all visitors out by sunset. We were determined, however, to see the building entirely cloaked in darkness, and once we had done so, celebrated our day at one of the Wonders of the World back in the restaurant at which we had eaten lunch. We had drunk quite a few Kingfishers before we returned to the station to collect our packs, and make our onward journey to Delhi. Tired from the excitement of the day and one too many beers, we used our packs as pillows and settled down for a nap on the platform while we waited for our 1am train to depart. We woke only to the shrill blow of the station master's whistle, and just about managed to hop on to the train as it slowly pulled away from the platform.

Finding ourselves in the nearly empty, air-conditioned compartment of First Class, we decided not to argue with fate, and got our heads back down for a few more hours' kip, our unreserved tickets tucked safely in our back pockets. When we were finally caught, we were led to our rightful standing positions in seventh class, where a notice screwed onto the wall of the toilet read, "Please do not soil the seats in western-style lavatories".

We pulled into New Delhi Station just after seven in the morning, and in an attempt to avoid the hundreds of touts waiting for us, lingered in the carriage as long as possible, hoping for an unblocked run for the exit once we got off. The plan kind of worked, but we still had to fight our way through the scrum outside to escape the persistent cries of cheap everything. Layered in travel grime and trying to ignore the pester of rickshaw drivers slowly cycling alongside us, all the shouting, and grabbing hands suddenly got too much for me, and I turned around to the nearest pestering driver and chucked the contents of my water bottle over him. He sped off cursing, while Simon, in hysterics now, made to copycat my attack on his nearest assailant who quickly backed off, leaving us be at last.

We found the area of Paharganj, just west of the railway station and prime backpacker territory with its numerous budget guesthouses, hippy clothing shops and travel agents. Exhausted, we found a dive of a room and slept until the evening, and on waking, I took Simon out to introduce him to a proper Indian bar.

Because drinking is somewhat frowned upon in Indian society other than at weddings or religious festivals, Indian bars are pretty seedy, and you feel like you're committing a sin just by going inside. The bar we went to was down in the basement of a shopping arcade and upon pushing open the heavy soundproofed doors, we were greeted with darkness. It took a good minute for our eyes to adjust to the blackened, smoky room, lit only by a handful of lights and a strip of neon tubing running along the floor. It was a bit of a sad lonely place with booths filled with depressed and broken-looking men sipping away their sorrows, but at least it had air conditioning, so we took a table away from everyone else, and sat with our backs against the recesses lining the wall. We began to make our individual lists of things we needed to do in Delhi.

It was late by the time we were heading back to our accommodation, and we were forced to walk down the centre of the road, since all the pavements were taken up by homeless families curled up to sleep beneath the gloomy specks of streetlights. We then spent 10 minutes trying to get into our guesthouse, before realizing that in our drunken states we had gone to the wrong one. It was a wonder therefore that next morning we were at the doors of the Iranian Embassy when they opened for the day. We were told that to enter our next destination, Iran, we needed written permission from our own Governments, and once we had that, we could apply for a visa. So, I headed off to the British Consulate, and Simon to the Swiss Embassy, which were each located on opposite sides of the city.

The British Consulate in New Delhi was the biggest I had ever seen. It was a grand old building with immaculate gardens and well-dressed guards. A highly polished Rolls-Royce was parked outside among other equally shiny and expensive cars. In the foyer, I sat in a leather armchair below two British flags as I waited for instructions on who to speak to. There was a heavy red book on one of the nearby tables, which on closer inspection I found was a visitors' book for passing dignitaries. Inside were the names of the former Prime Minister John Major and Foreign Secretary Robin Cook. Other entries began with "Sir", "Lady" and "Colonel", while some were simply signed, "Queen's Messenger". Before I left the foyer to collect my letter of recommendation to the Iranian Embassy, the most recent entry in the book read: "Ben Harris, Never-Never Land, Occupation: Pirate."

The letter it turned out was rather extortionately priced at £30, and after having a rant at the woman behind the bullet-proof glass about how as a tax payer (kind of), I shouldn't be charged a penny, I got into a conversation with a guy who was there because he had lost his passport for the seventh time. After I suggested he get himself a money belt, he asked why I was there, and I explained I was after a visa to get in to Iran.

He smiled. "That's like trying to get blood out of a stone, mate," he said. Then went on to explain how he had previously waited eight weeks in Delhi for an Iranian Visa, only to have it denied. He did, however, scribble down the email address of a middleman in Iran who he said might be able to help me out. I thanked him, pocketed the piece of paper, and then sped back across town in a rickshaw to the Iranian Embassy. On the way, I asked the driver for the time. He proudly showed me his watch, and then told me he couldn't believe I didn't own one, as in India, a watch is a huge status symbol. As if to confirm this information, I then immediately spotted a man sifting through rubbish on the side of the road who was shoeless, yet wearing a silver timepiece on his wrist. When we reached the Iranian Embassy, it was nearly 2pm, and having been open for nearly four whole hours, it had now closed for the day.

Instead I went to the nearest bank to complete what I thought would be a simple task of exchanging a 100-rupee note with a burnt edge, that had been slyly passed to me in Varanasi, and which no one was now accepting. Inside the first bank I was simply palmed off and given instructions to go elsewhere. This happened twice more at different banks, until I headed for the Bank of India. Surely the people who printed the money could swap it, I thought. Inside I showed them the note and explained the problem. The teller disappeared to speak to someone else, who went off to speak to someone else and so on. I couldn't believe how long it was all taking – it wasn't even a huge sum of money, a little over $3 US, although this would be worth one night's accommodation here. Its value was no longer the point though, and it was the principle that had me running around the city determined to swap it. Eventually I was called over and ushered into the bank manager's office. Inside, a group of bank employees were pouring over tatty books with thick spines. I was told to sit on a chair by the door, where for some time I was ignored. Then after much debate, the group turned to me and announced that they were unable to change the note as it was burnt.

"I know it's burnt," I said. "That's why I'm exchanging it."

"No, we cannot sir, I am most dreadfully sorry," the manager said.

It was at this point that I lost my patience and said in a rather loud voice.

"Can't you just stop being awkward and just change it? That's what you're supposed to do!" The note was perfectly readable, no codes or security stamps were damaged, it just didn't make sense. My loss of calm, however, didn't go down well, and I was eventually escorted from the building by an armed guard following a little bit of a scene. I stood outside the bank incensed, ranting about my predicament to anyone who would listen. Eventually, an Indian man approached me and proudly told me he had been educated in England.

When he heard the palaver I had been through trying to change the note, he said, "Sir, the biggest mistake your country made when leaving India, was to leave behind its bureaucracy!" He took the note from my hand, tore off the area that had been burnt, thereby reducing it to a third of its original size. I stood there in disbelief; the cursed note was now even more damaged than it was before! But the man just smiled at me reassuringly, told me to wait there, then went inside the bank from which I'd just be ejected. Five minutes later he was back out again, holding a brand-new 100-rupee note.

"How?" I said simply.

"Well the problem is, there is nothing written down about how to deal with burnt notes, only ripped or torn notes, and without any direct instructions on how to deal with a burnt note, they can't exchange it. They're scared to think out the box in case they get it wrong!" he said, tapping his head with a smile.

It had certainly been a stressful and educational afternoon, so I went for a junk-food fix at McDonald's and ordered a Maharaja Mac meal. It was good, but not cheap, although the price was made up for by the fact that despite the filth that encircled the building, McDonald's' hygiene standards apparently didn't waiver, even in India. The place was spotless, and I was the most scruffily dressed person in there. Apparently McDonald's was quite the place to be seen and something of a status symbol, since all the locals appeared to be wearing their finest attire; men in pressed white shirts and women in fine, brightly colour saris with armfuls of bangles hovering dangerously close to dollops of ketchup.

Back at the room I found Simon experimenting with some street food. I confessed where I had just been and he teased me about it, calling me a package tourist. I had the last laugh though, when his local delicacy sent him back and forth to the toilet for the rest of the night, with truly authentic Delhi belly! But one delicious food treat that I did discover around the corner from us, was honeydew melons. At just 10 rupees each, these were all I ate for the next few days.

The next day, the employee at the Iranian Embassy was blunt but thankfully honest. He explained to me that due to Tony Blair and George Bush's new-found friendship, Britons were no longer particularly welcome in Iran, and if I was to submit my application, it would probably be denied after a very long wait. He advised me to try at a different Iranian Embassy. Simon, on the other hand could get a seven-day transit visa to Iran if he wanted, but he decided to wait and see if he could do better elsewhere with me.

Later that day, while I was wandering around the market, I randomly bumped into a young Nepalese guy called Raj, whom I had met in Pokhara. It was quite incredible that he should spot us in a city of however many millions, but I guess as two very tall white scruffy westerners we kind of stuck out. As he came running over to me, I immediately realized he looked very different to how I remembered him – rather than neat, clean and well-groomed, his clothes were filthy and his face unshaven. He had tears in his eyes as he struggled to explain what was wrong, and it took a while for me to calm him down sufficiently to understand him. He explained that he had come to Delhi a week before in the search of work, and that two Indian men, who spoke Nepalese, had befriended him. Trusting them, he had left all his belongings with them for an hour, while he searched for a room to rent, and they had stolen everything he had. He'd been sleeping rough on the cowshit-covered streets for days hoping to spot the men who had taken his stuff. He was clearly distraught, with no money and no idea what to do. I pointed out that this was not Pokhara, it was Delhi, there were millions of people here and that it was highly unlikely he'd ever see those thieves again. He nodded at me sadly, knowing that what I was saying was true.

Raj was probably four or five years older than me, and although he came from the second largest city in Nepal, it was so isolated that I could understand how he could be so duped in his innocence and naivety. No stranger to having been ripped off myself, I gave him 500 rupees, enough to get a shave, buy some new clothes and a ticket back to Pokhara. He wanted my address so he could send the money for the ticket to me when he got home. "I don't really have one," I said, which left him looking confused and unsure, so I took his address and told him that next time I was in Nepal I would call him and we would go out for beer and he could pay. He hesitated for a second, worry spreading across his face.

"But I cannot drink beer for I am a good Hindu. But cola I can drink?" Trying hard not to laugh, I said, "Yeah, Coca-Cola is cool."

Greatly relieved, he pressed his palms together, and with a slight bow of his head said, "May Shiva protect this man!" I laughed out loud this time.

"Well," I said to Simon, as I watched Raj hurry away in search of a barber, before beginning what would presumably be his rather reluctant journey home. "I reckon we'll get those visas somewhere else down the road; I've just topped up our karma!"

When we'd only been in Delhi for a week, I'd already had enough of it, and I wanted to move on to some-where less polluted. I'd read that one day living in Delhi was the equivalent of smoking 20 cigarettes, and the evidence of this was apparent each time I picked black clumps out of my nostrils before I went to sleep at night. Simon couldn't get enough of the daily chaos and wanted to stay a while longer, so I spent one more day trying to enjoy western amenities before I would catch an overnight train and leave Delhi and Simon behind. I visited the Pizza Hut, but was disappointed after I ordered a family-sized pizza for myself, only to receive one no bigger than an English medium. More disap-pointment followed when I tracked down The Pegasus Tavern, reputed to be the last English pub in India.

While the style of the place was pretty authentic, you could neither sit nor order at the bar, which was instead used to pile up the dirty dishes. I drank one pint ordered from a waiter at my table, and left, missing England for the first time in a long while.

Taking a boat down the smelly ganges

Gun cleaning in Pakistan

Simon and I near the Afgan border, waiting on visas

An Afghan street kid

Afghan children with little sister in playpen

Children in the caves of Bamiyan

Man selling single shoes

Fixing my UN bicycle in exchange for an english lesson

Me in disguise cycling around Bamiyan in Afghanistan,
the Budda caves in the background

Me in a Russian tank

IRAN

The bridge at Esfahan

16

The Divide

Pokhara to Delhi = 933km

The overnight journey north was a long one. The carriage was packed solid with passengers, most of whom stood in the aisles between the beds, eyeing my reserved bunk with envy. The fans above my bed, however, only worked in short spurts, and the breeze they occasionally produced passed me by, so the combined heat of all the bodies on board plus the stale uncirculated air, meant the next 12 hours were spent lying in a puddle of sweat. Everything in my pockets was drenched, and I later discovered all the stamps and visas inside my passport were smudged beyond recognition.

The other thing to make the journey rather tiresome was the neglected child in the berth below me, who howled and screamed for the entire night. His parents seemed to be the only people on the train unaffected by this, and were sleeping soundly on the other side of the carriage. As I lay there quietly seething, the noise suddenly stopped. I swung my head over my bunk to see if another passenger had perhaps given in to an urge to throttle the kid, only to see that he had now wet himself, and a yellow trickle of urine ran down the plastic bedding of his bunk and was collecting in a puddle in the corner. After this brief respite, his wailing then continued until about half an hour before we reached my destination, Pathankot, when he closed his eyes and fell asleep. I slid down from my bunk and eyed the child's parents resentfully, they were just waking up and stretching their well-rested limbs. I felt like yelling at them, "Oh now the little b***** can sleep, can't he!" But I was so badly dehydrated and exhausted, I didn't have the strength. From Pathankot I still needed to get a bus a further four hours north to my final destination of McLeod Ganj, where the Dalai Lama and his Tibetan government lived in exile.

After I had revived my shrivelled insides with a few litres of water, I boarded the correct bus, and was pleased to be given the prized seat up the front, parallel to the driver. He was a friendly man, aside from his excessive and unnecessary use of the horn which, placed only inches above my head, left my hearing impaired for hours. After weaving our way up hairpin bends for the final 10km of the journey, we arrived in McLeod Ganj where I agreed to take some photographs of the driver posing in front of his bus. Then after he had given me a very solid pat on the back, I entered McLeod Ganj, otherwise known as Mini Tibet. At first impression, it seemed more like mini Israel than mini Tibet to me, as there seemed to be 10 Israelis to every Tibetan. I began trying to find accommodation, but everywhere was overpriced or full. I was then told about the hamlet of Bhagsu, a further two kilometres down the road, and began to make my way there on foot. The route took me along a pine-covered ridge where the settlement of McLeod Ganj and Bhagsu sit, and I admired the surrounding views of the valley below, and the almost vertical walls of the Dhauladhar range behind me.

At Bhagsu, I found a family home with a few spare rooms to let for a reasonable price, and here I met a young Australian girl who told me that the reason McLeod Ganj was so crowded, was because the biggest trance rave in India was happening nearby in a few days' time.

"You'll have to be quick if you want to get a ticket," she told me. I smiled and nodded. I wasn't there for that kind of experience. When I later heard that the event had been designated by the Israeli organizers to be a foreigners' only event, and that natives had been banned from attending, I was especially pleased that I hadn't bothered to get a ticket.

The area did empty out though after the rave had taken place, and while some tranquillity returned to the setting, I was left with the feeling that it was a place I had arrived to a few years too late. The Dalai Lama was away in Europe spreading the word of his people's persecution and his country's occupation at the time I arrived, but I was pleased to hear that when he returned in 10 days' time he would be giving teachings and everyone was welcome. I felt it would be worth the wait and decided to hang around. I spent the time wandering around looking in at the numerous retreats. There were yoga and reiki courses and I found it odd that although people went to them in order to be cut off from the rest of the world, they were still able to order Marmite or Nutella on toast and other western luxuries.

Most of the cafes were filled with backpackers and fake hippies, smoking weed and painting rocks, while the owners turned a blind eye to people openly snorting Ketamine off the stone tables. One evening, I sat chatting to some travelling British students, and growing bored with their conversation that seemed to largely revolve around university courses and brands of moisturiser, I asked them what they thought of the Dalai Lama's forthcoming teachings that would be happening on his return. Blank expressions were exchanged.

"What exactly is the Dalai Lama?"

After that I imposed exile on myself, and spent most of my time alone, reading and frequently checking my emails to find out when my salvation would arrive, in the form of Simon. Having not heard from him since leaving Delhi, I was beginning to wonder if he was okay, since I knew he'd been planning to go and explore the slums on the outskirts of Delhi. There was no answer from him for a few more days, but I did get some pleasing news from our middleman in Iran, who informed us that he was writing us letters of invitation to visit him, claiming we were long-term friends. He would attach and send these to us via email and this, we hoped, would help us greatly with our visa applications. If our visa applications were approved we were to pay him $35 US when we reached Iran.

Meanwhile, the local family from whom I was renting a room, were hosting a three-day wedding, and so I spent a lot of the next few days watching dance moves stolen from Bollywood movies, and listening to a trumpet play all day and well in to the night. I was pretty sure the wedding band was almost certainly composed of relatives or close friends of the bride and groom, as there was no other way they would have been given the gig.

One lunchtime I was just wondering where Simon had got to, when I turned the corner of the compound in which I was staying, and nearly bumped straight in to him. We immediately went for a beer, after which Simon declared that it was too touristy here, and since it was a further three days before the long-awaited Dalai Lama's teachings, he was going to get back on the bus the following morning and move on. I understood, but continued to wait it out, and spent one of the following days visiting the museum where I saw photos of the young Dalai Lama making his escape to India. I also got my security clearance and photo ID from the Tibetan Welfare Office, and purchased a small radio and headphones so that I would be able to understand the Dalai Lama through translation on the day.

When the day finally arrived, I walked down to the temple and went through the security checks. First, I was scanned for metal objects and then patted down for concealed weapons by a man whom I felt took far longer than was absolutely necessary around the inside of my legs. Once I was admitted inside, there must have been about 3,000 people sitting on mats all around the grounds, patiently waiting for the teaching to begin. I greeted an old woman in Tibetan. She was seated near to where I was standing, and smiled and gestured for me to share her mat with her. While the Dalai Lama was not visible, I understood that he was inside the temple, and there was a great feeling of excitement in the air, just from the knowledge he was there. When his voice began to sound throughout the grounds, I tuned in my radio and began to listen.

The man making the translation was obviously sitting too close to one of the speakers that were placed all around the temple, as his voice was half drowned out by interference, but what I could understand, I soon realized was far too in-depth for me. The English words being used to translate the teachings were not even in my vocabulary. I turned off my radio and instead sat listening to the Dalai Lama's calming voice. This was enough for me. I hadn't gone in some feeble attempt to gain enlightenment; solely for the experience. As he spoke fluently for the next three hours, with only a brief pause for lunch, monks walked around handing out bread and water. When the speaking ended, I wasn't sure what to do and so went to stand up, but the old woman stopped me and motioned for me to rest on my knees. As I did so, the doors to the main temple opened, and the head lamas appeared and walked down the steps, at the bottom of which they formed a line, like a guard of honour. Then His Holiness appeared, and walked down the steps before climbing into the back seat of a waiting car. Everybody in the grounds, now also on their knees, turned to face him, their eyes cast downwards, their heads bowed. As the car began to move, I realized I was in prime position, and it was going to pass right by me, and unable to hold back my curiosity, I sneaked a look up at the vehicle. My eyes locked with the Dalai Lama's, and for two seconds we stared at each other. He smiled, and I felt an indescribable warmth float over me. Then, remembering my insolence, I lowered my gaze back downwards. I was stunned by how I felt – I could not put it down to his celebrity status, for I had seen many a famous face before now and never had I felt anything like that. The sheer presence of the man was so strong, it seemed to almost radiate through me. I left the temple on a natural high and headed back to my accommodation. In fact, I was on such a high, that I was actually enjoying the Hindi music that I had tuned into on my new radio.

The bus for my return journey in the morning was driven by the same driver who had brought me to McLeod Ganj over a week before. This time I didn't have to suffer the blaring of the horn though, as the lucky seat was already taken by a chap who appeared to be a close friend of his. When we arrived in Pathankot, the driver reminded me not to forget to post him his photos, then kindly walked me to the train station. I'd begun to get sharp shooting pains in my mouth and I realized my wisdom teeth were coming through – all down to the Dalai Lama I thought!

After standing in line for close to an hour and gritting my teeth every time someone jumped the queue ahead of me, which seemed to be a constant occurrence, I purchased my ticket to Amritsar. My patience was rewarded somewhat on the train, for I managed to get a seat before it became really crowded for the four-hour journey south. The downside to this, however, was that all I had to look at for the whole time was a row of elbows and wobbling bottoms.

Amritsar is the Sikh's holiest city, and is the largest within the Punjab. Among the heavily congested streets sits the fabled Golden Temple. This was the only place I really wanted to see here, as I was now keen to cross into Pakistan. It was 46 degrees when I arrived in the city, and having travelled down from the climate of the north, which was more like the mild summers of England, I was really beginning to feel the heat.

I left the station, crossed over a bridge and began walking downhill along a crowded pavement. There seemed to be a bottleneck ahead, where people were filing past some kind of object that was blocking the walkway. The closer I got the more intrigued I became, as everyone seemed to be having a good look at whatever it was as they passed. When it came to my turn, I felt a sickening jolt of shock: sprawled out across the pavement and into the gutter was the swollen body of a dead man. I could tell from his clothing he had been homeless, but what really shocked me, was not the sight of a rotting corpse, this unfortunately was nothing new to me, it was the fact that everyone was walking past seemingly without a care. I wondered how long the body would lie there decomposing before someone complained about it and the authorities would be forced to remove it. How sad to die alone in such a crowded city, I thought. I hoped that when my time came, I would not be in a place where people just walked around me.

I spent three hours searching for a room and reached the stage where the heat was making me feel physically sick and dizzy and I was forced to steady myself on the walls as I walked. When I did find a vacant room, I headed straight for the shower and lay on the floor under the cold water for some time. It was hotter in the room than it had been in Varanasi, and I downed litres of water mixed with rehydration sachets, then swallowed a few Ibuprofens for my headache and toothache. I had a dinner of glucose biscuits and Coca-Cola before attempting to go to sleep. This was not an easy task. I had three cold showers throughout the night, and only managed to get to sleep after I poured a bucket of water over the bed. Amazingly, I woke quite early and apart from my ever-persistent toothache, I felt fine.

Gold isn't really my colour, but the Golden Temple was more like a diamond in the rough. Its domes soared high above the crowded network of dirty streets below, the early morning sun shining off its bordering rectangular lake in which the temples' mirror image was reflected. Before I could enter, I had to remove my shoes, wash my feet, and cover my head, then almost immediately a young boy latched onto me, desperate to be my guide. I declined, but it seemed I didn't have much choice in the matter. Inside, Sikhs bathed in the temple tank, which was like a hot tub or paddling pool within the lake, only more holy – the Amrit Sarovar or Pool of Immortality-giving Nectar – while keeping their heads above the water, careful not to get their tightly wrapped turbans wet. I could hear a string instrument playing. My guide pointed out the bullet marks that scarred the sacred building, left from the siege of 1984.

He told me that the temple had been the sight of a massacre, after heavily armed fundamentalists led by Sant Jarnail Singh Bhindranwale, had occupied it and the surrounding complex, as part of a bloody campaign to set up a Sikh homeland. The siege was brought to an abrupt end, however, when the then Prime Minister Indira Gandhi, ordered an inept paramilitary attack on the building, called Operation Blue Star. Heavy weaponry was used, including tanks, and both the temple and the buildings around it were hit heavily, resulting in huge damage to the religious structures and a great loss of life. Bhindranwale, along with more than 2,000 others including pilgrims trapped inside, were all killed. I knew it had not ended there: four months later Indira Gandhi was shot in the head in retaliation, by her own Sikh bodyguards, which then provoked the worst riots in the city since partition. Sikhs were mercilessly killed in towns further north of Amritsar, all of this resulting in the animosity which continues between the Sikhs and the Hindus to this day. Despite expensive restoration work since, the temple was still scarred by mortar damage and pockmarks from bullets.

Having had my fill of the Golden Temple, I decided it was time to cross the border in to Pakistan. Amritsar has three bus stations: I inevitably went to the wrong two first the next morning. Finally on the right bus, I watched as a few rows ahead of me, a man with one hand stubbornly tried to open a jar. Refusing any help offered by others, it took him around 15 minutes to complete the task, and when he did, he turned around grinning at everyone at his accomplishment.

I arrived at the border town of Wagga a few hours later but the border was still shut, and given that I was about to enter Pakistan, a country where alcohol is illegal, I thought it best to have a last few bevvies before I began my new teetotal lifestyle.

When the gates opened an hour or so later, I saw I was not only going to be the first person to cross that day, but I seemed to be the only one crossing at all. As I entered the Indian immigration office where they were as power-mad and bureaucratic as ever, I felt excited. They searched my bag, and I complained at the lack of respect given to my possessions. I was asked more than five times if I was carrying hashish, as if my reply might suddenly change to a yes, and once they were content that they had sufficiently annoyed me, I was waved through.

It was quite clear that there was no love lost between India and Pakistan. Along the border, both sides had evidently done their best to outdo the other, flying their nations' flags high above every available rooftop and painting their national colours wherever possible.

I walked past stands around which, I later discovered, crowds gathered every evening to cheer on their countries as the border was closed for the night. This was a daily ceremony I would like to have seen, as it was meant to be quite a spectacle with guardsmen dressed in outlandish hats and sporting ridiculous moustaches, speed-marching with perfect synchronization as they slammed shut the gates and lowered their flags until the following day.

I walked through the orange, green and white gateway to India, and on the ground in front of me the borderline was quite clearly marked with white paint. I paused for a second, then took a running jump and leapt from India into Pakistan, which prompted a shake of the head and a frown from a guard posted nearby.

After walking through the Pakistani gates, which had the Islamic symbols welded into the metal framework, I entered their immigration office. Their border house was very welcoming; a burst water pipe created a peaceful waterfall outside. The official came out to greet me, took my passport and paperwork and told me to wait in the garden while he dealt with it all. When he returned, he asked me if I was carrying any drugs or alcohol, and then welcomed me into Pakistan.

Just down the road a man was running an outdoor bookshop, which consisted of two neatly tidied shelves leaning against a wall. I happily exchanged a few books with him which I had been carrying for far too long, and when he asked if I had a guidebook I might want to exchange and I told him that I didn't carry one, he produced a card with the details of a place to stay in Lahore, my next destination. I found the bus stop, and when my bus arrived, I was amazed at just how immediately different it was from India. The men and women on the bus were completely segregated, the females getting on at the front, while the men boarded at the back, and the two sexes were completely separated by a metal divide two thirds of the way up. From what I could make out through the gaps in the partition, the women had far less space and very few seats. Some of them were fully veiled in burkas, lines of sweat ringing the cloths around their heads.

The men, all of whom were comfortably seated, stared at me without blinking. Most of them were clutching sticks or scythes and didn't look all that friendly. They mumbled things to each other, their eyes fixed firmly upon me, and to say I felt uneasy was an understatement. But the adrenaline was pumping once again, and I was looking forward to my travels in Pakistan.

17

Mary Poppins

Delhi to Dharmsala to Amritsar to Lahore = 733km

Once I'd left the bus I began searching for the road on the card I had been given. There was little point attempting to blend in and not look like a lost tourist; if my white skin and lack of facial hair didn't give me away, my western clothing definitely did. Every man in the city was clothed in the shalwar kameez, the pyjama style national dress which consists of a long loose shirt over a pair of light baggy trousers in various shades of beige, and held up with string. It was like everyone was on their way to a mass sleepover. I wandered around trying to make sense of the map I had picked up at the border, but soon got hopelessly lost and hailed a rickshaw.

As it turned out, The Regal Internet Inn, was the only real budget place to stay in the whole city and every traveller in Lahore, which totalled about seven, was booked in. It was a real retreat from the madness outside, and was run by a man called Malik, a tall man in his 50s who had a neatly trimmed moustache, and always carried a comb in his shirt pocket to keep his slicked-back hair tidy at all times. He was an educated man who had once been an adviser to the former Prime Minister, and I think he ran the guesthouse more as a hobby than anything else, and having travelled the world in his previous career, seemed to understand us westerners, or at least have a handle on our way of thinking. He was able to see the funny side of his country-mens' roundabout way of doing things, but still leapt to their defence over those quirks and peculiarities that we just could not understand. Everything was up for debate with Malik. He was always asking questions, but one question we always learnt never to raise was that of religion. He actually asked that it not be dis-cussed too much around the hostel, and I wondered if it was because there had been a past discussion that had turned nasty. Discussing religion in a country so pas-sionate about theirs is a risky business, especially if you are not going to be showing anything other than respect to their extremely conservative views. In fact, I noticed that he rarely had other Pakistanis at the hostel other than his sons who he didn't encourage to hang around. I suppose what went on at the hostel would, to your average Pakistani, be quite shocking, with the women sitting around in shorts and T-shirts and their heads uncovered, chatting to me and Simon and the other men in the hostel, easily and freely. I guess Malik didn't want to advertise his allowing such un-Islamic behaviour, in case he became a target for extremists.

On my first evening I was reading up on the rooftop, which had been converted into a cosy relaxation area, when the power suddenly went and we were flung into darkness. We sat there, for a few minutes wondering what was going on, when suddenly Malik appeared, holding his hands up to the sky and declaring, "Kite flying!"

"What?" We all asked.

"Kite flying is such a problem in Pakistan, it's actually illegal," he explained.

"But people love it so much they still do it."

"But what's wrong with that?" I asked.

"The kites hit power lines and short entire blocks of the city." He indicated the darkness that now surrounded us and then went on to explain how Sundays, like today, were the most common time for the crime to be committed, and that at that very moment, special government teams would be racing around the city. One would be responsible for trying to catch and fine the offenders, while another would be busy pulling abandoned kites from the power lines.

"Come," said Malik. He indicated that I should climb higher up onto his water tanks to get a better view, and when I did so, I saw the most spectacular sight; a sky so full of kites, they could easily have been mistaken for flocks of birds.

I spent the rest of that evening chatting to a group of travellers who were travelling "overland" like me, in that not a single one possessed a plane ticket. One of them, an Icelandic guy, told me that he was still celebrating his recent triumph of crossing the Iranian border, where he was told he was the first person from Iceland ever to do so; unfortunately it had therefore taken them four hours to work out how much to charge him.

Apparently, I'd just missed the "The Swordsman", an American man who, after losing friends in the terrorist attacks of 9/11, was travelling around the tribal areas of Pakistan armed with a Samurai sword in an

attempt to single-handedly track down Osama Bin
Laden and behead him. The story went that everyone
who met him wanted to hold or kiss the sword that
would either kill Bin Laden or, as some worried, The
Swordsman, himself.

There seemed to be a few of these legendary characters drifting around the overland travelling community
network; I'd also heard about a woman known as Lady
Penelope who moved around the tribal areas of Pakistan
under the cover of a burka, always wearing heavy
makeup and pink nail vanish beneath; while another
man was riding a horse around Pakistan and back to
Europe. Despite never meeting any of these individuals,
everyone I spoke to knew of them, and most knew their
current whereabouts. I always seemed to have just
missed them though, which made them seem almost
mythical.

My first full day in Lahore was mainly spent eating
beef and all the different foods I could lay my hands on.
Cows were now considered to be cows again, rather than
sacred beasts, and instead it was pigs that had been
removed entirely from the menus. Not far from where
I was staying was Ice Cream Street, a road dedicated
purely to the sale of milkshakes and ice creams. It was
here that all the men congregated to meet with friends
and unwind in the evenings, presumably due to Lahore's
total lack of bars. As I watched the men sitting around
slurping their banana sundaes, I couldn't help but wonder
if they knew that something was missing from their night
out but couldn't quite put their finger on what it was.

I decided to try to work my way down the entire
milkshake menu, and after my fourth visit to the same

parlour, I was given an ice cream on the house. This did not go unnoticed among the other men, and I was consequently invited over by a group of the parlour's hardcore ice-cream eaters, and spent the next few hours with them as they excitedly awaited my opinion on the various milkshake and ice-cream concoctions they insisted that I try at their expense. Perhaps this wasn't so different to men drinking in a bar after all, I thought.

After a week in Lahore, Simon finally arrived fresh from the slums of Delhi, summarizing them as "very smelly". Together, we visited the old fort and the mosques around the city, and got ourselves geared up in the national dress. While our new attire only helped us blend in marginally, it certainly helped with the intense heat. I quickly learnt not to sit on plastic seats for too long though, as the material was so thin it became translucent with sweat, and made the chequered pattern of my boxer shorts plainly visible.

Outside one mosque, things became uncomfortable when an older Pakistani man took it upon himself to convert us to Islam, presumably because the Koran states that the conversion of a non-believer will guarantee entry into Paradise. After starting off quite calmly, our lack of compliance led to him eventually lurching towards us, his arms flailing around in a flurry of erratic gestures, as he demanded that we "must convert!" When we politely tried to walk away, we found ourselves penned in by a group of younger scholars, who seemed equally keen to see us converted, so giving up on the pleasantries, we pushed our way through the crowd, flagged down the first taxi in sight, and returned to the sanctuary of the guesthouse.

When Malik had the time, he was happy to ferry me and Simon around to places he thought would be of interest to us; all he charged was our share of the petrol money, and he didn't seem to mind our endless barrage of questions. He took us, to what he modestly called his garden, but which actually turned out to be an orchard where we picked enough lychees to feed everyone at the guesthouse for two days.

Malik had a lot of important contacts around the city, and everyone he spoke to showed him a great deal of respect. This was not just those who had high-ranking status or those of considerable wealth, for when he took us to meet the gypsies who trapped venomous snakes for a living and resided in a dusty camp in a patch of ground in the suburbs of the city, there was genuine affection in the greeting they gave him upon our arrival. They ushered us out of the hot sun to the cover of their temporary home, a mishmash of ripped, dusty sheets suspended from bamboo poles. Here we sat drinking tea on homemade camp beds, one of which was occupied by a severely malnourished-looking elderly man who lay comatose for the duration of our visit. His thighs were not much wider than his calves, his upper body virtually skeletal, and gently smouldering beside him was a large water pipe with a long copper tube running off it within a few inches of his mouth. He was evidently an opium addict, but from the steady smile that stretched across his sleeping face, he seemed to be a content one. A podgy man, who I guessed to be the son of the old man, sat down on the dusty ground and chatted away to us in good English, while fiddling about with small vials. He had a big round belly protruding from his white robes, and I wondered if his father's weight loss had more to do with him not being quick enough at meal times.

He explained to us that they earned a living by collecting venom from snakes and selling them to hospitals, as well as charging small fees for removing the reptiles from peoples' homes. He got up and began opening the pots and baskets that lined the tent, one by one from which, he began to pull out various snakes. While holding a black and red banded snake, he showed us how he extracted the toxins by firmly gripping it behind its head, and placing its upper jaw over the edge of a glass beaker. We watched as the small droplets ran down the inside and collected at the bottom. Once all that could be withdrawn was taken, he carefully released the snake back into its box, and as he replaced the lid, it could be heard hissing angrily inside. He then rolled up his sleeves and showed me his arms which were covered in scars from past accidents while handling the snakes. While most were just two small white teeth marks about an inch apart, there were also a few deep grooves crisscrossing the skin.

"What are those from?" I asked.

"If I'm bitten but do not have the right anti-venom, I slice my arms with a knife to drain the bad blood," he said.

I was sure that I had read in the past that this was not the best way of stopping the venom from a poisonous snakebite, but here he was sitting there in front of me, so who was I to argue? I pointed to the five or six baskets containing different species and asked if he had anti-venom for all of them.

"Most of them, I think," he replied. I asked if I could handle a few myself. He agreed, and after he had demonstrated a number of times the correct way in which to hold them (with your fingers around their neck and your thumb pressed down on the back of the snake's head so its jaws are held shut between your thumb and curled forefinger) I found myself excitedly holding a rattlesnake, its tail rhythmically quivering in warning.

Later that afternoon, we returned to the city and Malik led us through miles of twisting alleyways through the old town, to where the food market was held. As we wove our way through the market, we were careful to keep him in our sights, for we knew if we lost him, we'd be searching for the way back for a long time.

One evening, as we sat on the roof terrace with Malik, and bemoaned how much we were craving a nice cold beer, he informed us that as foreigners, he could get us licences to drink and buy alcohol from a "permit room". This was a revelation to us, and the next evening Malik took me, Simon and four other guests, all armed with our licences to drink, to the permit room. This turned out to be a bottle store inside one of the upmarket hotels, where I was surprised to discover that while alcohol was officially illegal, Pakistan still had at least three independent breweries. I bought one of each of the different beers, but when I got them back to the hotel to try them, I found that all of them were weak and disappointing, and regretted not buying the bottle of Martini I had considered while still clutching my "License to Drink".

The highlight of my stay in Lahore, was when Malik took Simon, myself and two of the other males staying at the guesthouse to a Sufi night. Sufism is a mystic tradition within Islam, which encompasses a diverse range of beliefs and practices dedicated to divine love and the cultivation of the heart. A 15th-century Sufi, Malik explained, had described Sufism as "a science whose objective is the reparation of the heart, turning it away from all else but God". While a Sufi night is a predominately "Muslim only" affair, thanks to Malik's standing in the community, we were readily accepted as guests.

No women are allowed at a Sufi night, however, and the event was held at a shrine surrounded by tombstones. It was already dark when we arrived, the only light came from the dozen or so fires that burnt among the crowds and cast eerie crooked shadows across the cemetery. Men sat on the edges of tombs and across graves, their backs resting against the headstones, and I was immediately reminded of the voodoo scene in the James Bond movie, *Live and Let Die*.

A plume of bluish smoke rose from the hands of nearly every man, and a sweet-smelling cloud of hashish hung in the air, while plastic bottles of illegal homebrew were being circulated. Drummers sat around the main shrine beating a continuous rhythm, while the dancers sat in preparation, taking long inhalations on their dedicated water pipes, which were presumably filled with opium. There was a truly magical vibe in the air; everyone was welcoming, even when they asked me what my religion was and I told them that I had none. I did, however, receive a frown or two over my responses about religion, when I said that I felt a lot less wars would have been fought and a lot less time wasted if there were no organized religions in the world but they quickly passed this off with a shrug, and the offer of another swig of the bottle of warm grog.

I had been standing on the edges for some time, trying to take in the spectacle before me, when I was invited over to sit down by the fire at the heart of action. My eyes quickly began to stream with water from the smoke, but I couldn't complain, for I was aware of the honoured position I had been given, as most men were forced to stand at the back, craning their necks towards the action.

As glowing joints of opium and hashish constantly circulated, so did the men who seemed to be taking turns to sit close to me. They all asked the same questions as their fellows before; what was my religion (I have none), do I like poetry (no), what instrument do I play (air guitar?), and the inevitable, are western women really easy? To this last, I explained that sex was less of a big deal in the UK since women were free to do what they wanted, and people didn't wait until they were married to have sex. They were all quite keen to come to England after hearing this. In return I asked them as much about Sufism as I could, but strangely they were unable to elaborate much on the subject, perhaps because it was so deeply ingrained in them that most questions were simply answered with, "Because that is Sufism!"

When the dancers began, I was struck dumb. A shirtless man with a double-ended bongo secured around his neck, spun round and round on the spot without pause or stumble for more than five minutes, his momentum propelling the drum horizontally out from his chest as he pounded out an incredible rhythm with his outstretched arms. While still in sync with the musicians, his drumming slowed and he came to a stop. He then raised his arms and looked up at the starry sky, and swaying slightly in a trance-like state, he spoke. Whatever it was he had said was repeated humbly by some of those around me, and while he stood there in apparent ecstasy, perhaps feeling closer to God, or perhaps just dizzy, others began dancing. Those unable to enhance their performance with musical talent, stood there and began to circle their heads violently. It was almost as if their necks contained no muscles as their heads were soon flying around so fast it was impossible to focus on their faces. This was taken a step further when they began rotating their whole upper bodies at the same speed, keeping their feet stationary for as long as they could, before spiralling out of control and either crashing into the crowd or regaining their balance. The drummers, dancers and spinners continued for hours in perfect unison. Every now and again, someone who had had too much to drink would stagger into the arena to have a go. They would be given about 10 seconds to prove themselves worthy of the spotlight, and if not (which they never were) they would be unceremoniously dragged back into the crowd to a chorus of boos and hisses.

This was undoubtedly one of the best nights of my trip, and proved that even in Islamic countries, men still find a way to go out, get wasted and listen to music. As we made our way home just as dawn was breaking, I wondered if the women all got together while the men were at Sufi night to have a gossip and dance around.

For the next three days the monsoon rains were so torrential that we didn't venture far from the guesthouse. If we did, we had to be very careful walking the streets, as every Pakistani was equipped with an umbrella which would leave me walking along amidst a sea of sharp, eye-level spikes, ready to skewer me at any wrong turn. To relieve the boredom, Malik kept us entertained by inviting some well-known local musicians to perform privately for us on the rooftop. They were great, very swinging 60s and Beatles-esque, but he did ask the girls to cover their shoulders and knees before they arrived so as not to offend them.

Eventually, it was time for us to move on to Islamabad, and we did so in style; having missed our intended budget bus because we were too busy eating ice cream, we had to shell out for the pricier air-conditioned version instead. On arrival, we found we were unable to match any of the road names with those on our maps, so on meeting a minibus driver who claimed to know where Islamabad's one and only campsite was, we climbed in. He of course had no idea, and just drove round and around in circles in the hope that he would spot it before us. After the fourth time around the same roundabout, we told him to stop, which he reluctantly did outside a hospital entrance. A huge argument broke out as he wanted us to pay the full fare which we had agreed when we got in, despite us being no closer to our destination. A mob soon gathered around us, and we were forced into paying up before hurrying inside the hospital to safety. There we found an English-speaking doctor who we asked for directions. He was busy, and confessed to not knowing the campsite's location himself, but determined to help us, assigned one of his personal porters to take us there. The porter didn't speak any English, but drove us straight there without hesitating. We climbed out with our bags and thanked him, and in response he spoke his first and only words, which turned out to be the full names of what I later learnt was the entire English cricket team, before grinning and driving off. I've never seen a game of cricket in my life, and it took me about a fortnight to figure out what on earth he was going on about, but incredibly, the same thing happened to me again a few weeks later in a store in Peshawar.

Inside the campsite, three privately owned overland trucks were parked among the grassy knolls. We nodded a greeting to the foreigners relaxing outside their mobile homes, and then approached the five Pakistani men guarding the campsite, who sat around with AK47s held loosely in their hands. After asking them if there were beds to sleep in, we were led to a tiny, oval-shaped room, its walls scrawled with messages from what looked like generations of travellers. Inside on the floor a sleeping bag was unrolled over flattened cardboard; at the end of the room, a newspaper was unravelled and on top some marijuana lay drying. There was nothing else besides an old backpack and a pile of books, and only enough space for one more person to lie down. There was no toilet and, unsurprisingly, no shower.

When we looked at the man standing by the door in his blue government uniform, he smiled and motioned for us to make some space. We shrugged our shoulders and lent our packs against the wall, and as we did so, a short man, who if it wasn't for his ginger hair could have easily been mistaken for a local, came storming inside. He was dressed in a shalwar kameez, and had an impressive colonial moustache. On his head sat a small but heavily decorated hat with little mirrors sewn in to it, and he was clearly not happy. He looked at us and said, "Don't worry, its not you I'm angry with," and turned and began shouting at the gormless guard in the doorway. He was clearly annoyed at us being put into his room without being consulted. Even though there were no locks on the door anyway, he complained that we could have "nicked his stuff". As he said this, I looked around the room my eyes resting on what app-eared to be his only possessions, a neatly stacked pile of books on Quantum Physics.

The guard wandered back to his deck chair, seem-ingly unsure as to whether he had just been praised or reprimanded, then our new roommate introduced himself as Neil. Apparently, Neil was an unemployed soil scientist from Jersey, who was in the middle of writing a book which would "explain some of the great-est mysteries of our time." In fact, he claimed to have answers to questions that Einstein himself had struggled to solve. But it was while writing this book that a vision came to him in a dream and told him he would find the truth by visiting a specific church. The only problem was, the church was in Kashmir, and no one had ever heard of it. After doing some research in Jersey, he came across records and photos of a church in Kashmir that was exactly the same as the one he had seen in his vision. The next problem was that no westerner had laid eyes on the church for 60 years. It was also doubt-ful that the church was still standing, as it was right on the front line of the fighting. Unperturbed however, Neil had set off to find it anyway. That had been three months ago. He had tried to enter from India but the army wouldn't let him close to the disputed border, so he was now attempting to reach it from the Pakistani side, but first had to wait for an No Objections

Certificate (NOC) from the government which would allow him into no-man's-land.

For the next three nights we spent our evenings with Neil excitedly talking Quantum Physics at us, despite me repeatedly telling him I had left school with a "U" in Science and had no idea what he was talking about. He also confessed that the flowers talked to him and that he often saw spirals, shapes and bright lights hovering in the air.

"But," he said, with a joint bouncing between his lips, "that's not unusual for scientists like me."

At bedtime, we left our bags in the room with Neil, but slept outside. I had a one-man tent, but Simon had to make do with his hammock in which he was feasted on by mosquitoes without mercy. Although the campsite was right beside a four-lane highway it was surprisingly peaceful first thing in the morning, and surrounded by trees, the birds sung and the occasional mongoose darted through the undergrowth.

On our first morning we headed out early for the Iranian Embassy. We found that most were inside a secure area called the Diplomatic Enclosure. It was quite a fiasco just to get inside. We had to pay for a special bus to drive us inside the enclosure, and everything but our wallets and our paperwork were taken from us and held in storage and for each object we had to pay 10 rupees.

The bus drove a total of half a kilometre before dropping us off outside the Embassy, and yet cost the same as a 100km journey. It seemed that we were not allowed to actually enter the Embassy, as there was no visible door. Instead there was a small window in a razor wire-topped wall. In front of the wall was a sun shelter with two benches and a machine that dispensed cold drinking water, and neat lines of colourful flowers grew on either side. As I sat on the bench waiting for the window to slide open, I felt like I was queuing to get into heaven.

When the man behind the mysterious wall finally appeared, we slid our piles of paperwork through the grill to him. After some examination of our letters of invitation and recommendations, he gave us a bank account number into which we had to pay the visa fee, and explained that we were to return once we had the transaction receipt. I had to pay $40 more than Simon which brought the total for my visa for Iran to $200. When we returned hours later, the window was shut once more. We knocked quietly but persistently until the man could ignore us no longer. He took everything from us and told us to return at 4pm the next day. We asked if that meant that our visas would be ready by then, and received the predictable "Insha'Allah" meaning, "If God wills it." We walked out of the compound, but on the way stopped to try and get inside the Canadian Embassy, as we'd seen a red umbrella poking out from a balcony above us and were convinced it was a bar. The guards assured us it was not, and refused us entry.

Islamabad seemed to be a very modern and tidy city. We wandered around, stopping frequently to enjoy cold fruit juices. It was very neatly laid out in blocks, and there were no rickshaws, only taxis available, which made a huge difference to the noise pollution. Lots of people stopped us in the street, but they were only interested in talking to us, not in seeing what they could get from us, which took a while to get used to after India. I finished some conversations feeling quite guilty for being suspicious and defensive, but it's hard to be friendly to everyone when you're trying to keep your wits about you.

There were a lot of beggars lining the streets, and very few of them were able-bodied. Those that weren't lepers were badly deformed with things that would never have been allowed to reach the stages they were at in a developed country. One man's face was completely blocked out by a bulbous growth that was drooping down from his forehead. Others were missing limbs, and all were well worthy of charity. One benefit for them in Pakistan was that the Koran commands that a percentage of every person's wage is given to the poor, and most appeared to abide by this.

It seemed that the government's answer to those who were unemployed but able-bodied, was to equip them with a blue uniform – the same worn by our guards at the campsite, hand them a gun and tell them to go and stand somewhere, because it seemed that every shop and business had their own armed guard outside, and those without a store front, just hung around idly on street corners.

When we returned to the Iranian Embassy the next day, we received our visas, but were devastated to find that after the lengths we had gone to to get them, they had only allowed us 12 days. We were even more devastated when looking through the paperwork, discovered that it was partially our own fault. When we had been asked to provide an exact itinerary of where we would be going and for how long, we had written down 12 destinations from a map, but not how long we would be in each place, since we assumed all tourist visas lasted 30 days. As a result, we had been given just one day in each place, a feat that would be next to impossible, but it was now too late to do anything about it unless we wanted to submit another application for a visa, which neither of us could afford, in money or time.

We spent the afternoon in the camp, chatting to the guards as they polished their guns. They let us hold the guns and take photographs, and laughed when we pulled Rambo style poses for the camera. At first I had felt very lucky to have so many armed guards watching over us at night, but then Neil explained that the previous year the campsite had been invaded by rioters in an "anti-western" rally, they had assaulted the campers and ransacked their belongings; one overland truck had been burnt to the ground. After I heard that, I looked at the guards and realized that if anything like that happened again, they would be the first ones escaping over the back fence.

That evening two of our Japanese friends from Lahore arrived. We'd nicknamed them "Full Power", as when we had commented on their ability to smoke untold amounts of hashish in a single sitting, that had been their reply. They spoke very little English, but I enjoyed talking to them just for their hilarious facial expressions and repetitive, "Ooohhs" and "ahhhhs", which made them seem so excited and interested in everything. That night, as we lay among the trees looking up at the stars, Neil baffled us with big words we didn't understand, while Full Power sniggered like Beavis and Butthead.

The next morning Simon and I departed for Peshawar. When we climbed aboard the bus we asked if it was going where we wanted. "In sha'Allah" was of course the reply. Four and a half hours later we had arrived. We checked in to a hostel where the reputation of the owner had preceded him. Unfortunately, that reputation was a bad one. It was the cheapest place in town though, so everyone seemed to end up there anyway. The fact that it was right behind a baker's certainly seemed to help.

Almost as soon as we had put our packs down, we got chatting to a guy from the Bronx in New York. His eyes announced with a challenging stare that he was a tough guy, he had dark ginger hair and a scar running down his cheek. He told us he was a writer and I clearly remember that one of the books he had written was rather unforgettably called RAPE. He told us that he was on his way to talk to a man about entering Afghanistan. He said we were welcome to join him if we wanted, so purely out of curiosity, we did. The man he was meeting explained that to get to the border you would have to hire a jeep, a driver, and an armed guard or two. Then you needed to gain permission to enter the tribal areas, where Pakistani and International law is redundant. But all this was only possible if you had a visa for Afghanistan. On the way back, Simon could already tell I was thinking about going, and before I had said a single word he said seriously, "I'm out."

Back at the guesthouse we settled down on the sofas and relaxed for the rest of the day, finding out the gossip on the travellers' network from three Japanese who had been in Peshawar for two months. The first wisdom they imparted to us was to try the fresh local yogurt in the bakers at the front of the building. It was only plain, but you could also buy a small jar of locally sourced honey. These, mixed together into a 1l tub, became my breakfast, and sometimes lunch and dinner for the entire time I was there. I later wondered whether our new Japanese friends were perhaps relatives of Full Power, as they seemed to be in Pakistan purely for the hashish as well. We were lucky to see them on that first day, as it soon became apparent that they were practically nocturnal, rarely rising from their beds before sunset, and when they did, they would begin all night smoking sessions. Sometimes they would be so stoned that I would pass them on my way out in the morning still lying on the sofas, their eyes partially open, but their brains clearly closed.

The owner of the guesthouse was aware of the bad vibe surrounding his name, but never seemed anything but nice to me. Maybe he had turned over a new leaf. Malik had seemed to suggest that our new host had a bit of a reputation for theft and trickery, which I never really saw, although once, when I was alone with him, he did offer me $500 for my passport. When I turned him down, he upped his offer to $700. At that point I had to act offended and say there was no way I would ever sell my passport, because I knew that if he put the price up one more time, I would probably have said, "Sold!"

One evening, while absent-mindedly flicking through my passport, I took a closer look at my Pakistani visa and noticed a stamp across the corner. It read, "NOT VALID FOR CANTT AREA". I looked up and asked everyone where that was. '

"You're in it!" was the unanimous response.

"Oh!" I replied.

18

London Bombs

Lahore to Peshawar 486km

On one of our first days in Peshawar, we went to a yard on the outskirts of the city where the old Bedford trucks they used as buses, were being restored "Pakistani style". We'd ridden around in the back of these heavily adorned vehicles for some time, and although they were a little cramped and dull on the inside, the outside of the buses made them the coolest mode of transport available. At the yard we watched as the trucks were stripped bare and sanded down. The next step, was for the entire truck to be painted in bright lurid colours, then on top of that Koranic verses, lines of poetry, pictures of mountain scenery, birds, Roman numerals and even pop stars were painted. But that was not all. Mirrors, flashing lights, chrome strips and mini windmills were added randomly, the windows were replaced with blue tinted glass, and beads and multicoloured chains were hung from every available edge. Even the bumper didn't escape the fancy dress. Finally, the hubcaps, were removed, repainted and refitted so that they protruded slightly from the wheels, and the end result was a cross between a Romany Gypsy caravan and a Christmas tree.

Later that day, we headed to the fruit market in the old town where it felt a bit like I'd walked through a gateway into the past, if you ignored the plastic kitchenware and mobile phones present on most stalls. Hours slipped past as we strolled around the carpet, leather and tailor shops, often being stopped and offered refreshments by the traders. As we sipped a cup of tea, they never gave us the hard sell, just let us know what they had to offer and I ended up buying some hand-made leather sandals, which must have been good quality as they were stolen within a week.

Eventually the alluring aroma of the fast food kebab stalls drew us over and we stood and watched the animal carcases being stripped of their fat and grilled. The succulent slices of kebab were served on leaves, and came with the option of a seasoning of a dozen different spices or herbs.

There were so many traders packed into the tiny outlets which made up the old town, that it was hard to know who owned what. There were entire roads dedicated to dentistry, and to make the surgeries easily identifiable to the high percentage of people who were illiterate, enormous plastic moulds of lips and teeth hung off pieces of string in the windows. Outside each practice were dozens of second-hand dentures displayed on rickety rain-damaged tables, priced using a colour system rather than numbers. Whether they had a try-before-you-buy policy, or you just had to pick one and hope it fitted, I wasn't quite sure.

The men out-numbered the women by twenty to one. Those women we did see were well covered or shrouded completely under their light blue burkas. As I shuffled along a narrow causeway taking great care not to step

on anyone's exposed toes with my size 13 feet, I passed
three women draped in burkas. As I looked down again
to position my feet, I noticed how carefully and beauti-
fully decorated their feet were. Their nails were painted
and neatly trimmed, and their toes were adorned with
expensive rings, as bangles slid seductively around their
ankles. Surprised at this, I looked up at the grill that
covered the eyes of the first woman I passed, and I could
just make out a pair of powerfully green eyes. She knew
I'd noticed her feet and I'm sure she was smiling.

Over the next few weeks, I became aware of just how
much excitement the hidden women could bring to the
men, simply by exposing an arm briefly, or flashing an
extra half-inch of ankle. These spectre-like creatures
draped in blue remained somewhat of an enigma to me,
and I soon found myself looking at the veiled women in
the same way as the local men, trying to catch even the
slightest glimmer of character from behind their
disguise. I had to be careful though, for I knew these
women could be punished far more severely than I
would be if they were caught making eye contact.

As it turned out, the three Japanese who had been in
Peshawar for months, had actually been in India or
Pakistan for the past five years. As a result of not doing
much but smoking, drinking and talking, they spoke
fluent Urdu. This came in very handy when they took
me to visit the place I wanted to see next, the Smugglers'
Bazaar. Although it was possible for us to visit half the
bazaars during the day with an authorized guide, the
other half were forbidden for foreigners to enter at all.
At this particular Bazaar on the border of the tribal
lands, you could find everything from Sony Plasma TVs
to children's toys, but as it was exempt from Pakistani

law, it was also the place to buy all contraband, from guns and drugs to diamonds. Our enticement, however was far less illicit or extravagant.

The road that runs through the centre of the Bazaar leads up to the Khyber Pass and then on into Afghanistan. On the way the Japanese explained that we would have to move like lightning when the bus stopped, to avoid getting busted by the guards and having to pay a bribe or simply be sent back. As we neared the last stop, I was amazed to see that in the middle of this dusty no-man's-land, was a shiny and well-kept KFC restaurant. It looked like it had been plucked straight from the city and plonked back down in the desert. The only noticeable difference was the bold sign above the doorway, which read in English, "No Smoking, No Guns" and outside, two teenage boys sat on brand-new Chinese bicycles, with bubble wrap still covering the frames.

When the bus pulled over, the race was on. Directly ahead of us was the checkpoint where a few guards stood idly by a barrier which blocked the road and had scrawled across it "No Foreigners". We ducked straight off the road and dived into the crowds out of the guards' view. The Smugglers' Bazaar was a seemingly endless maze of shacks and canopies and makeshift workshops, and I was almost running to keep up and not get lost. We sidestepped from one meandering ally into another, so that before people could really register our presence, we had gone again. The stench of raw sewage hung in the air as it dribbled through gaps between shacks, dogs scrounged everywhere in the rubbish for scraps. The only time I paused was at a stall selling weaponry, and from where I stood, I could see through an open doorway in to a room where lines of young children sat stitching footballs in silence.

When we made it to the rendezvous, we were deep within the Bazaar and a long way from the checkpoint. The man we had come to see sat cross-legged behind three glass cabinets inside a tiny shack. He got to his feet when we entered, and greeted us like long lost sons. Once formal introductions were over, we climbed up and sat down on a ledge that ran around the perimeter of the room, and he resumed his position behind the three cabinets. In front of him was a large set of scales which I came to see over the course of the day, he used to weigh his goods which were mainly heroin, hashish and opium. His customers came in quietly, mumbled their orders, then threw down the correct money on to the cabinet before hurrying back outside with their packages and disappearing into the crowd. The owner was well protected – he had three loaded guns within arm's reach at all times, but he was quite happy to pass them around for us all to look at, and laughed as we handled them like eggs.

We were not there for the drugs though, but the cold cans of Heineken. The fan that rotated on its pedestal was weak, but gave just enough of a breeze to keep us awake, and as we sat there chatting and drinking, I told Simon that I had decided I was going to try to enter Afghanistan. He wasn't surprised, but didn't think it was one of my best ideas. He turned down the invitation to come with me, but then said that he was going to head south to Karachi, a city rated as the third most dangerous in the world! We enjoyed quite a few cold beers in the near darkness of the drug dealer's shack, which necessitated several trips to the loo which was quite a nerve wracking experience, since the toilet – a roofless building reserved just for peeing – was a fair distance away, and required very thorough navigational and safety instructions to get there.

Several hours later, as yet another customer arrived, the door opened and this time revealed that daylight was swiftly fading. We had clearly lost track of time, and Full Power leapt to their feet in panic – this was not a wise place to be in the daytime, let alone after dark. We all rose to leave immediately, and attempted to head back to safety at the same speed with which we had arrived, but it was soon clear that we were all far too unsteady on our feet. Luckily it didn't matter so much if we were seen leaving as we had already accomplished what we had set out to do and in the end with no bus in sight, we shared a taxi directly back to the guesthouse, eased by Full Power's fluency in Urdu.

Back at the guesthouse, bouncing with energy from the day's activities, Full Power cooked up something slippery, oily, noodley but delicious for dinner. It was shared and enjoyed by everyone, even the guesthouse owner, although he did say it needed more spice. This was also my last meal with Simon in Pakistan, as he was leaving to head south the following morning.

After seeing Simon off at the bus station, the next day, I was just heading back to the guesthouse when a man stopped me in the street and asked where I was from. I told him London, England and, to my surprise he said, "Oh, I'm sorry, I hope your family is good!"

"What are you talking about?"

"The bombs, the bombs, in London! Bang!" he replied, motioning dramatically with his hands.

Feeling a little worried, I hurried back to the guesthouse to find out what he was on about. Someone there had a copy of the local newspaper, *The Frontier Post*. The headline declared that terrorists had set off bombs in train stations all across London. The rest of my day was spent hunched around a world radio listening out for updates. To my relief, I soon received an email from my mum explaining that everyone we knew was okay. But now my decision was cemented, if I was ever going to see Afghanistan, I had to go now before the borders closed down and it was too late.

For the next three mornings I went to the Afghanistan Embassy. Each time they told me they weren't taking visa applications at the moment. I felt really sorry for two Americans staying in the guesthouse that night, as they had succeeded in gaining Iranian visas, only to then have them revoked thanks to George Bush's "Axis of Evil" speech that had occurred a couple of days before. The Iranians had not surprisingly been offended at this, and blocked all entry into Iran by American citizens, which meant for these two, their overland route to Europe had just been drastically messed up. I just prayed Tony Blair could keep his mouth shut long enough for me to get inside.

I sat around making lists of things I needed to get and do before I crossed the border. After a lot of scouring the streets, I found a bookshop which stocked books in English. There I bought a large but rough map of Afghanistan, and a book about the Taliban. I started asking a lot of different people the same questions, until I knew if it was possible to reach the border without a guard or a jeep. I learnt that there was an early morning local bus that ran to the border, but finding out where this left from, was not so easy.

On the fourth morning I returned to the embassy and again they told me the same thing. This time I wanted more of an answer and said I wanted to know when they would be submitting applications for visas, or if they were just going to keep making excuses in the hope that I would go away. Although I was deadly serious, I said this with a charming smile, and the official confessed that they'd run out of visa stickers and were waiting for a new batch to be sent from Islamabad. He said it would be quicker for me to return to Islamabad and go to their other Embassy there than wait here, so that day, I reluctantly backtracked to Islamabad.

Arriving back at the campsite we'd stayed in before; I was pleased to find Neil was still there he told me he was a little closer to bribing the right people to get him his NOC certificate. That night Neil introduced me to three Pakistani men who had become his friends in Islamabad. We went to one of their homes and drank tea. Two of them could recite every word of the Koran and were surprised that I could not recite a single word from the Bible. It was a nice evening, but unfortunately the main things they wanted to talk about were religion, women and poetry, three things about which I knew nothing.

They were a little forceful with the religion, but not in an extremist way, more in the way that comes from having no doubt that your religion is the correct and only one. Apart from being a sinner in their eyes, I was just someone they simply couldn't understand. They were desperate to class me as an atheist, but I wouldn't allow it, saying that I just didn't conform to any particular religious club.

"If I believe in anything," I told them, thinking of my experiences back in Thailand. "It's the force of Nature." That was my God.

The poetry was frankly weird for me. I had never before had a man recite verse to me with his hand on his heart and tears in his eyes. When they finished, I didn't know how to respond, and so just offered up an awkward, "Very nice."

They were all very emotional and talked a lot about their souls and their heavy hearts. I thought this was maybe due to the lack of females in their lives, as the only real contact they seemed to have with women until they got married was with their mothers. As a result, they seemed to view women as foreign objects, who were only there to produce sons. Even in the Pakistani movie industry of Lollywood (yes, Lollywood), kissing between the sexes was completely forbidden.

One of the men was going to go to Birmingham in England to attend university, and they all had hundreds of strange questions to ask me about women, few of which I had the answers to. After the subject of sex before marriage had passed, and they had all professed to being strongly against it, the one headed for Birmingham asked me quietly what was the best way to "woo" western women. I was no help there either, and sometimes wonder how he got on seducing the women of Birmingham with heartfelt poetry, in a strong Pakistani accent.

In the morning I went to the Diplomatic Enclosure only to find that the Afghan Embassy was not enclosed in the special area, but back in the centre of town from where I'd just come. I grabbed a taxi and was glad I had, as I would never have found it on my own. The

Embassy was a rundown building, marked only by a wonky rusty sign that pointed towards the ground. The walls were splitting and shabbily repainted, the guttering was broken and an orange stain ran down from it to a window, behind which an official sat. I explained to him through the cracked glass that I wanted a visa for Afghanistan, and that my intentions were innocent. He told me that I would need a letter of recommendation. Wanting to scream, I calmly explained that I really couldn't afford another letter of recommendation, not after Iran. He didn't seem to care and sent me off to try regardless.

Jumping in another taxi I shot across town to the British Embassy. There they told me what I had feared, that they were not recommending any unnecessary travel to Afghanistan. They didn't want to know about my plight, but I felt I might be able to persuade them if I could talk to the Ambassador, who wasn't available until the following day. I continued my preparations anyway and got all the photocopies and photos the Afghan Embassy had also asked for in addition to the letter.

That evening, Neil, myself, and a Canadian girl also staying at the campsite, went out for dinner with my new Pakistani friends. They insisted on going somewhere quite smart, and on picking up the bill afterwards. On the way, one of the men took my hand and held it as we walked down the road. While I was aware this was perfectly normal in Pakistan and India as a sign of friendship between two men, it didn't make me feel any more comfortable. Then as we walked in to the restaurant I felt even more uncomfortable; not for the first time on my travels, I was clearly totally underdressed.

It didn't seem to matter though, as all the other diners seemed jealous of our hosts having western friends to dine with and show off, even if one of them looked a little rough around the edges. We must have been served around 10 courses, and I was expected to eat from every dish. I managed it, but did wish they had warned me how many there would be from the start, and I wouldn't have stuffed my face quite so much with the first few.

First thing the next day I returned to the Afghan Embassy to plead my case once more. I was the only one waiting when they opened, which I decided was even better as it gave me more time to grovel. It turned out; I didn't have to.

When I explained that the British Embassy was advising against travel to Afghanistan, the official stared at me for a full minute, tapping his pen on the edge of his desk distractedly. I was just about to push my point when he said, "England won't help you, but Afghanistan will!" And he took my passport and my $30, and told me to return the following day.

I hurried back to tell Neil the good news about the Embassy official's bizarre change of heart, but wasn't far from the campsite when I began to hear shouting. Coming down the main road towards me was a rabble of protesters. Unsure at first what it could be about, I ducked into the corner of a shop to let it pass, but as they got closer, I saw they were burning an effigy of something and there were two news teams filming them and running about 10m ahead of the marching crowd.

I still couldn't understand what they were shouting, but as I crept closer, I could make out the words on the placards reading, "Don't punish us, Blair!" and "No to Terrorism!" Most of them had spelling mistakes, but the message was clear enough. They were worried about reprisals for the London bombings. I felt safer when I saw this, thinking it was unlikely they were going to attack a British westerner, as that would be a bit contradictory to their message. Still, I wasn't taking any chances, and took cover in a shop until the whole episode had passed. Back at the camp, I forgot about the march and got on with celebrating my visa success with Neil over mango shakes.

I was sad to leave Neil in the morning, for meeting people like him make me feel sane. I kept in contact with him via email quite regularly over the next few months. Then an earthquake hit Islamabad, and I never heard from him again. I sent a number of emails to him to see if he was okay, but never got a reply.

I picked up my visa without any further complications, and thanked the man behind the chipped window repeatedly, before catching the bus back to Peshawar.

Back at the guesthouse I took great pleasure in telling everyone how I had got my Afghan visas in Islamabad, with no letter, and particularly enjoyed relating what had happened to the two French guys who had been there before I'd left, and were still waiting patiently for the visa stickers to arrive at the embassy in Peshawar.

I spent another two days in Peshawar preparing; I went to the bank two mornings in a row to withdraw the maximum daily allowance, knowing that once I crossed into Afghanistan I would have to carry all the money I needed for up to a month on my person since there would be no banks.

I went to the Office of Tribal Affairs to be granted a letter of permission to enter the lawless territories. I arrived early in the morning and was kept waiting for ages. Then I was told that for an extra fee everything could be sorted out a lot quicker. Refusing to be baited into a bribe, I told them I was in no hurry and could wait all day if necessary. Another hour passed before I was finally given handwritten permission, and I left the embassy to pack. I sent an email to my brother Sam, to tell him of my plans for entering Afghanistan, just in case something went wrong. I then sent another email to my parents telling them that I was going into the mountains for a bit and would get back in touch in a few weeks, to be sure they weren't going to start getting worried.

I had no idea what day of the week it was when I walked back through town, and wondered why all the shutters on the shops were being pulled down and everyone seemed to be hurrying to get somewhere. Then as I turned the corner to the main road which was normally heaving with traffic and stalls, I saw that it was deserted too. There was not even a bullock cart in sight. It was of course, Friday prayer, the most important prayer of the week. All around me, personal prayer mats were being placed on the ground and men were kneeling. People were still arriving when the praying began to the soundtrack of protracted wailing that came from the speakers mounted on the top of the nearby buildings.

The whole city had come to a standstill, rather surreally I was suddenly surrounded by over 1,000 men prostrating themselves in the middle of the dusty road. I wasn't sure if it would be disrespectful to walk past them while they were praying or not. I did know it would certainly draw a lot of unwanted attention my way, so I settled down in a doorway with a fruit smoothie, and waited for them to finish. It took well over an hour before the worshippers had dispersed and the road had returned to its normal level of activity.

When I got back to the guesthouse hours later than I had planned, the Japanese immediately said with a smile, "Friday Prayer?" I nodded.

19

Mecca Cola

Peshawar to kabul = 290km

The bus to the border left at 7.30 the following morning. I was up by 6.15am, bleary-eyed from a broken night's sleep thanks to the mosquitoes. Already sweating from the early morning heat, I grabbed a quick shower in an attempt to cool myself down. Downstairs, I passed Full Power, who were still seated on the communal sofas smoking, just as they had been when I'd gone to bed the night before. They offered me a joint, but telling them I had somewhere I had to be I headed out of the door to the crossroads, with a mixture of nerves and excitement.

I was just beginning to get a little anxious that I didn't know where the bus stop I needed was, when a taxi appeared. I hailed it and tried my best to explain to the driver where I wanted to go. He nodded and we started driving away from the old town which is where I had thought the bus was leaving from. Slightly concerned something had been lost in translation, I said again, "Afghanistan bus?"

"Yes, yes, yes," he replied. When we began heading down the road that I knew led to the Smugglers' Bazaar, I was now sure that he wasn't heading for the bus stop but not wanting to ask him for a third time, decided to wait and see. As we approached the "No Foreigners" barrier that marked the entrance to the Bazaar, there were two guards manning it, who were just slouching around chatting. I was a little tall for the front seat of the taxi, and my head was already being pushed into the roof, so as we drove through the open checkpoint, I turned my collar up to hide my neck and pushed my head up at an angle. The guards glanced at us without pausing from their chatter, and on we drove. A couple of kilometres further down the road I noticed that everyone seemed to be on foot, and coming from the direction in which we were headed. A few were carrying microwaves and TVs on their shoulders; another was pushing a shiny new drum kit along in a wheelbarrow. We passed a second Border Police checkpoint, and this time I was spotted, and the guards came running out of their hut waving their arms for the car to stop. They ordered me out of the taxi and my papers were checked, and it was then explained to me that my driver thought he was taking me to the border.

It suddenly all made sense; he'd clearly been thinking in the hundreds when we'd held up fingers bartering for the price, while I had been thinking in the tens. I explained that I was trying to get the bus and had never wanted a taxi all the way to the border. I was told I could go on the bus, but I had to have an armed guard. Having paid the taxi driver a fair amount to cover my journey so far, I turned back to the officials, determinedly. "I'll be crossing in to Afghanistan on my own, I don't need a guard to travel 35km to the border," I said.

The official held up my papers and pointed to some small print, and it became apparent that I had unknowingly already agreed to this at the Tribal Affairs Office. "I don't care if you get shot in Afghanistan, but until you get there, you're the responsibility of Pakistan," he said.

Begrudgingly realizing my hands were now tied, I agreed to allow a guard on the bus with me, but said I would only pay for his bus fare. The guard assigned to me was an older man with grey wispy hair who I guessed had somehow missed out on his chances of promotion to a better post earlier in life, and once aboard the bus, insisted that we sit at the back. I thought this was a security precaution, but it turned out he just knew that those seats had more legroom. We hadn't been travelling very long when a man a few rows ahead of us produced a large chunk of some brown substance, which he pulled a piece off and began to chew. On spotting this my guard shouted out something to him in Urdu. I guessed that he was reprimanding him for such blatant drug use, for this was hashish it seemed. It had a, by then familiar, sweet and potent smell that was drifting our way. The passenger turned to look at the guard and, jaw still circulating, he handed the lump back to him. My guard smiled, pulled off a piece, lifted it to his nose for a sniff, and then chucked it into his own mouth before handing the remainder back to its owner. A few minutes later he was gazing out of the window, his chin resting on the exit end of his rifle. It was at about this point that I realized that if anyone was going to shoot me before I reached the border, it was going to be the one supposed to be protecting me, so I shuffled a few seats away from him and spent the rest of the journey staring out of the opposite window.

I was excited to be crossing the Khyber Pass, as few places have witnessed such action. The shells of bombed-out houses were visible from the road, while higher up stood the remains of an old, possibly British, fort. I could easily imagine the likes of Genghis Khan passing through here, but struggled to visualize British soldiers as they just didn't fit in with the surroundings. When we reached the border, it was more like a giant market filled with beggars from the nearby refugee camps. I waved off my armed guard at the immigration office and approached the man behind the desk, who was sitting reading a newspaper. He looked up, annoyed to be interrupted, and after stamping me out said irritably, "Go away."

I did as I was told, and outside briefly paused to examine my visa which now had the word 'USED' stamped across it. I felt a huge rush of adrenaline; my only option now was to head to Kabul.

I didn't actually cross in to Afghanistan. I just kind of wandered through the crowds until I suddenly found myself there. Realizing I had accidentally crossed the border, I had to backtrack 50m in search of the immigration office, where I was greeted very warmly and sat and drank tea while they checked my papers. I was then asked to sign at the bottom of a document that I couldn't read, and once everyone seemed happy with the administrative side of things, I was welcomed to Afghanistan and taken directly to a moneychanger by an official who assured me this particular moneychanger gave the fairest rates around. It turned out to be a boy who can't have been more than 14 years old, but had the manner and confidence of an old hand. My money now changed, I was shown to the bus stand, where

I was lucky enough to get one of the last seats on a minibus headed for Kabul. Every male passenger on the minibus shook my hand, and then we were on our way.

Unfortunately, the seat I had managed to snag was one of the folding variety which come down in the middle of the aisle and have a back that only reaches a few inches up your spine. This meant that after bouncing along the road to Kabul for several hours, I was left with a very bruised and sore back. On the route, we passed what appeared to be a well-organized scrap yard which was where, I was told, all the stolen cars were brought so that their number plates and engine numbers could be changed within the safety of the Tribal Lands, before being driven back across the border. Not far into the journey, the man next to me offered me a bottle of water. I gratefully accepted, assuming he had more in the huge bag upon his lap. When I later saw him buying more, I realized that this was not the case and as was the custom in Afghanistan, he was simply being very generous to someone he saw as a guest.

Near the front of the bus a little girl sat fidgeting between two very stiff looking women. She had beautiful long black hair that hung down past her shoulders, and hazel eyes. She kept turning around to stare at me inquisitively while she chatted away to those around her non-stop for the full eight hours to Kabul. Thinking of her now I feel very sad to think that in a few short years after that journey, she would have had to don the burka like all the other women on the bus; those beautiful eyes and bubbling personality hidden from the outside world forever.

After about two hours we stopped for prayers and breakfast, and I realized that my stomach must have shrunk in size over the past month, as I was still struggling to finish my first Afghan meal of meat and rice when the others were already getting back on the minibus. As we drove up and down through the passes, another man shared some really sour red berries with me, while yet another offered me some juicy watermelon.

Our route seemed to be roughly following a river which was sometimes flat as a swimming pool, and at others, a torrent of white water. More than once we passed through villages where kids attacked us with water guns, ambushing us from both sides and squirting water through the open windows. Being the tallest and seated right in the middle of the minibus, I got hit every time, much to the amusement of everyone else. Soon the driver was deliberately slowing down each time we passed through a village, giving them time to reload, but since it was like an oven on board, I didn't really mind too much.

As we slowly climbed one of the passes, we overtook a truck with a P&O container on the back, the same company that ran the ferries which crossed the English Channel, and I took this as a good omen. We squeezed passed a few UNWFP (United Nations World Food Programme) trucks on their way to deliver aid, and a large petrol tanker, clearly marked with "highly flammable" symbols. I wondered what would happen if it went over the edge on this narrow road, and no sooner had this crossed my mind than Mr Watermelon pointed out of the window to the remains of a truck a few hundred metres below us. It must have flipped and rolled a dozen times before coming to rest. As we continued on along the crumbling road, I made a mental note of all my available exits and hand holds.

As we came down from the mountains a little community of tent dwellers appeared on the plain ahead. They were miles from anything and completely exposed to the elements, but the camp seemed quite well established as each tent had its own yard penned in by a thatched fence. Whoever they were, our driver felt it necessary to pay them a fee before we could pass.

Once across the plain, we were stopped at a checkpoint, and as soon as I was spotted, I was pulled off the bus. When I saw my pack was being unloaded and I was still being told nothing, I began to feel a little worried. None of the people at the checkpoint were in uniform, and I was a bit concerned that the minibus was going to continue without me. When they began roughly handling my pack with the intention of searching it, my worry turned to anger. It was the one constant on this long journey, an old friend, and I had become very protective over it, not even liking people moving it without asking. So, when they started unpacking it and laying my semi-clean clothes down on the dirty, dusty ground, it was an effort not to say anything I would come to regret. I ground my teeth together as I watched them handle all of my gear, then have a long debate over what my cooker was actually for, before putting everything back inside. They only managed to fit half of my possessions back in before the pack was full to the top. Tutting and sighing repeatedly, I unpacked and repacked everything once more, giving them a running commentary as I did so and exaggerating the dusting down of the clothes they had dropped in the dirt. By the time the cramped minibus pulled away with me back on board, they were kicking at the dirt like scolded children.

A little further down the road we passed the decrepit remains of a VW camper, which looked ever so lost amidst the ramshackle debris of a tumble-down village. Perhaps its hippy owner had left it there in the 60s when Afghanistan had been a safe country to drive through, and I was still musing on this a few hours later when the outline of the city of Kabul began to appear on the horizon across the plains.

Suddenly, the other passengers began winding up their windows and making sure all the doors were securely closed. I followed everyone's gaze out of the window to our left, yet I couldn't see what all the fuss was about. All I could see in front of the barren mountains in the distance was a quivering haze of orange. But as I stared harder, I began to notice the wall of orange was rapidly growing in height and heading right for us. Just before the dust storm struck, the driver slowed to a halt, and as the grit swirled around us, scratching and clawing at the minibus, the visibility was reduced to no more than a few metres. Our attempts to keep the invasion outside, however, were in vain, as the dust sneaked in through every available crevice. Everyone began coughing and spluttering, and I pulled my shirt up over my head to protect my eyes, nose and mouth. Then as quickly as it had started, it was all over. My eyes were itchy and watery, and for the first and last time, I envied the women seated near the front, under the protection of their burkas.

The bus dropped me off in the heart of the capital, and accompanied by Mr Watermelon who had offered to ensure I found somewhere safe to stay, I hailed a cab to take me to the UN compound. The building itself looked as though it could withstand nuclear attack. On the front line, outside its heavily fortified walls, were two Afghani guards, alert for trouble. I approached them with my hands in the air, and explained that I needed help finding one of the hotels that the UN allowed foreigners to stay in. Unfortunately, their English was no better than my Pashto, so they radioed through for assistance. The blue razor wire-topped gate slid open, and a black American solider strutted through dressed in full desert camouflage, his eyes hidden behind mirrored Oakley sunglasses. He held his machine gun cocked and seeing me dressed in my shalwar kameez exclaimed, "What da Hell?"

Resisting the urge to tell him to shove his gun where the sun doesn't shine, I held up the address that I'd scribbled on a napkin back in Peshawar, an address that had come from the "untrustworthy" guesthouse owner.

"Do you know where this is?" I asked him.

"Ain't got a clue," was his helpful response.

I later heard that the Americans had changed many of the road names to make it easier for them to remember, hence the ever so sensitively renamed Washington Street, for example.

I climbed back into my cab and we drove around the block to the European enclosure where I found two Brits just entering the building. Unfortunately, they were also unable to help as they explained that they lived inside the compound, and never really went into the city. Eventually, with the help of a dozen taxi drivers we found the hotel, only to be told at reception that they could no longer accept foreigners as the UN had not granted them the new required permit. This permit was something that had only recently been introduced for security reasons and meant that foreigners could only stay in places designated by the UN so that in the case of an emergency it was easier to locate and evacuate everyone. It occurred to me that this also made it easier for terrorists to target them.

Eventually we found a place just around the corner where I was able to stay. I thanked Mr Watermelon for all his help and at his insistence, took his phone number in case I needed anything more. We said goodbye, and I turned to make my way up the steps of the hotel, where I was immediately passed by a westerner in wraparound sunglasses and a baseball cap, presumably to disguise his identity. I stopped him to ask about the hotel rates. He was clearly in a hurry, but quickly told me that the rooms at the front of the building with the windows were the cheapest. I frowned, and slightly irritated at my obvious lack of experience in war zones, he elaborated. "When the hotel gets bombed it takes the worst impact from the front. So, you should stay away from windows as they could slice you up real bad if they were shattered."

"Okay, thanks for that," I said, and feeling sufficiently alarmed, I walked inside.

The receptionist was on the phone, so I stood around in the foyer waiting for her to notice me for a few moments before there was a sudden loud pop from outside. Given my recent conversation, I nearly jumped out of my skin, and I turned to see a group of people forming on the front steps of the hotel, their heads craning upwards. Then there was a zzzzwwwpppp sound, and a fireball fell from above. I cautiously followed the receptionist outside to find that the hotel's electric sign, which ran down the front of the building, had burst into flames, and was now rapidly melting, large blobs of bubbling plastic streaming down in front of us. For the next 15 minutes hotel staff threw buckets of water through the open windows above, while hoses were sprayed from below. As the last of the smoke drifted away and the hotel owners turned their attention to the plastic which had dried and hardened on the ground outside the entrance to the lobby, the fire engine arrived. Everyone began clapping and cheering sarcastically, but not wanting to lose face the firemen, whose blue uniforms looked as though they had fought a few hundred fires since their last wash, proceeded to carry out an inspection of the building.

Crisis over, my check-in resumed accompanied by firemen running up and down the stairs behind me. As it turned out, I wasn't forced to choose between a cheap room and a safe night's sleep since the place was practically empty, so I was given a room at the back of the building for the same price as one at the front, $15US a night.

I let myself into my room, dumped my bag on the bed, and went straight back outside for a wander. The streets were busy with traders and men sitting around drinking tea. Going against all my better instincts, I went down a subway to cross the road and was immediately offered drugs by two men perched on old wooden crates down there. I declined and walked on as the dealer shouted after me something that was certainly not very complimentary. His words echoed around the mildewed walls and followed me up the steps as I made a hasty exit. I explored the locale for another half an hour or so, but didn't feel all that comfortable walking around. By now I was more than used to having everyone stop and stare wherever I went, but this was different. I realized that I didn't know if any of these people were Taliban sympathisers or worse – Al Qaeda operatives. It's quite easy to become paranoid in situations like that, and I walked back to the hotel in the twilight, and this time took the overland route rather than the subway.

Back inside the relative safety of the hotel, I went for dinner in their rooftop restaurant where I found the chef-cum-waiter asleep on the floor. I woke him up and feeling a bit guilty, asked if they were open. "Yes, yes, yes," he said.

I sat down and he passed me a menu faded from being left in the sun too long. It did, however, offer a good variety of dishes, and I ordered something relatively simple and inexpensive. The waiter nodded and went off into the kitchen, and I sat looking out at the city which was almost entirely in darkness now, with just a smattering of lights powered by generators. When the waiter returned, he brought me a bowl of rice piled with some pieces of badly chopped chicken. I looked at him in confusion as this was not even vaguely what I had ordered. He mimed drinking something, and I realized I couldn't complain as the guy didn't speak any more English than I did Pashto.

"Yes, yes, yes," he said, when I continued looking blank. I was beginning to see a pattern emerging.

"Coca-Cola?" I asked. Nodding, the waiter disappeared back inside the kitchen and returned with almost what I had asked for. The can of drink was called Mecca Cola, and had exactly the same branding and logo design as you'd find on a normal can of Coca-Cola. Sadly, I thought, as I took a sip and gagged, that was where the similarity ended.

20

Careful Underfoot

Distance from Khao Lak = 14,257km

That night, I slept so soundly nothing short of a not-so-unlikely bomb could have woken me. The first thing I did in the morning, was go and register at the British Embassy, which took me a long time to find even by taxi, for there were no signs or flags flying to identify the different embassies. Outside the British Embassy there were no pavements, just huge concrete walls wrapped in barbed wire, with guard towers on each corner and everybody who approached was treated with the utmost suspicion.

I got out of the taxi and began walking towards the front gate, simultaneously rolling up my sleeves, before being told to stop before I was more than a few metres from the entrance.

"Your passport," a guard shouted. I pulled it out of my pocket and held it up. Unfortunately, the coat of arms embossed in gold on the front had rubbed off, so after the guard approached to take it, a rather meticulous examination followed. My ghostlike passport photo probably didn't help things either. It seemed to pass muster, however and once inside the main gates,

I was patted down, scanned and possibly even X-rayed. I was directed to walk forward and then wove my way through an assortment of concrete bollards before passing under the sturdy car barriers. Inside the first small building, a British man with a public school accent was explaining to some well-to-do looking Afghanis, what they would have to do to get back into England, as from what I could gather, they had been kicked out of the country for claiming false asylum.

The rather attractive Consul Assistant Tina, sat here behind a glass screen. Or perhaps she wasn't rather attractive at all, and she was just the first female I had seen in a long time whose head was not covered. Either way, this reminded me that I was technically on British soil within the Embassy grounds, and I felt safe for the first time since crossing the border.

Tina gave me a registration form to fill in. I had to leave a lot of spaces blank as the form was intended for NGOs and they didn't have a separate registration form for tourists. I filled it in as best I could, and then Tina came around the front to chat with me. I got the impression that she didn't quite believe me when I told her that I was just in Afghanistan to sightsee. She asked quite a few probing questions, but after a while she seemed to accept that I had nothing to hide, and she warned me that I mustn't walk around on my own or travel by taxi, as that was how most kidnappings occurred. I asked how I was supposed to get around then, and she replied, "Maybe you should just stay inside." She was clearly only half joking.

Before I left Tina, invited me around to her house for dinner, but said that it could take up to a week for her to get me the security clearance.

"Thanks," I said. "I probably won't be around in a week's time, but we should definitely have dinner next time I'm in town." Tina definitely was quite attractive after all.

Before I left, I managed to get from Tina three photocopied versions of English newspapers which they had lying around the back office, and over the next week I must have read each copy front to back a dozen times. One article claimed that there were members of Al Qaeda within the CIA, which seemed unlikely but also quite possible I thought. After all they were both interested in the buying and selling of weapons.

As I was leaving the Embassy, four men strode through security towards me, holding up matchbox-sized ID cards to the guards on shift as they did so. All of them had shaved heads, were built like tanks, and the shortest of the four must have been at least 6ft 2in. I stepped aside for them as they strutted past, but I doubt they even noticed me.

Once back at the hotel, I went for a shower and a shave in the communal washrooms. I had to use a shard of glass in one of the broken windows to hang up my clothes, and the water was far too cold to call it refreshing, but I looked better for making the effort. Back in my room I laid out my map of Kabul on the bed and studied it intently. Once I'd made a mental note of exactly how many lefts and rights I needed to make to reach my intended destination, I set off, but five minutes after leaving the hotel I was hopelessly lost. I found myself in a bustling food market that sold anything and everything that was edible. I noticed a lot of the stuff for sale was marked, "Aid, not for resale" and some of the goods were still wrapped in their UNWFP packaging. The women in their burkas had to hold every item up close to the mesh through which they could see out, just to identify what each item was, while on another stall, young men watched slyly as the covered women revealed their forearms to try on bangles. I was being equally as sneaky by taking quick shots with my camera that was half concealed up my sleeve. Every stall had a tarpaulin tied above it which was connected to their neighbour's which provided one huge shade from the sun. Unfortunately, the strings were all tied quite low, and I nearly decapitated myself several times.

I followed the wall that ran beside the dried-up river of Kabul. Young children were running around barefoot in the marshy riverbed. I noticed that they were carrying old rice sacks in the hope of retrieving something of value in the mud which they might exchange for food. Hanging over the wall were dozens of old hand-woven carpets, and near the end, a man was sitting under the shade of an antique umbrella. He was selling shoes, which were all laid out on the wall beside him. There must have been over 60 designs. None of them, however, were pairs and they were all in random sizes, styles and colours – and more bizarrely most seemed to be for the left foot. I can't imagine that he had many customers apart from the odd landmine victim, but he was quite content just sitting there on his wall.

A moneychanger spotted me crossing over a bridge. He was wearing one of those middle-aged-man safari waistcoats that only seem to come in beige. Money was bulging from his many pockets and he tipped his Indiana Jones style hat in my direction. Before he could offer, I told him I didn't need to change up any money.

"Can I walk with you then?" he asked, and I nodded. He spoke good English and proudly told me he had gone to school in Iran. He was clearly still angling for a sale though, and told me it was best for me to change up all my money in Kabul, as I wouldn't be able to once I left the city. I told him if that was true, I would come back and find him before I left, as all my money was back at the hotel. This was a lie, but he soon gave up on this tack and instead produced something I really did want; a handful of Iraqi money from the toppled regime. He saw my eyes widen at the portrait of Saddam Hussein on the bank notes. This made it quite hard to haggle down the price, as he knew he had already sold them before we started. I consoled myself that I still bought them for a fraction of what they will be worth in the future though.

Back at the hotel I consulted my map a second time before setting out to find Chicken Street which had been a must-see for all tourists since the start of the hippy trail. It was where all the carpet and jewellery stores were located, and it was here I bought my Afghan hat as seen modelled by Osama Bin Laden in most of his videos.

A little further down the road from the hat seller, two western men stood outside the doorway to a jewellers. Both had earpieces in. As I approached, they gestured with their guns for me to walk out into the road and around them. Someone of importance was obviously inside, perhaps an ambassador buying his wife some new earrings. I tried to peek through the doorway but the smartly dressed men deliberately blocked my view. As I reached the end of Chicken Street, wondering why there were no chickens, I looked across at the next street, and was taken aback by the vibrant colours that greeted me. This road was appropriately named Flower Street, as every shop was bursting with blooms of all shapes and sizes. A group of giggling women, possibly a wedding party, came out of one of the florists and got into a waiting car. With so much brightness and life around me, I forgot where I was for a while, but was soon brought back to reality when a convoy of UN vehicles cruised past, their enormous black aerials wobbling over the bumps in the potholed road.

I had a meat and rice dish for lunch in a small restaurant with a back-lit picture of Mecca on the wall that changed colour. While I ate, I watched a group of women walk carefully down the road, their billowing burkas flapping behind them like unpegged tents. Shortly after them a line of tanks trundled past, each with soldiers positioned on the roofs, fully armed and scanning the crowds for trouble.

On the way back to the hotel I passed a line of photographers in the street, equipped with the old-fashioned studio cameras complete with a black velvet backdrop. They asked me if I would like to have my picture taken. Instead, I offered to reverse roles and took photos of them instead standing in front of their museum pieces, pulling poses borrowed from western boy bands.

I had another meal of chicken and rice at the rooftop restaurant that evening before getting a good night's sleep, but this was entirely counteracted by the worst possible 30 seconds post-waking I have ever experienced. I'd put a portable swivel head fan beside my bed before drifting off, which I had forgotten about as I slowly opened my eyes and swung my legs out of bed next morning. My legs, still wrapped in the sheets, knocked the fan over which then started dancing its way around the room. Panicking, I reached out to grab it, but in my dazed state, didn't gauge the width between the bars that covered the fan, and accidentally stuck my fingers straight into the rapidly spinning blades. The fan still spinning and bouncing around the room, and my hand now pumping blood from three deep cuts, I went for the socket to unplug the fan, and was promptly electrocuted and thrown back across the room to the foot of the bed. In shock, I lay on the floor for a few moments staring at my hand, before rushing out of the room to get to the sink in the communal bathrooms, deeply shocking two female cleaners on the way, since I was still only dressed in my boxers.

Once I'd patched myself up, I headed out in the hope that all my bad luck was over for the day, but halfway down the stairs I stopped, noticing there was something stuck to my sandal. I lifted up my heel to see that it was the sticker that had been positioned on the floor of my room. It was an arrow and supposed to be pointing in the direction of Mecca. I quickly went back to my room, worried that I had just committed a huge sin, and using my compass in order to get the direction correct, I fixed it back as best I could onto the carpet.

Outside, I found a taxi driver and asked him to take me to the Kabul Museum which was once one of the greatest museums in Asia. Unfortunately, throughout the Civil War, the Mujahedeen repeatedly plundered the place, then in 2001, the Taliban destroyed most of what was left to punish the Hazara people for rebelling against them. It's estimated that less than a third of the original collection remains.

I paid my 10 Afghanis entrance fee (43 Afghanis equal $1US), and began to look around. Within a quarter of an hour, even walking slowly and reading all the notices thoroughly, I'd seen everything there was to see. The restoration work was impressive, but compared to the photos showing the objects in their original glory, it was like looking at a pile of broken bricks and trying to picture a castle. In front of one of the windows there was a plaque detailing the history of Afghanistan's one and only train, which was displayed outside on the other side of the glass. Wanting a closer look, I left the building to go around the back. It looked lost and lonely and very rusty. I climbed in to the front cab, and looking out through the driver's window, I could see the Darul Aman Palace which was built by the King in the 1920s to be the seat of the future parliament. Due to a combination of fires, coups and shelling over the past decades, however, it was no longer fit for anything. If it wasn't for its size and strategic location, it would have been unrecognizable from any of the other bombed-out buildings that littered Kabul.

After a search by the guard for any concealed artefacts, I left the museum grounds, crossed over the road, and jumped over the wall that must have once bordered the palace's magnificent gardens, and began walking across the rubble-covered ground towards the building. Halfway across I heard a shout from behind me and turned to see four men from the museum waving in my direction. I waved back and then continued walking, but their shouts grew louder and I turned around again and this time I realized that they were wanting me to go back over to them. Slightly annoyed, because I thought they were just calling me over to practice their English, I returned to where they stood on the other side of the wall, and to my surprise they all looked extremely relieved. Then pointing urgently at the ground over which I'd just walked, they said, "Minefield."

"Oh."

They pointed out a safe path that led around the back of the building, and I dutifully stuck to it this time. There were signs all along it reading, "No photography of Military installations", which I took to mean the rolls of razor wire that surrounded the palace and the guard tower that was posted on one corner, rather than the building itself. I walked around the outside of the palace, held back by the spiked fencing, yet still close enough to see the bullet-ridden structure properly. The sun was shining through the gaping holes in the roof where the bombs had dropped. There were no walls at all on one side. Among the destruction, some parts lay preserved though. Marble columns stood unscratched by shrapnel. Along the stone ceiling borders, detailed carvings were intact. I could see why the place was still being guarded.

As I completed my circle of the palace and made my way round to where the guard tower was, I assumed that the soldiers had already seen me and weren't bothered by my presence, otherwise they would have said something. But as I walked closer, still taking pictures, but being careful not to include them in the frame, an order was shouted from above. I looked up at the hut on stilts to see a gun pointing directly at me. A soldier on the ground then came over and demanded my camera saying, "No photos, no photos!"

The sign on the fence said it was the Canadian Army guarding the palace, yet the flag on his uniform suggested he was Hungarian. I explained I had taken no pictures of military installations, only of the palace itself. I took off my hat to emphasize that I was western, but he insisted that I delete all the pictures right there in front of him. I was pleased I wasn't using film. With our hands carefully positioned between the reels of razor wire, I deleted them one by one under his watchful eye, shooting the odd glare up at the trigger-happy guard who continued to watch me through the sight of his gun. Once they were happy, I was offered reluctant thanks for my cooperation. As I walked away, I looked back at the palace and saw that it sat on a rise. Anyone with a zoom lens could have taken the same pictures I had.

Not far down the road, a shepherd and his flock were crossing. He can't have been more than 12 years old, but he controlled them as though he'd been doing it for a lifetime. He was happy to be photographed, and didn't notice that I positioned him to include various angles of the palace as the backdrop. I couldn't help but hope the guard in the tower was still watching.

I was 10km outside the west of Kabul. The surrounding area had been on the front line of the fighting in the 1990s, so I decided it would be interesting to walk back. I made my way along the side of the main road, passing friendly locals who were building stone walls. Nearly every building either side of me was incomplete – there was kilometre after kilometre of broken houses and derelict buildings. I came across four young sisters outside their crumbling home, happily playing among the rubble. They stopped as soon as they saw me and called inside the house to their parents.

Their dresses looked homemade – not in terms of their quality, simply from the fact that they were all made out of the same red fabric. The two smaller sisters shielded themselves behind the tallest, as we waited for their parents to appear. The youngest child was no older than three and sat nibbling on a boiled sweetcorn in a playpen made entirely out of fallen bricks.

A man appeared, and sized me up silently for a while, probably not sure what to make of the first foreigner he had seen not wearing fatigues or carrying a gun.

He then invited me inside for tea. They lived on the third floor of the otherwise abandoned building. As we walked up the stairs, I found myself stupidly thinking how dangerous it was that the stairs had no banisters to stop you falling, completely forgetting that they were living in a house which could topple over at any second. Inside their living space, he didn't introduce me to his wife when she appeared out of one the side rooms under the cover of a burka. She quietly made the tea at the far end of the room, making as little noise as possible, while his children, still young enough to be allowed a presence, giggled behind me and talked about me to each other. He showed me a tin of photos, clearly his most prized possession, and from the look of the clothing and backgrounds in the photos, I sensed that he was trying to show me that he had not always lived in poverty. I drank about four cups of tea in the end, as he continually kept topping up my chipped cup. We exchanged lots of nervous laughter and smiles as we watched his pretty daughters whispering behind their hands, their sparkling green eyes darting shyly in my direction. I gave up trying to explain what had happened to my fingers, as they had no electricity so there was no fan for me to demonstrate with. Whenever I looked over at the mother who remained a ghost at the far end of the room, her head movement suggested that she looked to the floor, ashamed to have been caught looking back at me. As I left, I took a quick peep into the room she had originally appeared from. Their bed lay on the floor in the corner. One of the outside walls was completely missing, leaving a clear view of the city in the distance. Only half the roof remained, which just about covered their bedding. It reminded me of an album cover I had seen once. I wanted to take a picture but knew I couldn't, and left, offering a thousand thankyous for their hospitality.

After such an eventful morning, I decided it was time to track down some alcohol. I headed for the Mustafa Hotel which, with its popularity with journalists, I knew would have beer. Here I found my Icelandic friend from Lahore relaxing on a leather sofa clutching a cold can of Heineken, and watching a badly-dubbed kung-fu movie. He explained that he was in Kabul trying to get a visa for Tajikistan, but was so far being denied on the grounds that it was too dangerous there. I spent the rest of the daylight hours that day drinking and watching terrible movies with him.

I checked my emails and saw that I had received one from Tina at the Embassy. While her personal message was friendly, funny and informal, the official attachment was serious but laughable. It listed the eight restaurants in town that were currently approved as safe to eat in, all of which I could tell by the names were well above my budget. It then proceeded to tell me how to act when visiting these places. These were the instructions:

1. *Contact the restaurant prior to your arrival and ensure the place has a rear exit.*
2. *Ensure your driver is on standby to pick you up or waiting outside in the car.*
3. *Make sure you are seated at the back of the restaurant with your back to the wall. Be aware where all the exits and fire extinguishers are located.*
4. *Ensure your hand-held radio is with you and on at all times (carry a backup i.e. mobile phone).*
5. *Use common sense and do not stay in the restaurant any longer than is necessary.*
6. *Do not become complacent and forget the environment you are in, stay alert and be aware of suspicious behaviour.*
7. *Know what to do for emergency procedures (fire, rocket/bomb attack), and what your immediate action drills are.*

This didn't sound like a recipe for a very relaxing meal to me, and I decided to stick to the local restaurants, and sent a friendly email back to Tina saying as much.

After leaving the Mustafa Hotel I headed directly back to my accommodation with a heightened sense of danger, aware that my judgement was perhaps a little impaired. I had another meal of chicken and rice in the rooftop restaurant but for a change was offered a Pepsi rather than a Mecca Cola.

With no real plans, I spent the next day wandering aimlessly around the city. Using landmarks to guide me, I now had a pretty good idea of where I was around the city. When I got lost, I didn't show it, I just kept walking until I spotted an area I knew. Kabul has a local bus called the Milly Service. I decided to do a lap of the city on it and was sitting contently on a bus minding my own business when we pulled over at a stop somewhere in the city centre. Suddenly someone yanked hard at my hair from behind, pulling my head into the metal bar that ran across the seats. I spun around to catch the culprit, only to see him and his group of mates scampering from the bus by the rear exit. Counting to 10 in my head, I thought better of retaliating and turned back round to face the front. We had stopped in a small market and there was a large crowd around the bus. I was looking ahead trying to forget about the incident, when a fist came through the open window and caught me behind the ear. I jumped from my seat to go for the door, but the bus had now begun to move and the door closed in my face. I sat back down again and scanned the crowd outside for the perpetrator. The gang were lost in the crowd, so taking deep breaths I again tried to ignore the situation. Then out of the corner of my eye I saw someone in the crowd approaching the window, but coming covertly at an angle. This time I was ready. As the bus slowed once more to pull back out on to the main road an arm shot through the window. I lent back out of its trajectory, grabbed it by the wrist and began to pull it further inside the window, then slammed the sliding window hard into his elbow before releasing him. The bus was pulling away now and the gang ran beside the bus shouting abuse at me. Knowing I was safely on the moving bus, I kept my silence and responded with the international middle finger salute.

When I got off the bus a few roads away my jaw was still quivering from a combination of adrenaline and fear, so I quickly found a taxi to take me to the Mustafa

Hotel. I needed a beer. My nerves a little more settled, I continued my exploration of the city and tried to forget about the events of the morning. As I wandered, I noticed how every new school, hospital and charitable building was built or run, either by Japanese, Germans or Italians. I saw nothing built by the two nations who maintained the headlines and took the credit for anything constructive being achieved. It seemed to me that all the aid work seemed to be carried out by those who rarely made the news at all where Afghanistan was concerned. The Americans certainly made their presence felt wherever possible though, and I saw yet another patrol of infantry pass me by, marching with an enormous air of arrogance, their guns pointing indiscriminately towards small children and grown men alike and generally treating the Afghani people like they were an inconvenience in their own city. When the patrol saw me, they were completely thrown off guard, and I got nothing but dirty looks from them as they passed.

I decided it was time to move on from Kabul and head to Bamiyan. As there is no government assisted public transport outside of Kabul, the only way to get around is by privately run minibuses, which only depart if they have enough passengers. All the minibuses left from the same road in town at around 5am each morning. Since I had smashed my last alarm clock to pieces months before, I went to sleep that night repeatedly saying to myself, "Must wake at 4 o'clock, must wake at 4 o'clock."

I woke at 4.05am, and complimenting my own body clock, packed up and headed down to reception to check out. I first had to find the receptionist. When I did, I got him to write down in Afghani where I wanted to go. Outside I was overrun with taxi drivers fighting for my business. Most disappeared when I produced the scrap of paper on which my intended destination was scrawled. The problem was, that after 25 years of war and no public education, not many Afghans could read or write their own language, which meant that this particular strategy was useless. I repeatedly attempted to pronounce the road where the buses left from, following it with the word "Bamiyan". Eventually one of the few taxi drivers who was still bearing with me, guessed what I was trying to say from the Bamiyan part, although when he said the actual name of the road, I wanted to shout, "That's what I said!" but I guess I hadn't got the intonation quite right. As we walked over to his taxi, I was still a little suspicious of his slightly shifty behaviour and failure to make eye contact with me. I became more worried when we got into the unlocked taxi and he started to hotwire it. It took five minutes for him to successfully get the engine ticking over, and every time he failed, he gave himself an electric shock, and threw me an embarrassed look of apology. I trusted him a bit more after this, but made sure he glimpsed the blade I was carrying in my waistband when I made a show of tightening the drawstring on my trousers.

As we drove along, I was surprised to see that even at this early time in the morning, the streets were alive with people. The steel shutters were up and business had already begun for the day. When you live in a capital with no electricity, you had no choice but to live your life by the rise and set of the sun.

When we pulled onto the correct road and I saw all the white minibuses lining it, I breathed a big sigh of relief. But when my driver obligingly pointed out the correct minibus for me, I had to pay him and climb out of the taxi as it was still moving, so he didn't have to stall and hotwire the car all over again. I exchanged the word Bamiyan with my new driver a dozen times before I got on the bus, as he repeatedly pronounced it differently from the taxi driver and myself. As we set off, I was still double-checking with the other passengers where exactly was our final destination, and still unconvinced I was heading to the right place, I introduced myself to everyone on board. Although Bamiyan was only 90km away as the crow flies, it was going to take 12 hours to get there due to the appalling condition of the road. Within a few hours I was struggling not to lose my temper as we bounced from one pothole to the next, my head crashing from roof to window every few seconds. Then as we wound our way through what I think was the Panjshir Valley, there was a loud bang followed by a scraping sound to the side of us.

21

Frosties For Breakfast

Kabul to Bamiyan
return = 480km

I looked out of the window to see our rear wheel over-taking us. Luckily, we hadn't been able to go faster than 10km an hour for ages due to the condition of the road, so we came to a grinding but controlled stop. As we piled out of the bus to assess the damage, I was immediately aware that we were going to be here for some time, when the three women who had sat in silence beneath their burkas at the front of the bus up until then, calmly retrieved their dirty laundry from the roof rack, made their way down to the shallow river which ran alongside the road, and began scrubbing. Four of the men then commenced a forensic style search along the part of the road we had just travelled. From the automatic way everyone set about their tasks, I guessed this was not an unusual occurrence. Twenty minutes later, the men returned with every nut and bolt we had lost along the way. In the meantime, those of us left by the bus, together lifted it to allow the smallest man, who was evidently extremely trusting, to roll underneath and place large rocks beneath the chassis to prop up the axel. The only tool they had was a large spanner, which over the next hour they used to hammer everything back into shape incredibly well. While we were waiting, the Afghans amazed me with their almost childlike love of nature. They took me up into the surrounding mountains where they found different stones to show me. They cracked open a few for me to see. Some were hollow inside and sparkled with a type of precious stone. One rock weighed five times more than it looked like it should, while another was jet black and, as they demonstrated, good for sharpening knives. There were also these small pellet-sized rocks which when you scratched off the surface, revealed a shiny silver sub-stance beneath. These were true men of the mountains.

As they kept handing me these different types of rocks, I was unsure if they were giving them to me as gifts or just to look at. Not wanting to cause offence by dropping them, I therefore ended up returning to the bus with my pockets weighed down with stones and spent the rest of the journey, surreptitiously dropping them out of the window.

In under an hour and a half, the bus was fixed and ready to go again. We reached several wobbly old wooden bridges, where we were all made to get out once more so the driver could rev the engine and accelerate full speed over the top of them, before we all climbed back inside. The bus continued on its way up and over eroded passes until eventually we entered the Bamiyan Valley. It had been declared a World Heritage Site in 2003 and it was easy to see why. The road followed a river that ducked under and around the encasing mountains. Tall green trees surrounded us on both sides backed by sandy orange cliffs. I could easily imagine it being the location for the shooting of a thousand movies, but sadly until the country is a little more stable, I think Spielberg will be looking elsewhere.

The small town of Bamiyan had once been a place of Buddhist pilgrimage, and an important point on the Silk Road. Two statues of the Buddha were carved into the sandstone cliffs in the 6th century. The figures were hewn from rock before being covered in straw and mud to create the smooth lines of the robes. The statues were then painted and the faces were concealed behind gilded masks. The sides of the niches where the Buddhas stood were covered in detailed paintings and carvings.

Standing at 38 and 55m tall respectively, they were the tallest statues ever made, and survived for centuries, until in March 2001 the Taliban destroyed them using dynamite and tanks for being "un-Islamic". Those of us with a slightly more cynical view on life, would say it was not until this happened that the world sat up and started to care about what the Taliban was doing to the people of Afghanistan and more importantly to some, its heritage.

As we slowly crept closer to Bamiyan, my mineralogist friends pointed out a settlement high above us on the cliff top. It seemed to be carved straight into the mountainside out of rock and sandstone. Clearly it had long since been abandoned. Everyone, including the driver, strained their necks to look up at it as we passed, they repeatedly looked back at me for my reaction. When I gave them the thumbs up sign, they beamed with pride. A few kilometres outside the town we were forced to swerve around an abandoned tank that was just sitting in the middle of the road, either left by the Russians or the Taliban.

When we pulled into the one and only road that made up Bamiyan town, I said heartfelt goodbyes to my new friends who were being met by family members at the bus stop. I had only known them for 12 hours and hadn't been able to verbally exchange more than a "hello", but I was going to miss them now that I'd arrived friendless once more in yet another unfamiliar town. I began asking around for the guesthouse I had been told to look for, only to be told that the place I was searching for had either burnt or closed down. I couldn't work out what had exactly happened through the frantic hand gestures, but it didn't sound good and the upshot was that there was only one other place left in town to stay. When I was shown to the one room available there, I found that my accommodation for the night was on the roof of a parade of shops, half the size of an average shed, with a broken window covered by a plastic bag. There was no lock on the door, and if I needed the toilet or a shower, I had to walk five minutes down the road and pay 20 Afghanis at the public hamman (bathhouse). As I stood staring into the dark room, wondering how many diseases I was going to catch from sleeping on the flea-ridden camp bed, a black cat jumped out from under it and shot out of the room between my legs.

I asked how much the guesthouse owner wanted.

"$10US," he said. I laughed.

"I'll give you $2US."

He wouldn't budge below $9 though, so annoyed, I left. I had no problem staying somewhere rancid, but I wasn't going to be ripped off in the process. As I walked away, he yelled that it was the cheapest I would find, and that I would be back. I ignored him and tried to remember if it was good luck or bad to have a black cat cross your path.

As I got closer to the end of the road wondering where I was going to sleep, four United Nations cars came rolling through followed by an armoured vehicle. Curious as to where they were going, I watched as they made their way up a road that led upwards to the top of the nearest mountain. This gave me the idea that I could camp in the mountains for a few days, but given that there were mines scattered all over the mountainsides, I thought it best to go and check with the UN first as to where was safe.

I tried to follow the road up which I had seen the UN disappear, but lost them when the road forked. I took a short cut up the side of the mountain and made it to the top, but slipped halfway and cut my knee in the process. It took over an hour of wrong turns to find the UN base, as none of the locals seemed to know where the mysterious cars went to or even seemed the least bit curious. The compound was spread out across a village and all of the walls of the buildings were built with mud and sandstone. I approached a guard who was in charge of a sturdy barrier blocking access to the metal gates marked "UN" with white paint. He spoke some English, and understood when I explained that I was looking to get some advice on the non-mined fields in the area. He called someone out to take his place and disappeared behind the gates. When he returned five minutes later, I was invited inside and taken into a room where I was patted down and asked to fill in a form. Once that was completed, I was issued a pass to continue into the neighbouring room, where a tough looking man, with a chiselled jaw, met me.

He introduced himself as Cyril and offered me a seat at his desk. I had assumed he was a soldier from his appearance and as it later turned out, he had in fact been in the army for 20 years before starting work for the UN. I apologized for troubling him and explained my predicament and we chatted for some time. To be honest, I think he was happy to talk to someone of no importance about irrelevant things for once, if for no other reason than to have a break from the piles of paperwork stacked up in front of him. Behind him he had three separate phones plugged in and the walls were plastered with maps on which drawing pins pulled strings taught. Once I had answered a lot of questions, which I guessed were for the purpose of sussing me out, he clearly concluded that I was not a threat, just a foolhardy traveller. He picked up one of the phones and rang someone. Whoever it was seemed to have given me the all clear also, as he then invited me to stay at the staff compound with him. He said he finished work in ten minutes and told me to wait in the conference room. While I waited I amused myself by reading the staff notice board which was covered in aerial maps with arrows and notes saying things like "staff robbed here".

When Cyril was ready, I climbed into his marked UN vehicle which seemed to have a lot more buttons and gauges than your average four-wheel drive, to my new digs, which only took about five minutes. A man stood outside the large gates and the moment Cyril vacated his seat, the man got in to it and drove the car away. From the outside the place looked exactly the same as all the other surrounding buildings – a one-storey house with simple mud walls. I only got the feeling it was going to be different inside, when Cyril ran his hand along the side of one of the mud walls and pushed a concealed doorbell. Rather than your average "ding-dong" sound, a nice little melody rang out. "Nice touch," I said. Cyril smiled slightly.

Inside the quarters were painted in the United Nations colours of blue and white. In the centre of the compound was a swimming pool, albeit a small one, and around it was well-watered green grass. Under a sheltered section at the end there was a table tennis table and in the four corners of the canopy were speakers. These were connected to the lounge area, where there was a sound system, a PlayStation 2, Sky TV and a huge collection of DVDs, CDs and computer games. There was an internet connection and a satellite phone also available. He explained that there were only ever four of them staying there, and at that time just two, as the others were off on a mission. They had their own cook and cleaner and were sent care packages of imported food every fortnight.

Cyril showed me down to the basement where I was to sleep on a mattress, and once I had come back up with my dirty pants to put in the washing machine, I sat down with Cyril in a deck chair and cracked open a cold beer. We were on our second beer when his work colleague Matt arrive. He was from Africa and spoke with a strong Afrikaans accent. I suggested I could put my fingers in my ears if there was anything they needed to talk about that I wasn't allowed to hear, but the conversation turned to my trip and my plans to travel overland through Afghanistan. They thought it was a stupid idea even though at that time there was not believed to be any Taliban presence in central Afghanistan. Although they were equally concerned about highway robbers as the Taliban, and said I should fly across instead as it would only cost $50US. I tried to change the subject numerous times as they didn't understand why I couldn't fly. I settled on the excuse that I couldn't afford it, which was pretty weak, as it would cost me the same, if not more, to travel overland. At 9pm they considered it late and suggest we turn in.

When I woke up in the basement the next morning, for a good minute I was very confused as to where I was. Cyril and Matt had already left for work when I came up from the basement, squinting in the bright sunshine. The cook offered me a hot breakfast, but I opted for a huge bowl of imported Kellogg's Frosties and a fresh coffee, then set off to see the remains of the Buddhas for myself. The huge niches in which they stood were visible from miles away, so it wasn't hard to get there. I went to the Foreign Affairs/Tourist Information Office on the way, because Cyril had said there was a small chance it might be possible to get a visa extension there, for it could take anything from three days to three weeks to travel overland, all depending on luck. Inside the tiny UN sponsored office sat five Afghans drinking tea. There was not a pen or paper in sight. I aborted the idea as soon as I realized that no one spoke any English, and left them topping up their teacups.

My explorations showed that there was very little remaining of the small Buddha, aside from the alcove it sat in, but what I found far more interesting were the passages and stairways that were dug deep into the cliffs and linked a warren of chambers and halls all around the Buddhas. In the past, these had been monastic cells that honeycombed the sandstone cliff walls. While no monks now remained inside, there were several families occupying them. A group of children came nervously out to greet me, and I was amazed at how Tibetan they looked. Perhaps their ancestors had arrived on a pilgrimage and never returned to their homeland, I thought. I wondered if they knew, but sadly had no way of asking.

I walked down towards the niche where the big Buddha had been. A guard came out and said I needed a ticket. I knew this was not the case as Cyril had told me it was free. I went inside the "ticket office" and was told it would be $5 to see the Buddha.

"What Buddha?" I said, and turned on my heel to leave. A guard blocked my exit with his arm. I pushed him out the way and passed, but he followed me, slapping his gun in the palm of his hand and shouting. I walked away from the Buddha and the office, trying to understand why everyone seemed to be picking on me. I looped around a couple of fields and came back to the big Buddha from the other direction. This time I reached the niche without being seen. It seemed some sort of restoration or preservation work was taking place as half the niche was covered in scaffolding. I spent a while longer climbing among the network of caverns, entering through the miniscule doorways. Inside one, I found the remains of a sculpture in the wall. It resembled a horse without legs. When I left, I couldn't help but wind up the fake ticket collectors further, by walking past the window of their office and waving before power walking off.

I headed back to the compound to meet Cyril for lunch. I told him what had happened and he said I was right not to have paid and that he would be reporting it to their superiors. I felt like a spy. I neglected to tell him I had also deliberately wound them up afterwards.

After we'd eaten a lunch which included the first green peas I had enjoyed for close to a year, Cyril told me about another sight worth seeing, if not just for the view – an ancient settlement on top of one of the nearby mountains. Although guarded, this was also supposed to be free and accessible to the public. He leant me his pushbike to get there, and I soon discovered as I began rolling down the road I had attempted to climb up the day before, that the brakes were completely useless. Unable to stop with my flip-flops scraping along the ground, I attempted to shout a warning to anyone who was coming up in the opposite direction, but the bumpy ground turned my calls in to more of a yodel. It took some skillful steering to make it to flat ground, where I was finally able to stop, and curse Cyril for not warning me.

When I reached the top of the footpath that led to the settlement, I wrapped a chain around the back wheel of the bicycle and leant it against a boulder. A group of teenagers were coming towards me as I began to climb the zigzag path. There was something about them that I didn't trust, and after we'd passed each other, I ducked behind some rocks and watched them approach the bike. Sure enough they attempted to steal it, and so I ran back down the path shouting and hurling badly aimed rocks in their direction. At this, they gave up trying to drag the bike away and ran off without looking back. Shouldering the bike, I took it into a field of crops and hid it among the foliage instead, to protect it from any further opportunists.

At the top of the mountain I was first greeted by an incredible view, and then by a guard who predictably demanded that I pay to look around the ruins. *Not again,* I thought, then simply replied, "No."

I walked around inspecting the ruins and taking photos of the surrounding natural and man-made wonders. As I looked out across the plains at the Buddha niches in the distance, I tried to imagine the amazing civilization which had once existed here, and of Genghis Khan invading by horse through the valley. Then the guard reappeared accompanied by another guard with an AK47, so my daydreams cut short, I gave up and started to make my way back down the mountainside. Halfway down, rocks started falling close by. At first, I thought the cause was erosion, but then as I looked up, I saw the guard and his friend attacking me from above.

Hoping they were as bad shots as myself, I looked up at them and stood with my arms spread wide, motioning with my hands for them to give me their best shot. They did, but thankfully the three I let them throw before I continued downwards all missed. I successfully recovered my bicycle and decided to make the most of my new mode of transport by peddling off to check out the tank I had seen on the way in.

It was a hell of a lot further along the road than I remembered and my clothes were like used grease paper by the time I reached it. There was no one around, so I climbed inside the turret and made stupid imitation shelling noises for a while. To my amazement, I discovered I could still move the long shell barrel around, and turned it right around to face Bamiyan.

On my way back to town I got a puncture almost immediately, and was forced to walk a number of

kilometres in the blazing sun. A grimy young boy fixed
the wheel outside his family's mechanics business while
I sat on an old tractor tyre and drank tea. Before I'd finished half the cup the repair was complete, so I sat with
the boy until I had finished and he took the opportunity
to produce a school textbook that was almost as grubby
as he was. Sitting in the shade of the corrugated iron
workshop, we spent the next hour trying to improve his
English. When I left him to head back to the compound,
my faith in the people of Bamiyan had been restored
and I had forgiven everyone who had been unwelcom-
ing to me that day.

That evening, over a western dinner and a bottle of
fine French wine, Cyril and Matt told me how the town
of Chaghcheran in central Afghanistan was currently
overrun by the Taliban. This was a particular problem
for me, because if I was to travel across the middle of
the country it was where I would need to change buses.
This was very depressing news, so changing the subject
from my plans once more, I mentioned how I had
managed to swing around the turret on the tank. They
exchanged a silent look, and I could tell they didn't
believe me.

"That's impossible," said Cyril. "That tank has been
sitting inactive for years." But determined to prove my
story, I told them to take a look tomorrow and they
would see for themselves that the turret was now facing
the town. Matt said he would be leaving town for the
day in the morning and would have a look but hadn't
noticed which way it had been facing before. I dropped
the subject then, quite hurt that they didn't believe me.

The next morning, they had once again already left
for work when I came up from the dungeon. Once the

chef had cooked me breakfast, I caught some rays floating on my back in the swimming pool, rejoicing in the fact that I could bare some flesh without fear of reprisal. After a relaxed morning lounging around the compound as though I was on a package tour of Europe, I headed down to the town on the bicycle, this time walking the downhill part while pushing the bike. After asking a lot of people, I gathered there was not going to be a bus heading west for at least another week, which was not exactly the news I had been hoping for. But I cheered up instantly as I cycled through the town and saw the man who had tried to overcharge me for his stable of a room standing outside his guesthouse looking bored. I made sure to slow down as I passed so he could see me wave.

From there, I cycled all the way back to the tank and swung the turret around again, and after another cup of tea with the mechanic family, I went home to await Matt's return. It was well worth the long cycle, for I got an apology from the pair of them. Apparently, Matt had been completely confused when he had driven back to see it had moved again from its position that morning.

I accepted their apologies graciously then said, "I'll be moving on in the morning, I think. I'd like to buy you both a beer to say thanks for all this, but I can't because you're the only people with beer in Bamiyan." They stayed up later than their normal 9pm curfew that night to have a few drinks with me. When they asked me why I hadn't made use of the free internet and telephone services there, I told them that I couldn't as my mum would kill me if she knew I was in Afghanistan. They both burst out laughing at this, and then told me "off the record", that Osama Bin Laden was believed to be hiding in Russia. Before we turned in, they gave me a sewing kit to patch up my clothes which were looking a little the worse for wear. It was a joke of course, but I took the hint and decided to buy a new shalwar kameez when I reached Kabul.

I had to be down in the main town by 6am to catch the return bus, so for once, after sleeping outside, I got up before anyone else in the compound. What I hadn't allowed for, however, was the fact that the heavy gates were bolted and locked shut. I tried to wake the chef as I knew he was in charge of these tasks, but he was sound asleep and wouldn't stir. Instead, I let myself into his storage room where I had seen all the keys were kept, then found that all the key hooks were labelled in Pashto. I took a handful of keys and began trying them in all the different locks. With the clock ticking, I felt like I was on some sort of quiz show. I cracked the correct combination surprisingly quickly considering how many keys there were. Then wedging my pack in the now open doorway, I returned all the keys to the room. Unfortunately, I had no idea which key came off which hook, and ended up putting them all back at random, and feeling very guilty for the trouble I was undoubtedly going to cause later slipped out of the gates.

I made the bus just in time it seemed, as there were only one or two spaces left to fill. As we set off, I pulled the sewing kit out of my top pocket and opened it up and was shocked to find $50US with a note written in capital letters along the bottom: "FLY!"

I took in the last views of the Bamiyan Valley and then the bus began to climb the passes again, and so I rested my head against the window and slept. A few hours later, I was woken by a sudden burst of pain in my left ear. For the rest of the journey I had severe earache accompanied by a sore throat and a general feeling of sickness. We reached Kabul just as the sun was setting, and I made my way back to where I had stayed before and was impressed to see that they had already acquired a new sign. When I walked over to reception, the same man as before greeted me and said, "No buses from Bamiyan then?" He'd told me there wouldn't be any before I'd left and was now being cocky about it. In too much pain to respond, I headed up to my room, opened the door and collapsed on the bed. The earache had intensified tenfold and was relentless. The feeling that my brains were being nibbled away from the inside only subsided slightly if I pushed my fist as hard as possible into the affected ear. It felt a bit like when you dive down too deep in a swimming pool without pinching your nose and you feel that uncomfortable pressure. The difference was that I was sinking deeper, unable to reach the surface. Gripping the mattress, I pulled my face down into the pillow and screamed. I couldn't concentrate on anything and it hurt so badly I wanted to cry but had no energy left for tears. I hadn't eaten all day and yet I wasn't hungry. I'd had a lot of burns and broken bones in the past but nothing compared to this much pain. I felt helpless and alone. I wanted my mum.

22

Babysat

Kabul to Herat = 1,162km

I didn't sleep at all that night and in my agony and desperation had taken nearly a whole packet of ibuprofen, which had barely touched the sides of my pain. I got up and out as soon as it was light and walked around town in a dangerous daze, unsure of what to do about my ear or my travel arrangements. I bought a new shalwar kameez for which I almost certainly was overcharged, but I was beyond caring. I caught a taxi to the office of the AAA which stood for Ariana Afghan Airlines, and hoping that their planes ran on more than just batteries, decided that if the price of the ticket was less than $50, I would fly. At the offices of AAA, the assistant told me that there was a seat available in two days' time on a plane departing for Herat at 8am costing just a fraction under $50. Herat was on the other side of the country the last major city before the Iranian border. She stared at me expectantly while I sat there with my head pounding, unsure of what to do. In the end, I couldn't bring myself to buy the ticket, so thanked her and told her I would come back later.

I walked a few blocks and found a badly-stocked chemist where I bought another packet of ibuprofen. As I swallowed another couple of pills vainly hoping they would do the trick, I tried to tackle my "to fly or not to fly" conundrum.

With a healthy portion of self-loathing, I reached the conclusion that I couldn't do it. I knew if I did, I would regret it forever, no matter how much discomfort I was in right then. I had come too far to give up now. As fate would have it, a week later I read that a bomb had gone off in the departure lounge of Kabul airport, not only on the day of the flight she had suggested, but at 7.30am in the morning. It had killed a policeman and badly injured a journalist.

Back at the hotel, I spread my map out across the receptionist's desk, and with the help of him and a few other men who always seemed to be loitering in the foyer, we went over every marked and unmarked road in Afghanistan in search of an available route for me to take. The conclusion was that, time-wise, safety-wise and transport-wise, there wasn't a preferable route available.

I had two options: the first was to head south and around, but this meant stopping in Kandahar, the Taliban headquarters; the second and only real option left it seemed was to head north by bus to Mazar-e-Sharif, Afghanistan's biggest northerly city. They didn't know what I should do from there, but there was a small airport so flying out was an option. The bus left at the same time in the morning, but from a different location to the one to Bamiyan. That evening I managed to go out and force down some meat and rice even though it hurt to swallow and the pain had left me with no appetite. But I just knew it had to be done, as it had been nearly two full days since a morsel had passed my lips. I had another night with no sleep at all, and around 2am my ear began oozing brown sludge. I was really worried now, as I had already used up the antibiotics I'd been carrying, and had finished all the painkillers after once more taking far above the recommended daily dosage. I hadn't slept for days. I was paranoid and scared. I honestly thought I was going to die.

I was in no state to do anything but breathe by the time I had to leave in the morning, so the receptionist helped me to get a taxi and made sure it was taking me to the correct departure point. The bus to Mazar-e-Shariff was cramped, but the road was in far better condition than the road to Bamiyan, and we covered twice the distance in half the time. I attempted to care when we passed through the famous 6km-long tunnel which the Russians spent 12 years building straight through the 3,363m high Salang Pass. I tried to take in the views from the top of the passes but I was in too much pain to register anything other than the fact that I felt like I was about to meet my end in Afghanistan.

The other passengers on the bus were very sympathetic, and insisted on hydrating me with their drinks and feeding me small snacks. The man on my left continually chatted to me in Pashto, probably trying to distract me from the pain, which now felt as though someone was forcing a large spike down my ear canal. The fact that I was now deaf in my left ear and didn't speak a word of Pashto, didn't seem to bother him in the slightest. Just rabbit, rabbit rabbit. . .

As annoying as this was, Rabbit, as I subsequently named him in my head, would be the first person to save me over the next few days. As I stood to climb out of the minibus, I felt the world shift violently around me; during the last few hours on the bus, I appeared to have now completely lost my sense of balance. Standing up straight was enough of a challenge, so there was no chance of being able to carry my own bag.

Rabbit instructed me to sit by the side of the road before scampering off and returning sometime later with his muscular son. Muscles, as we shall call him, shouldered my pack with ease, and helped me to my feet. I had no idea where they were taking me, but I had no choice but to trust them. We arrived at their family home, and I was laid on a futon in the front room from where I didn't move until the following morning. Throughout the evening people came in and out of the room, some just to stand and stare at me, others to offer advice. I have a vague recollection of someone rubbing a green cream on my chest to supposedly help my ear. I ate a small meal, and think I must have got a couple of hours shut eye during the night.

Mazar-e-Shariff is home to the shrine of Hazrat Ali, which dominates the centre of the city and is the final destination for many a pilgrim. I only never imagined it would be mine. Its mosaic-covered walls and blue-domed rooftops are something I'd been told in Kabul I really couldn't miss. I did miss it though, for the next morning I was bundled off in a Land Cruiser. In my more lucid moments, I had told Rabbit that my intended destination was Herat, the most westerly town before the Iranian border. I desperately wanted to reach there now, as I knew it would have a hospital, and all the time I had lain incapacitated on his sofa, he'd clearly done all he could to organize my transport there. Everything was happening so fast, or so it seemed in my hazy state, that

I never got a chance to thank him before I left Mazer-e-Shariff. I had very little control over anything. Even as my pack was being tied to the roof rack, I was still trying to work out where I was going. I was already in the car moving when I eventually established that we were in fact going to Herat via a few other places, and that it was going to take us three whole days.

Due to my size and condition, Rabbit had thoughtfully booked me two spaces in the Land Cruiser, to give me more space. Probably also so that no one else had to sit too close to my dribbling ears, as the infection had now spread to the other. The two other passengers in the Land Cruiser wore western clothes and to my eternal gratitude, were kind and friendly and helped me wherever they could over the next three hellish days.

The journey was tough. Just an hour outside of the city I realized why there were no minibuses running this route, quite simply because there was no road. The car rocked violently from side to side as we bounced over the rugged terrain, and I barely stayed sitting in my seat for more than a few seconds at a time. About the only advantage of this, was that it at least put thoughts of highway robbers and the Taliban far from my mind, as we made our slow progress across the desert.

It was dark by the time we reached our final stop on the first day. We parked around the back of what appeared to be a restaurant, which I was helped through and up some stairs at the back. There, in a large and basic room apparently solely for the use of overnight travellers, a dozen mattresses were laid out on the floor, and in the corner was a large sink with three taps. I laid down on one of the half-inch thick beds and stretched out my aching body. I think a special allowance was made for me, as I was the only one who had food brought up to them. Everyone else had to go downstairs to eat. It got bitterly cold during the night, which wasn't helped by the fact that although someone had closed the balcony doors, there was no glass in the windows. I didn't sleep at all. Without an alarm clock going off, the two drivers and the businessmen all woke in the night at the same time. They stood up and began splashing cold water on their faces in the moonlight, and I guessed we were off again.

The second day we must have driven for more than 18 hours, stopping five times along the way for prayer. I was more of an object than a person by then, and remained curled up against the window, staring unfocusing out at the landscape. I wanted to be anywhere but there, preferably intensive care. That night was spent in the backroom of a family home. I noticed that despite us being surrounded by dirt and dust and no means of showering, my two companions, who I now assumed were businessmen, took great care in folding their clothes and hung their shirts on coat hangers from the ceiling. Apparently keeping up appearances mattered, even when you were being thrown around in the back of a car like livestock. I don't think I spoke more than three words that day. Before we went to sleep I saw one of the businessmen and one of the drivers, of the two that took turns staring at me with real looks of concern. I was convinced they thought I was going to die during the night, but instead I somehow managed to sleep for at least four hours before we set off again and once we got back in the car I was feeling marginally better. This may have been because I knew this was the last day of the worst journey of my life, or maybe I had crossed some pain barrier where I no longer felt much at all.

We were entering the outskirts of Herat by mid-afternoon and I could see the towering minarets ahead. As we hit tarmac once more and started driving down a straight road lined with tall pine trees, the driver put his foot down, and we hit about 40kmph, the fastest we had driven in three days. Even I managed to raise a smile and join in the chorus of celebratory shouts as though we had crossed an imaginary finish line. Everyone kindly opted to take me straight to the hospital. Finally there, my western status and the fact that I looked like I had risen from the dead, got me to the front of the queue and after a doctor took a quick look in my ear, he told my driver to whisk me across town to an ear specialist. The specialist's room was incredibly basic and small, but he spoke English and knew medical terms I didn't, so I trusted him. Before the examination began, I thanked all of the guys who had helped me so much over the last few days, and insisted they get on their way. We exchanged Afghan handshakes, which differ from a western handshake as the hand is placed over the heart and the head is slightly bowed as you shake hands.

I felt sorry for the doctor as he pulled his stool close to me and began pulling and probing in my ear, for it had been six days since I had last changed my clothes or washed and I not only stank, but was covered in an orange film of dust and sweat. After he had given my ear a fairly brutal clean, I felt a huge rush of hot liquid pour from it. I went dizzy and had to grip the corner of the table to stay on my seat.

"You have ruptured your left eardrum and have a severe infection in both ears."

"Both?" I asked.

"You could have passed the infection from one ear to the other even with a brief touch of a bacteria-covered finger."

"How could I have burst my ear drum and not known it?" I asked, bemused. He quizzed me about where I had been when it had all begun, and I told him about the bus journey on which I slept and he concluded it probably happened on the way down from one of the passes.

"You had your ear against the window, yes? Possibly a vacuum came about between your ear and the glass which didn't equalise to the surrounding pressure as you came down in altitude." He indicated a popping motion with his hand, and I understood.

Never again would I opt to sleep rather than look at the scenery when travelling through mountain ranges. The doctor prescribed me 11 pills a day for a fortnight, and six eardrops a day for a week, plus a handful of painkillers. I was a little suspicious of the huge dosage, as he charged me nothing for the consultation, but directed me downstairs to a pharmacy where the chemist looked so similar to the doctor, I could only assume it was his brother.

I checked into the Jam Hotel in the centre of the old town. My room had a balcony which looked down on the crowded street below. I didn't know this for the first two days though as the heavy-duty painkillers kicked in quickly, and I went straight to bed once inside the room and didn't wake up for another 30 hours or so. With no watch or calendar, I was extremely disorientated, and it took a while for me to figure out exactly how long I had been out.

I began the medication properly the day I woke up, and once I had showered, shaved and changed my clothes for the first time in a week, despite still being deaf in one ear and finding myself veering to the right when I walked, I had never felt so revitalized. My appetite returned, and I spent the afternoon eating from the numerous food stalls that were set up along the road. There were hardly any cars in the old town compared to the number of donkey carts. A lot of the goods on offer from the tiny stores seemed to be imported from Iran. Entire roads were full of shops dedicated to the sale of herbs and spices with overpowering and unfamiliar smells and displayed in huge open sacks. In the gutter, boys sold imitation boxes of Oreo cookies, carpet and cloth salesmen fought each other for the best sales, and a kite seller injected bright pops of colour to the scene.

One thing I found odd was the fact that the roads were covered in discarded Persian carpets. They looked in good condition to me and could have been the centrepiece of any room in the West. Here though, the carpets were more common than wallpaper, so they were chucked out with the rubbish as soon as the colour faded or the weave began to wear.

It was movie night at the hotel that evening and the film of choice was a subtitled *Toy Story 2*. Locals arrived from outside the hotel to enjoy what seemed to be a popular weekly pastime, and some who arrived late just stood against the walls once all the floor space was taken. As the old TV was plugged in, and the play button pushed on the video player, all the men in the room (for there were no women in sight) began fidgeting in anticipation. As the only westerner, it was a very surreal experience to sit there surrounded by all these Afghans with their long beards and turbans watching a cartoon about talking toys. While the movie played, I glanced around and thought about how much these people had seen and experienced, and how just a few years before, TV had been completely banned by the Taliban. At one point during the film there was an inside joke that only a westerner could have understood and I let out a laugh and every face in the room turned to look at me suspiciously.

23

The Map

Herat to Tehran = 1,219km

I was up and out early in the morning. This was partly due to being woken by the sun coming in through the uncovered windows, and partly my excitement at being able to function again. I first headed to the 800-year-old Friday Mosque, famed for being Afghanistan's finest Islamic building. It was enormous. Two minarets dominated the centre of the courtyard, and every inch was covered in intricately detailed mosaic. Seeing this, made up for missing out on the shrine in Mazar-e-Shariff a little. I didn't venture far from the entrance though, because as a non-Muslim, I was unsure as to where I was permitted to go. I didn't feel overly welcomed either, and was fearful I was invading the worshipper's privacy. The last thing I wanted was another incident like the one back in Lahore with Simon.

I returned to the hotel for lunch and to take my next dose of pills. When I finally arrived back at the Friday Mosque later that afternoon having got a little lost down the alleyways of the Old Town, I found another westerner had arrived. We got talking, and he explained that he had cycled all the way to Herat from his hometown in Prague. I think I scared him at first, because I was so excited to speak some English that I couldn't stop talking. His name was Matthias or Matt as he told me to call him and it turned out, he was staying at the same hotel as me, which he told me, had rooftop access, something I had not yet discovered. So, after making our way back to the hotel together, we went up to the roof to sit in the sun and gaze out across the ancient city. Matt produced a pipe and began to smoke some Afghani hashish. "The heroin was cheaper," he said. "But I get addicted to things easily."

Conversation turned to his travel plans, and he explained that he intended to cycle across Afghanistan via the central route. He imagined it would take him no more than two weeks. I started to tell him that it wasn't possible because Chaghcheran was now occupied by the Taliban, but then I saw a familiar look come over his eyes and I knew he had turned on his selective hearing. Whatever I said was not going to make a blind bit of difference, so I just wished him the best of luck, and offered him all the travel advice I could.

I spent the rest of the afternoon on my balcony peo-ple-watching. On the opposite rooftop there was a small mosque where the workers who couldn't make it to the main mosque's call to prayer could go. Here, around 30 faithful Muslims came to prostrate them-selves towards Mecca five times a day, and each time a rather tall man in clean white robes stood motionless behind them, watching. He was obviously someone of importance, as everyone greeted him with respect as they arrived at the top of the crumbling stairs. I started thinking that Cyril and Matt were wrong and Osama Bin Laden wasn't hiding in Russia after all, but in fact living right opposite my room watching me slurp ice cream.

It was so hot in the room that night, that I stayed out to sleep on the balcony, and was woken by the stall traders setting up shop just before sunrise. As I watched the day unfold below me, I spotted my Czech friend from the day before busy securing his trailer to the rear of his bicycle and then giving the bike itself a thorough check.

"Good Luck!" I shouted down.

He looked up and nodded at me, and then shouted, "Got a light?"

I groped around on the table and found a packet of matches and dropped them down. He caught them, then giving me a thumbs up, lit a cigarette, mounted his bike and began peddling off towards the rising sun. I never did find out if he made it.

I took a cold shower and was just getting dressed when glancing out to the balcony I saw a shaving mirror attached to a stick being poked around the wall that separated my balcony from my neighbour's. I quietly moved to the end of my bed and crouched down while I waited for the mirror to find me, and when it did, I glared back at the intruder at which point the mirror shot back out of sight behind the partition. I then went straight to the hotel owner and demanded I was moved rooms.

The owner came with me to knock on my neighbour's door, and when it was opened, Mirror Man, who it seemed had donned glasses since using the mirror, an unusual sight in Afghanistan, opened up looking sheepish, and when confronted denied all knowledge of the incident. This denial was enough for the owner who then turned to me and said, "You are wrong, this is a good man, he is from Kandahar!" As if the fact that he was from the same area as the Taliban HQ was supposed to reassure me. Then he turned back to Mirror Man and using the international sign for crazy, circling his index finger around his temple, and apparently apologized on my behalf. Even if I wasn't going to be believed, I wasn't staying in that room, so after a while the manager reluctantly gave me a different room on the other side of the building. Once I had moved all my stuff across to my new room, I set off to enjoy the rest of the day.

I wanted to visit the Citadel, the foundations of which dated back to Alexander the Great, but with only a vague hand-drawn map that I copied down from a map on the hotel wall, it took me forever to find. I finally saw it when I was about 10ft from its walls, and I was amazed it took me so long, because it was enormous. The streets that lined it were full of traders selling the same things as their ancestors had probably sold in those very same spots for generations before. As everyone else walked past the Citadel without a second glance, I imagined it was like a castle from a story book, unseen by anyone but me. I was unable to go inside as it was being used as an army garrison, so I simply stood and stared at its fairy tale size and stature, while people milled around me. Many stopped and looked at me, followed my gaze to the Citadel, and then looked back at me in confusion, unable to understand that what I was seeing was in any way special.

After spending the rest of the day locating the minibus stand and once more losing myself in the maze of the old town, I decided it was time to move on to

Iran. All my efforts to plan my route to the minibus stand the day before turned out to be in vain, for I still managed to get lost on the way the next morning, and the whole time was accompanied by a beggar beneath a burka, who followed me around with her palm out-stretched. Finally on the minibus, I soon regretted not choosing one of the other dozen or so vehicles leaving the city that morning, since we broke down on the open plains just outside of Herat. As we stood by the side of the bus awaiting the repair, the wind was one of the strongest I had ever experienced. Not only were we forced to shield ourselves behind the bus, but those close to the edges were clutching handles to stop them-selves from being blown off their feet. With my eyes closed from the swirling dust, it was the sound of the engine roaring in to life that told me the bus had been repaired. It was only temporary however, as 10 minutes further down the road the engine groaned again and we sputtered to a halt. While the driver seemed to be con-vinced that he could fix it again, the other passengers braced themselves against the formidable gusts of wind and began untying their bags from the roof.

By now I seemed to have been adopted by a couple of men who helpfully told me how much to really pay the driver who was now stranded with his minibus and demanding the full fare from me. When another half-empty minibus came along, they then made sure I paid no more than they did for my new ride. The new minibus was in much better repair and the driver was cautious, slowing right down when the wind was at its worst, a marked difference from the last driver who had been speeding along with two of the wheels barely touching the ground.

I reached the border around midday, with a slightly orange complexion from all the dust. In the immigration office I handed over my passport, then stood by and watched as everyone behind me was stamped out while my passport remained at the bottom of the pile. I kept quiet and waited until there was no one else who could be stamped out in front of me, at which point the official picked up my passport and made a fuss over the fact that it didn't look like it had just been issued and he couldn't immediately work out where I was from. I apologized and after a couple of bizarre questions, such as, "What is your father's occupation?" I was stamped through, but just as I was heading for the door, I was called over to another office. Again, my passport was taken and a man disappeared with it into a backroom. Then through the glass I saw someone sniff it. You don't want to do that, I thought. It had been in my back pocket for months. When the guy returned, he said, "What's your name?"

"Benjamin Harris," I replied. He seemed disappointed that he hadn't managed to catch me out.

I had walked no more than 10m away from the building when a group of bored looking young officers called me over. At this point I should have kept going as I already had my exit stamp, but I obeyed and walked across to them. They asked me to empty the contents of my bag onto the dusty ground. I refused, saying everything would clearly get dirty or be blown away. So, they took me back inside the building I had just managed to leave, and began eagerly searching my bag. They removed the five books I was carrying as if they had discovered a haul of narcotics and flicked suspiciously through the pages, clearly unable to read a single word.

They took the books and my map away and I was told
to wait. After 20 minutes I was still patiently waiting, so
I asked what was going on and where was my stuff.
Someone went off to find out and returned with another
man who was holding my confiscated items. He handed
me my books with one hand, but kept hold of the map
with his other.

"No chance, you're not having my map for your
wall!" I said, and catching him by surprise, snatched the
map from his grasp. A bit of a struggle ensued during
which his hat was knocked from his head causing him
to call for backup, but by the time backup arrived in the
form of three more men, I had the map back in my pack
and was now sitting on top of it. Five officials now
surrounded me all growing increasingly irate as I refused
to give up my map and remained seated on top of my
bag like a stubborn child.

"I'm not in a hurry," I said, indicating that I was
happy to sit there all day, so then they began waving
handcuffs at me. I shrugged and offered them my wrists.
Thankfully, as I'd hoped, they were bluffing. A crowd
had gathered and the stand-off continued. Then an
Iranian, who spoke fluent English (he later told me lived
in Holland), approached the semi-circle and offered to
be translator. He explained to me that it was against the
rules for maps to leave the country. I explained that
I had already been stamped out and that I hadn't
brought the map inside the country in the first place.
I added that I was in no hurry and would sit there long
after their shifts had finished. This was a little over
the top, but he bravely translated it for me anyway.
Their response was that I could buy another map of
Afghanistan in Iran.

"Exactly, so why do you want this one?"

We had reached a stalemate, and our discussion disintegrated to, "Give us the map!"

"No!"

"Give us the map!"

"Never. . . "

The Dutch Iranian kept going to leave, clearly under the impression I was insane, but couldn't quite seem to walk away entirely and instead kept returning to translate. After 20 minutes or more I told him he should go; I was confident I could win this one on my own. But he stayed, and began to fight my case rather than just interpret it. He explained to them that I didn't want to give up my map, not because it was of any real accuracy, but because it had been all I had to stare at for so many evenings. They wanted to know what all the little circles and pencilled annotations were, and I explained that I had added places myself that I'd travelled through but which were not marked. Things began to cool – they were starting to realize that maybe I wasn't just being a stubborn bastard...

The Dutchman took his leave around the time I was ordered to the General's Office. I was sure this meant I was about to lose my map entirely, but when I entered his rather nice office, he greeted me like an old friend, clearly intrigued to meet the person who had just fought with all his staff over something as insignificant as a loosely detailed and badly scaled map. Five minutes later I was out of the door grinning, map in hand. I passed all the henchmen including the one who had lost his hat in the scuffle and marched out of the doors. Bureaucracy: nil, Ben Harris: one!

It was a long way to the Iranian side of the border, and by the time I got there they had closed for lunch. Outside I saw the Dutchman who, along with a handful of others, was also waiting for Iran to reopen. He had evidently told the others about what had happened because when I approached waving my map in the air, everyone laughed.

The entry procedure for Iran was an absolute shambles and included one guard making a really open request for a bribe to speed things along. I refused and it took me an hour to get my entry stamp. I shared a taxi with my new Dutch friend and two others to the nearest city of Mashhad, which I was surprised to find was very westernized. The roads were in excellent condition and litter free, the men were all dressed in jeans and T-shirts; it was quite a transition from Afghanistan. A lot of the women were decidedly Middle Eastern though: while their faces were uncovered, the rest of their body was draped in black, reminding me of the wicked witch who delivers the poisoned apple in Snow White.

Before we parted, the Dutchman invited me to stay with his family for a few days, I declined with thanks and was instead dropped off at the bus station. I took some convincing to get on the correct bus to Tehran, because although I knew fuel was cheap in Iran, I didn't realize just how cheap. The 14-hour overnight journey was going to cost just $4US. All the buses were air conditioned and looked relatively new and I shook my head when they indicated which one I should board, saying, "No, I don't want the luxury service, I want the local one."

"This is the local service," they replied.

On board, everyone was friendly and excited that I was from England. They showed no aversion to my nationality, which was a very different reaction to what I had come to expect from my own government's propaganda on Iran. Once outside the city, we entered the desert, and I watched the sun slowly dip out of sight beyond the endless plains of sand. At dusk, the conductor came along and handed me my complimentary goodie bag of food. It seemed that the government was trying to encourage the people of Iran to eat a lot of bananas, as inside the bag of snacks was a pack of banana cream biscuits, a doughnut with a banana cream filling, and of course, a banana milkshake with which to wash the revolting concoction down.

I arrived in Tehran around 10am the next morning, and it was certainly a metropolis. The city sprawled with freeways and noise, and I spent 10 minutes at the bus station just trying to find out which of the four bus stations in the city I had arrived at. Once I had established I was at the southern one and had a rough idea of where I was in relation to my map, I realized it didn't matter that much anyway, as for the first time on my trip I could afford to hail taxis everywhere. I had been reliably informed that the Mashhad Hotel was the best place to stay in the city, but there were two hotels in Tehran which shared the same name. One had high standards and high prices, and the other had exactly the opposite – I was of course, heading for the latter. Inevitably my driver confidently drove to the wrong one first, and we only found the one I really wanted when I spotted a Korean guy walking down the street and shouted out of the window asking him for directions. He was of course staying where I wanted to be, and jumped into the taxi to give my driver directions.

After dropping off my stuff in the dormitory, I headed out to enjoy some Iranian food. After little more than meat, rice and yogurt in Afghanistan, I couldn't wait to tantalize my taste buds with something different. I noticed that none of the foreigners in the dormitory said anything when I mentioned this, and an hour later I saw why. All I could find were kebabs, rice and burgers. They did come with salads, but I nearly chipped my teeth on the pickled onions, and the salad dressing was a bright pink colour that stained my fingers for hours afterwards. I was more than a little disappointed at what was on offer in terms of food, so I thought I would make up for it by ordering my first Iranian coffee. What arrived, was Nescafe.

24

Kebabs and Carpets
Tehran to Tabriz = 1,343km

I checked my emails that afternoon and found Simon had left Iran the day before. He had been in a nasty bus crash in the south of Pakistan, which had left a nearby passenger dead. Luckily Simon had walked away unscathed, and in even better news the walking stick he had been carrying for months which he loved so much and I hated, had been snapped in half. I did feel for him though – he'd had it strapped to the outside of his pack since Tibet, it had never quite fitted into the boots of cars, and he was always getting stuck in doorways because of it. He did take great pleasure in telling me, however, that he was now enjoying lots of cold Turkish beer while he hunted for a replacement.

I'd stopped thinking about alcoholic beverages for a while until I read that email. I then had an instant craving – I had just arrived in a new country after all. I made some enquiries about acquiring some beer, but it seemed that no black market existed for beer in Iran. I could, however, get a bottle of Jack Daniels within 24 hours if I was willing to pay up to $150US.

That night, as I sat on the rooftop with a few other guests at the hotel, I drank three litres of a fizzy orange pop called Zam Zam, and by the time I went to bed that night I had mastered reading and writing the numbers 1 to 20 in Farsi, possibly aided by the amount of sugar and E numbers I had consumed. Learning the numbers certainly helped me a great deal over the next week when it came to paying for things, as it was 9,000 Rials to $1US.

I had been told the best place to exchange US dollars was with the carpet sellers in the glass-fronted stores on the other side of the city. I decided to get there using the city's Metro system. The signs at the station were thankfully all written in English and it was made even easier underground, for the separate lines were colour coordinated with the arrows. Standing on the busy platform awaiting the next train, I noticed how clean it was and how efficiently everything seemed to be running. The train arrived to the appointed second and as I got onto the crowded but immaculate train, I thought about the filthy London Underground and found it hard to believe that this country was the developing one.

In the carpet sellers' main street, it didn't take long to find someone interested in becoming a Bureau de Change. He drew out the process deliberately while his shop assistants tried to persuade me to purchase a carpet and then get cash back. Given that even the cheapest one would have bankrupted me, I left carpet-less but a millionaire as far as the Rial was concerned.

My next stop was the Tehran Bazaar which turned out to be like a city within a city, made up of one giant network of corridors with curved ceilings. It seemed there was nothing you could not buy; carpets, spices, paper, gold. Other than the things I expected to see, I came across humorous T-shirts depicting George Bush as the devil. Unfortunately, they didn't have any in my size.

Naturally I got lost quickly and spent the afternoon with some carpet sellers smoking mint-flavoured tobacco from a water pipe, while watching the goings on around me. There was just one more sight I wanted to see the next day – the former US Embassy from where past coups had been plotted. I got there by taxi, but was disappointed when I arrived because I was not allowed inside since it was now being used by the Iranian military. There are rumours that during the height of the Americans' paranoia that the building was bugged, a special room was built within a room that was transparent and sound proof and hung suspended from cables so it did not touch any surrounding walls, enabling the Americans to hold important conversations without the risk of any leaks. It was also here I read, that on the 4 November 1979, students supporting the Islamic Revolution, and angry at America for getting involved in the situation, had invaded and ransacked the building, then held 52 US diplomats hostage for an incredible 444 days. This was of course of great embarrassment to the Americans, especially when documents (which are still officially classified today) were discovered, which implicated them in further espionage in Israel.

While I couldn't get inside the gates, most of what I wanted to see was visible from outside. On the wall by the front gate you could still see the US seal, carved into the stone. While it had been badly vandalized, possibly by hammers, the bald eagle was still recognizable. All along the tall walls that enclosed the place, government sponsored anti-American murals were painted. One, which used the American flag as a backdrop, portrayed the Statue of Liberty with a skull instead of a face. Other murals simply read "America is the most hated state for our nation", and "We will make America face a severe defeat", in bold and colourful letters.

I left the city that afternoon on a bus headed for Esfahan, which along the well-kept road took no more than five hours. At intervals along the side of the road, pictures of police cars were painted on to cut out boards. The detail of the painting and careful position-ing of the boards was so good, that even the driver seemed not to have worked out a way to distinguish the difference between the real thing and the fakes, and therefore applied the brakes each and every time we approached one and drove slowly until we were able to spot their giveaway shadow. I thought the driver was overreacting at first, as although we were definitely speeding, the road was empty. Then when we passed a real police car that was parked in almost exactly the same position as the fakes, I realized he wasn't being overcautious.

Arriving in Esfahan, I walked out of the bus station and asked the first passer-by for directions. I knew I wasn't far from my intended hostel so didn't want to get a taxi. Instead of just giving me directions though, the man I had stopped insisted on walking me the 3km to get there. Then when we reached the door of the hostel and I was wondering if he was going to want money for his services, he simply shook my hand, did a funny little bow, and walked off in the direction from which we had come. I was having a hard time working out the Iranians, for in some respects they were incredibly hospitable and continually dragged me off the street for a cup of tea, then at other times I was asked outright for money, but not by beggars, by ordinary citizens. Even young professionals in designer western suits would ask me for money as I walked past. Bus drivers and restaurateurs would try to charge me extra for services that didn't exist. But it was almost as though they were light-heartedly trying their luck for when I declined, they simply said "Okay," and dropped the subject completely. I'm a great believer in, "if you don't ask, you don't get", but this was a little odd. How was it acceptable to ask me for money just because I was white, but unthinkable to receive money from me for a favour?

Thankfully, at the hostel a dorm bed was available, and I grabbed it instantly, as there were only one or two hostels in the city. In the dormitory I instantly recognized the packs of an Australian couple I had met in Tehran. The strange thing was, I couldn't remember what either of them looked like, but had subconsciously lodged their packs in my memory. When they arrived, I was further amazed at my inability to remember their faces, as Doug had long, almost albino-white dreadlocks down his back which he had been growing for 10 years. His pretty girlfriend Kim, was also quite memorable. We went out for a sophisticated dinner of kebabs, chips and ice cream and then returned to the hostel where we sat under the stars in the courtyard until the early hours, chatting and drinking Zam Zam.

The next morning, Doug, Kim and I combined forces with our cookers to make tasty fried egg sandwiches, and I then set off on foot to find Imam Square. While I knew it wouldn't be hard to find (as next to Tiananmen Square in China, it's the largest on earth) I knew that making it there without being run over would be a challenge. I'd discovered that in Iran it was normal for motorbikes to tear down the pavement at 60km an hour. Insanely, they also appeared to have the right of way, which meant you had to have eyes in the back of your head at all times. Crossing the congested roads was an art in itself. It went something like this: deep breath, step straight out into traffic, keep walking at the same speed frantically swinging head from side to side while narrowly avoiding cars, trucks, scooters and bicycles constantly swerving around you. To add to the confusion, the local buses ran in the lane nearest the side of the road but in the opposite direction to the cars. When I first arrived in Tehran, I just stood by the side of the road awaiting a break in the traffic. After three days of doing this, I realized this wasn't going to happen, and started copying the locals instead. But my view on their driving changed while I was there. At first, I considered them the worst drivers on the planet, but by the time I left Iran I considered them the best, because what in England would be called a near miss, is just called driving there.

I started in the covered bazaar that joined with Iman Square at one end. As one of the largest in the country, and with some parts dating back 1,300 years, it was quite a spectacle. It was a bit like a car boot sale with a touch of class. One thing that saddened me, however, was the fact that ivory was for sale. Word had apparently not yet reached Iran that this was now considered extremely wrong, and there were small boxes and ornaments made from it on many a stall. I tried not to encourage the sale of these objects, but couldn't help but inspect a few pieces because the craftsmanship was of a very high standard.

As I wandered around, I found my eyes kept being drawn upwards to the ancient vaulted ceilings. The only source of light in the great building was through star shaped gaps in this ceiling and it reflected off the smooth white walls. I stopped at a teahouse that overlooked the square, and sat puffing away on the complimentary water pipe they brought me while sipping tea and writing my journal. I sat there long enough to see the light slowly change my perspective on the things below. One thing I also noticed was a number of women with swollen eyes and dressings covering their faces. I commented on this to the tea boy, worried that I was looking at the evidence of serious domestic abuse. He laughed, and using a knife from a dirty plate, mimed the cutting off of his nose. I later found out, Esfahan is the number one place in the Middle East to go for plastic surgery, something that is often paid for by husbands as a gift.

Once the sun had lost some of its heat for the day, I made my way down to the other end of the square and went inside the Imam Mosque. As one of the most beautiful mosques in the world, the entrance way stands at a towering 30m high. While the mosque is covered in blue-tiled mosaics on the outside, the inside is filled with sunken porches framed by more mosaics of dark blues and deep yellows. The place had taken a total of 27 years to build more than 300 years before. Considering the tools they had to work with, it was almost unbelievable to look at the perfectly proportioned symmetry that had been created.

Early that evening, as I sat discussing my discoveries of the day with the Australians and a group of other travellers in the courtyard, and vainly trying to palm off some of the fowl-tasting green Zam Zam I had mistakenly bought, an Englishwoman in her late 50s arrived. She had recently converted from Christianity to Islam, and after talking to her for a while I came to the conclusion her motivation to convert was rather shallow. She explained to me that her ex-husband had been a vicar, and from what I could tell she seemed to have converted to spite him after he had left her for another woman. She babbled on about her new-found faith trying to sound wise, but just came across as laughably ignorant. Kim interrogated her mercilessly, and she countered these questions with questions of her own that made no apparent sense. But what was clear was that we seemed to know more about her adopted religion than she did. It felt like a very dangerous game to be playing in a country where faith and devotion is everything.

Breakfast the next day was the best meal I'd had in a long time. The hostel owner had given us directions to a baker's shop which only sold one type of bread the shape of your average naan, but five times the size. It was cooked inside a large kiln heated by a bed of stones. Half of the population of Esfahan seemed to be there that morning, and we arrived to a crazy scrum of people shouting out their orders. There was no noticeable queue, and after five minutes of politely standing and waiting, as a polite Englishman does, to catch one of the baker boys' eyes, I gave up and went Iranian, pushing and elbowing my way to the front where, after receiving three hot pieces of bread, I squeezed back through the mob, holding the trophies above my head. From there, again on the hostel owner's advice, we bought some fresh honey, so fresh in fact that large chunks of honeycomb were still inside the spread.

Back at the hostel we polished off the whole meal without pausing for breath, then the three of us left to locate the Zayandeh River, which we were told was crisscrossed by at least 10 ancient bridges, into the supports of which were built lots of tiny teahouses. Still a little bloated from our sugary breakfast, this was nevertheless to be our first stop.

Inside, the teahouse that we selected (for no particular reason as they all seemed relatively identical) it felt even smaller than it was, with the walls so heavily decorated with drapes, photos and Iranian objects. We sat down on a ledge that was level with the window, with the river only a few inches below the sill. The men on the ledge next to us were puffing away on a water pipe which filled the room with a sweet but not sickly smell of cherries. We shared a pot of tea. In Iran it is served without milk, in a glass no bigger than one you'd use for sherry and half filled with lumps of sugar through which you suck the liquid. Between the ZimZam and the tea I imagine Iran has a lot of very rich dentists.

From our window we could look out to see the other bridges further downstream which all seemed to be social hubs, with lots of people sitting chatting on the steps while children played around the river banks. Beneath the bridges themselves, a walkway ran in the shade of the arches. Here, I saw people had stopped to rest, and some were even sleeping between the pillars with the water gushing past either side of them.

Shooting up from the river in between two of the bridges was a jet of water, which must have reached more than a 100m in height. I thought this was amazing, and as we later passed by, I stood marvelling at it for ages. Kim and Doug laughed at how excited I was at this, compared to my relative lack of enthusiasm for the bridges.

We sat on the edge of the river and ate yet another lunch of kebabs, and I wondered how vegetarian Simon had managed in Iran. As we ate, two teenage girls chaperoned by their older brother approached us. While the boy remained silent, they began talking to us excitedly in near perfect English. They told us that they had an appointment to get to, but asked if it might be possible to meet up with us that evening for tea. We agreed. The girls looked delighted and before they left, they shyly asked if they could touch Doug's dread locks. I wasn't sure whether to be hurt or relieved by this, as for the first time it wasn't my hair people wanted to touch.

The girls arrived at our hostel right on time, but unfortunately, I was still in the queue for the shower. The manager was a stickler for the rules, and due to them being Iranian, wouldn't let them inside to wait. Normally I would have agreed with this rule, as it was nice to have a refuge to return to after a long day in an unfamiliar environment. On this occasion though, it seemed very unfair, especially after Kim told him repeatedly that they were good friends of ours. Being made to wait outside must have piqued their interest because once we had finally got into their car, they wanted to know all about what it was like inside the hostel, which was slightly bemusing. But we described it the best we could, trying to explain what made it different to staying in a hotel. It seemed what they really wanted to know about though was the sleeping arrangements and wash areas. They were shocked that men and women were sleeping in the same dormitories, even more so when we said that while the showers were inside cubicles, they were within the same mixed room. This of course was illegal for them, and it seemed unimaginable that it should be happening in their own country. There were a lot of, "But what happens if. . . " questions coming from the two of them, and they just couldn't fathom how we could be comfortable with it all. Their sullen brother was once again accompanying them, since it would have been forbidden for them to talk to men without his supervision, even though he did not under-stand what they were saying. This of course, did not stop him from hushing them when they got too excited over a conversation, which they did regularly. He clearly didn't like Doug and me at all. I suppose we were for him far too relaxed around his sisters, and probably weren't following all the protocols of male and female engagement.

They took us to a rather posh hotel. As always, I was underdressed – I was still in my shalwar kameez, while every other male seemed to be wearing Nike and Levis. The man in the doorway was dressed in a tuxedo, and greeted us warmly before leading us through to what looked like the set of a bad 70s gangster movie. It was a circular room within a room enclosed by glass, at the centre of which was a huge and ghastly water feature covered in fairy lights which flashed in time to the terrible Turkish pop music spilling from the speakers above. The seats were small but not uncomfortable, and covered, along with the carpet, in dated patterns and drab colours. We spent the next few hours answering hundreds of questions about the countries in which we grew up, where we had visited, where had the best food, the best fashion, the best transport, the best sports' stadiums.

Unfortunately, we were given very little chance to ask any questions about where they were from, as they would only answer briefly, before returning to their own lines of enquiry. They did, however, say that it was sad that in Europe it was frowned upon for someone in their mid-20s to still be living in the family home, as the only reason they would have to move out, would be when they got married.

At least a dozen thimbles of tea were drunk, and we smoked our way through three different flavours of tobacco in a water pipe. By the time they dropped us back at the hostel, it was surprisingly late, and we had all had a really good night. Plus, it was nice to know that I wasn't going to wake up with the customary hangover that normally followed.

They'd arranged to pick us up from the hostel again the next morning to take us back to their family home and show us some of the pictures they had drawn. I made sure I was ready this time. When we arrived, I was surprised at how tiny and basic their house was, considering how well-educated they seemed to be and the wealth they had displayed in taking us to the expensive hotel. Sitting in their front room, we were fed a breakfast of the most deliciously sweet watermelon, and I struggled not to make a mess as the juice ran down my chin. They were far more relaxed and confident inside their own home than they had been in public, especially once their glossy brown hair was uncovered, and their eyes were no longer in the shadow of their scarves. Their pictures they had wanted to show us were all drawn in chalk and charcoal, and all seemed to be of their mother, who by the look of the pictures was not someone whose good side was easy to capture. Next, they produced a guitar and a wooden flute, and began playing some pretty awful traditional music. I smiled politely and clapped with the others when it was over, but then as an encore we were treated to some singing. I closed my eyes and nodded my head like I was enjoying what I was hearing, all the while pleading silently for the torture to end. Doug was my saviour, as once they had finished and we'd all made the correct noises, he took the guitar from them and began playing Rocky Racoon by The Beatles, and it was my turn to sing what I could remember of the lyrics; there was no doubt that they were equally horrified by my singing, as I was by theirs.

Once all the musical entertainment was over, the sisters suggested that they take us to visit a tomb on the outskirts of the city. The idea didn't really appeal to me at first because I'd seen so many tombs already over the past months that I was somewhat bored with visiting them, but when they told me that if you pushed the two minarets there they swayed about, they couldn't have got me in the car faster. Sure enough when we arrived, after stopping briefly for them to buy us some minty nougat, we found that the minarets did indeed wobble. This wasn't even something that anyone thought particularly problematic, and the guard was the first to demonstrate their lack of sturdiness by leaning his body against them as we all looked up and watched them sway against the blue sky. I had a go myself, and as I did so, I imagined future historians writing, "Two minarets once stood around the grounds of the tomb, but people thought it was funny to wobble them and they eventually toppled over."

We spent a last evening with our new friends around Imam Square, which I discovered looked even more amazing as the light faded as it brought to the fore a secondary shade in the blue tiles of the mosque. Fountains were turned on in the centre of the square at night and horses and carts trotted around carrying families in circles for entertainment. We explained to the sisters that we would be leaving Esfahan in the morning so tonight would be our final goodbye. This was only partly true – the Aussies were leaving in the morning, but I hadn't decided what I was doing yet. When we left them outside the hostel that evening, they told us it had been one of the best days of their lives, which I thought so nice, that much to the annoyance of their brother, I forgot protocol, and gave them both a hug.

As I poured over my map the next morning, I struggled to find somewhere I still had the time to properly see. I now had only four days left to cross the border, which was still 1,400km away. By the time lunchtime came around, I was still undecided as to what to do so went out for a kebab and an ice cream which helped me reach a decision. I was going to cut my losses and head to Turkey so I could drink a beer with Simon.

I persuaded the owner of the hostel to let me only pay for half of my last day, grabbed my pack and walked to the bus station. I got the last ticket on the last overnight bus to Tabriz that night, which was the last big city before the border, and I took this as a good sign.

The 17-hour journey could undoubtedly have been completed far quicker, had the driver not stopped for tea every 45 minutes. During the night, I was a little annoyed when at a toilet stop, I was woken from a comfortable sleep and told I had to get off the bus.

"I'm fine thanks," I mumbled thickly with my eyes still shut. The conductor then grabbed my arm and told me that I had to get off as there were unaccompanied women on the bus meaning I had to wait outside in the cold until their chaperones returned from the toilet.

Finally, at Tabriz, I was only 400km short of the border, but it was five in the morning and there wasn't another bus until 10am. It was cold and I wanted to keep moving so I found a taxi, and instructed him to take me to the outskirts of the city from where I planned to hitchhike the rest of the way.

25

Under The Spotlight

Tabriz to Antalya to Paris to London = 6,583km

After a quick breakfast of yogurt and bread at a roadside café, I walked to the edge of the freeway and spent the next two hours in clouds of thick black smoke until the world's slowest truck stopped to pick me up. The driver, who was wearing a tattered cap from the 1994 Football World Cup, was a little disappointed that I didn't speak the lingo, but was happy enough to get by with sign language.

The truck was old and badly in need of a service, and each time we hit a slight slope the driver had to drop down to first gear as the vehicle very nearly came to a complete stop. After 200km spent looking out of the window at all the other trucks overtaking us, he dropped me off at a crossroads and turned left towards Iraq.

I continued walking straight on singing a Celine Dion song, I have no idea why, and had covered a good few kilometres past small houses outside which long grass grew and rusting farming machinery lay abandoned, before a car stopped. I didn't really want to get in, for it was clearly already too crowded inside, but they insisted, so I had to squeeze into the front seat beside another man, and we set off with me in a rather uncomfortable position with my right arm and head sticking out of the window. An hour or so later they reached their destination, a town roughly 20km from the Turkish border. There they asked for the ridiculous amount of $100US in exchange for the lift. I offered them $5, and they seemed happy with that. As I set off in search of some food I mused how once again, the truck driver had asked for nothing and had in fact bought me a cup of tea, while the man in the nice car had tried to take advantage.

After a final kebab for lunch, I began walking in the direction of the border. The whole way taxis continually pulled up alongside me touting for a fare, so when after about five kilometres yet another began driving slowly at my side, I didn't even look across when I said, "No thank you," for what felt like the 100th time.

I heard the back-window wind down, and then, "Ben!" I looked over at the unexpected sound of my name, and saw a Czech guy I had met briefly back in Tehran poking his head out of the window. "I'm going to the border. It's already paid up. You may as well jump in!"

Fifteen minutes later we arrived at the Turkish border where the taxi driver began saying we had to pay twice the fare previously agreed as there were now two of us. When we protested, he called over all the other taxi drivers who were hanging around to back him up, and then started grabbing at us and threatening to get the police.

"No, I'm going to get the police," I responded, and practically ran over to the Border Police waiting with their guns. Thankfully they took our side, and ignoring the huddle of abusive taxi drivers, instructed us to keep walking beyond their barrier towards Turkey, and not to pay any more than we already had. Strangely, as soon as the taxi driver saw he wasn't going to get any more money from us, he quietened down and really didn't seem all that bothered after all. And so, I left Iran, not with quite the emotional send-off I had planned, but it would have to do.

It was a long walk from the barrier entrance up to the immigration offices down a long windy road, and I began to realize as we walked, that the Czech guy was either a little weird or a bit simple. He was very tall and skinny and looked like a basketball player and so without being able to remember his name, I did my customary renaming and this time decided on Jordan.

Jordan was certainly clingy, and began asking me if I wanted to travel with him around Europe. When I explained I couldn't because I was meeting a friend in Turkey already, he was quite clearly devastated at my rejection and I was a little scared for a moment that he was going to cry. I needed to use up the last of my rials in the shop at the border, but couldn't find a single thing besides an ice cream that I wanted or needed, so instead ended up with four tins of frankfurters.

Getting stamped out of Iran had taken a matter of seconds, but getting stamped into Turkey took us quite a bit longer. We were held back while dozens of Iranians were stamped through in front of us. Jordan began getting annoyed and started tutting loudly in a very dramatic and camp manner. I had to calm him down because it was clear that at this border post, being patient was going to be far more productive than throwing a tantrum. We were eventually called over, and Jordan was stamped through quickly without paying a penny. I however, was charged 15 Euros. I of course only had dollars which at first, they refused to accept and the official had to go off and check with his superior since this was the only currency I had. As I pointed out, I'd just come from Iran where I had had no access to banks in order to get any Euros, and they finally let me through.

The stress of crossing over was all forgotten, however, when I saw that inches from the immigration office there was a bar. Jordan was panicking about reaching the nearest town before dark, but I persuaded him to drink one beer and relax before we moved on. This turned out to be an excellent idea, for inside we met a friendly Kurd who offered us a lift to the next town. After getting another round in to celebrate this offer from our new friend, we set off.

Jordan and the Kurd chatted in the front while I was crammed in the back of his very clean red sports car. To my left was Mount Arafat, which at 5,137m tall, was not only the tallest mountain in Turkey, but also where Noah's Ark is believed to have come to rest after the flood. This story is not only told in the Bible, but also in Hindu scriptures. As I looked at the shape of the mountain, it was believable, for I could see a curve where it looked as though an ark could rest. For the Armenian people, the mountain is extremely sacred, but as the mountain is on the Turkish side of the border and they are not allowed to cross, they are forced to live in its shadow, without ever being able to visit. I was lucky that afternoon, for its summit was visible below the cloudline and the snow-covered peak had a wisp running west from its tip. All I could think was how much I wanted to climb it.

We were dropped off in the town of Dogubayazit, which actually seemed to be pronounced, "Dog you buy is it". There I immediately found an internet café, checked my emails, copied down where Simon was staying, and fired back a reply telling him to stay where he was, because I was going to come and find him for a change.

Simon was in Antalaya, but as I had no map of Turkey at that time, I had no idea where that was. I assumed it would be within a few hours' drive, but I turned out to be very much mistaken. It was beginning to get dark, so I headed straight to the bus station, and all the way there Jordan was trying to persuade me to travel with him. I was beginning to feel like a childminder.

At the bus depot I learnt that the next bus to Antalya was not leaving until 8am the next day, so it seemed I had little option but to spend the night in town. After so long paying next to nothing for a bed, I was taken aback by the rate of the rooms here and announced to Jordan that I couldn't afford a room and was going to go and sleep in a field. I mistakenly thought this would shake him off, instead this sounded all very new and exciting to him and he happily decided to join me.

We walked out of town in darkness and passed a military base. I had to repeatedly tell Jordan to be quiet, as he was getting very over-excited and loudly broadcasting our foreign presence to all in earshot. I led us across a field and nearly down a 10ft trench as we were not using our torches for fear of attracting attention. On finding a suitable spot, I laid down my Chinese raincoat and curled up on it in my sleeping bag. Jordan only had a blanket, which he claimed was equally as beneficial as my sleeping bag. Tired from more than 24 hours' solid travel, I closed my eyes and ignored him. He had just quietened down when a bright light forced me wide awake again. It was the searchlight from the military base. I doubted they were looking for us, and even if they were, I was sure they wouldn't be able to pick us up from where we lay. Jordan however was paranoid, and began panicking as the beam scanned back and forth over our makeshift camp. I only just managed to calm him down in time before he stood up and put his hands on his head in surrender. I slept soundly after that. I'm not so sure about Jordan. He was still packing his stuff up when I set off in the morning. I wished him all the best and told him I was sure he would find someone to travel with soon and feeling a little guilty, I left him looking heartbroken and shivering in the middle of the field.

When I reached the bus station, I found I still had an hour to spare, so I went off and bought a freshly baked baguette, then sat down behind the wall of a car park to enjoy a frankfurter sandwich. I thought where I had chosen to sit was quite hidden, but then out of nowhere a little girl of no more than five years of age appeared carrying a tray. On the tray was a pot of tea, complete with a little glass and a bowl of sugar. She placed it down in front of me without saying a word, and then vanished around the side of a building. Speechless, I looked around, trying to work out what had just happened. Then I spotted an old man standing by a window a few floors above me. He waved and then saluted. I returned the salute, and he backed away from the window with a smile.

Back at the bus station, I couldn't believe how expensive the ticket was, but without much choice I paid and took my seat. Antalya, it turned out, was 28 hours away. By the time the bus finally arrived, I had given up all hope of it ever stopping. I think the person sitting next to me was pretty relieved too, as I'd been irritating him for the past 24 hours, asking if we were nearly there yet. I checked my emails using the internet inside the depot and picked up directions from Simon, before jumping on a local bus.

I was just beginning to think I had already managed to get lost, when I spotted the guesthouse fitting Simon's description. I asked at reception for Simon, but was told he was not staying there. It was then that I spotted Simon's pack leaning against the wall behind the reception desk.

"I'm looking for that man," I said.

"Oh," they said, comprehension dawning. "He sleeps on the roof."

I took a seat in the courtyard and had just ordered a beer when Simon walked in. He greeted me with a thousand questions, then showed me upstairs to where we were sleeping, which was indeed outside on a rooftop. It was at the top of two flights of metal stairs, where a number of forgotten old plastic sun loungers were scattered beneath a canopy of vines hanging from a wooden trellis.

"We have our own vineyard," I said.

"Of course," Simon replied with a smile. He explained that he had worked out a deal with the owner that we could sleep on the roof under the stars and bunches of grapes for just 10E a night. This included a Continental breakfast and the use of the shower in one of the rooms before 6am and after 6pm. Although it was a fantastic deal, I was a little disappointed at the terms of showering, as after more than three days on the road, I felt very grimy and undoubtedly smelt. Simon had a solution to this problem and led me down the cobbled streets to the harbour where we stripped down to our boxer shorts and jumped off the wall in to the water. We spent the next half an hour swimming around in the open sea. It was the first time I had swum in the sea since leaving Thailand and it felt amazing. We showered off the salt water with a hose we found on the jetty, and headed back to our new digs that I'd named "The Vineyard". When we got back, Simon began searching for something in the bottom of his bag and in the process pulled out two tins of frankfurters. I couldn't stop laughing – he had clearly found himself in the same predicament as me at the border and reached the same conclusion.

Although where we were staying was relatively unspoilt, Antalya was a real tourist town and it was impossible to escape the hordes of package tours. A lot of the tourists were English and truly owned the expression, "Brits Abroad". There was a McDonald's only five minutes from where we were staying, and shops everywhere selling tacky souvenirs, including boxes of the soft sweet, "Turkish Delight", which, when we looked at the back of the packaging, was actually made in Spain.

It seemed that the exciting part of the trip was over for now, so I declared that we should celebrate our life-altering experience and take a holiday. And so, for the next 10 days we were a little more than tipsy and very merry. During daylight hours we sat in the shade of The Vineyard drinking and listening to music, or swimming at the beach and off the harbour wall. One night, while wandering around town searching for something of interest in what now seemed a somewhat dull environment, we came across a nightclub hosting an enormous outdoor foam party. I had no interest in going in, but Simon had never seen anything like it before and wanted to experience it. The bouncers said there was a dress code though, and wouldn't let us enter. I thought this strange given that it was a foam party, but accepted their ruling and moved on. Simon, however, was deeply offended by the discrimination and I had to drag him away from the door before we got hurt. Given that Simon was wearing flip-flops and I had nothing on my feet at all, I could see the bouncers' point.

We certainly stuck out like sore thumbs compared to the other tourists. I was still in denial that I would have to conform to wearing less comfortable clothes again, while Simon was still dressed in his Jesus attire. The other residents at the guesthouse, who sat around the courtyard writing postcards and attempting to pick up a 10-month tan in 10 days, certainly viewed us as oddities. I imagine it did look fairly strange when every so often one of us would come down the fire escape from the roof with two empty bottles of Efes beer, disappear down the side road for five minutes, and then return with two more full ones. We had made a deal with the man who ran the bottle shop down the road; because we bought in bulk, he was storing the beers for us in his personal fridge, and then allowed us to wander in and out of his house at random intervals and help ourselves. I think it's fair to say that we were having trouble readjusting to the western way of doing things. We were quite content in our little bubbles though, dancing around on the rooftop, listening to the album by a Chinese band, which Simon had bought near the start of our trip in China a few months before.

One morning I woke to find Simon scrubbing frantically in a tub of soapy water. When I sat up and took a closer a look, I realized that he was hand washing his way through a pile of laundry that I was pretty sure wasn't his own.

"What the hell are you doing?" I asked, blearily.

He looked up in distinct embarrassment and then explained that during the night he had been caught by the manager, standing teetering on the edge of the rooftop and urinating down onto the hotel's laundry, which had been drying on a line below. Thankfully the manager had seen the funny side and so was making him hand wash all the guesthouse's dirty laundry as punishment, despite the fact that there was an industrial washing machine downstairs.

"I was sure I was in the toilet," Simon finished. Shortly after his explanation, the manager appeared on the rooftop. As we caught each other's eyes we both burst out laughing.

I then reached over to my bag and grabbed a handful of clothes, tossed them at Simon and said, "Do those while you're at it."

This made the manager laugh so hard that his eyes started watering. He then took Simon by the hand and led him downstairs and across the courtyard where, still laughing, he pointed the toilet out to him. He repeated this joke three times over the next two days. It only got funnier.

Two mornings in a row we attempted to leave The Vineyard and move on from Antalya, but one more cold beer kept getting in the way. Instead, we ended up leaving late one drunken evening and made it to Fethiye, chosen purely because the name sounded funny while we stood in the bus queue at the station waiting to buy our tickets.

As crowded cities go, it was very picturesque at night. The main attraction was its long, crowded yacht marina. There were many handsome boats docked there, some private, but most equipped for taking tourists on coastline cruises. We strolled along the wooden walkway that ran beside the boats and down along the coast where expensive restaurants dotted the water's edge. We found a fish and chip shop operating from a boat and there I had the best chips I had had in a long time. From there we just kept walking west, and eventually ended up sleeping in an abandoned bandstand on the beach.

In the morning we found lots of cafes along the shoreline offering traditional English breakfasts, and it seemed that you could pay in almost any currency you liked. It was, however, a massive let down. I then discovered a tube of tomato puree had split in my bag and covered all my possessions, so I decided it was time to get my clothes machine-washed for the first time since the UN compound. The nice old lady in the launderette said it would take four hours for our stuff to be washed and dried. By now, aside from what I was wearing, I only had one pair of trousers, two T-shirts and two pairs of boxers. Simon was in much the same situation. Not wanting to waste space in the machine, therefore, we asked the laundry lady to turn away while we stripped off and changed into our bathers then added those clothes to the load. She thought we were mad but promised to have them ready in a few hours and we returned to our camp and spent the day swimming, reading, writing and sketching.

After another peaceful night listening to the waves breaking on the beach below the bandstand and the sound of Turkish pop drifting down the shore, we took our bags of clean clothes, and headed further west along the coast to Dalayan which we had been told was the location of a turtle nesting site. The campsite we checked into backed right onto a lake in to which a jetty ran out for 10m. Over the next few days, we would perform hundreds of somersaults from that jetty, turtles surfacing inches away from us in the water. They were far off the attractive turtles I would swim with almost daily in Thailand. Turkish turtles were almost grey in appearance and their shells covered in white coral encrustations. Their heads were pointed and their jaws looked sharp and powerful. While the Thai turtles had a rounded end to their flippers, these guys had long claws that looked easily able to shred an arm. Something told me these turtles were not going to let me chill with them like my underwater playmates in Thailand and every time I swam a few laps of the lake, I found myself clenching my toes, paranoid one was lurking there, waiting to take a bite.

In the evenings we cooked up some excellent meals on my cooker, but usually would stand around for 10 minutes beforehand arguing over the best method of cooking, like a couple of middle-aged men at a BBQ. I slept well in my tent almost every night, while Simon slept in a hammock with the mosquitoes outside. One night we were woken by two English girls having a loud argument less than 20ft from my tent. Based on their choice of vocabulary I would hazard to say they were not the most ladylike of girls, and from what I could make out they were arguing over a man that they both wanted to sleep with. After a little while they stormed off and took their argument elsewhere, at which point I stuck my head out of the tent to grin at Simon who said with a smirk, "English?"

"Yeah, sorry about that. We'll leave tomorrow." I replied.

We did leave the next day, but waited until the sun had gone down so we could make the most of our last few hours of swimming, sunbathing and drinking on the jetty. It was 1am by the time we arrived at Izmir, our final destination together. The bus station could have been mistaken for a small airport. It even had a control tower that overlooked the four-storey terminal. The place was filled with shops, restaurants and of course half a dozen Turkish barbershops. The guesthouse we searched for turned out to be more expensive than we had been told and in worse condition. But by that time, it was 2am and we were both drunk, so we checked in regardless. We dumped our bags and then went back out in search of some more nocturnal activities. When we woke up in our room late the next day, we had a handful of red roses between us, and no idea where they had come from.

We'd headed to Izmir because one of us had read somewhere that you could catch ferries to Italy and Istanbul from there. After grabbing a cold shower in the communal bathroom we went out to see if this was true. After following a lot of useless directions from locals, we found what we believed to be the ferry port, only to discover the ferries no longer ran from Izmir, but from Cesme, which was 100km away. We drowned our sorrows in more beers, and avoided talking about what we knew was coming the next day – that this goodbye would probably be our last.

In the morning we headed to the bus station to go our separate ways. Simon was heading by bus to Istanbul and then was going to try to get to Hungary within 10 days, as his favourite band, The Cure, was playing a concert there. I was heading for Cesme to try and get a boat.

"So, here's our pact," I said, just before boarding my bus. "If we don't see each other in England or Switzerland, we'll come and find each other when one of us is heading for the North or South Pole."

"Deal," Simon replied. Then after a final handshake, I took my seat on the bus to Cesme, feeling very sad. I was going to miss my eccentric companion. As the bus pulled away and I looked back at Simon standing there, I noticed just how different he looked from the rest of the people filing past him – like a shepherd among the flocks, even without his stick!

It only took two hours to reach Cesme, and before long I was walking down towards the harbour. I made my way through the crowds of holidaymakers and gap-year students heading straight to the booking office for the ferries. There was a ferry leaving the following evening for the city of Brindisi in the south of Italy, and after hesitating briefly, I bought a ticket.

While Cesme appeared to be somewhere that would be really nice to explore when quiet, it was now the high season and crowded with more tourists than the place, or I, could handle. I walked as far out of town as I could, and sat around in local cafes, watching the clock tick. I returned to the seafront when it got dark and walked along the breakwater in the moonlight where I found the flattest boulder I could, and curled up for the night, the spray of the waves below me drifting up and settling on my face.

In the morning I jumped off the rocks and into the sea for a quick wake-up swim. The temperature seemed to have dropped by about 10 degrees since Antalya, which was far too cold for me, so I almost immediately tried to get back out. No sooner had my head resurfaced though, in my hurry, I put my foot down on a sea urchin. I hobbled about over the rocks cursing, the spines still poking out of my foot. Spotting a local fisherman, I indicated that I needed a bit of help, and he handed me some pliers so I could pluck the spikes out.

I spent the morning limping around town, waiting as long as I could bear before making my way to the port. I was still hours early for the boat but I was not alone. Also wanting to be among the first aboard was a Frenchman. He had a shaved head and the type of long goatee beard normally associated with bikers. His ear lobes were stretched in Swahili fashion with hoops. We discussed his ears for a while, and he explained that it had taken him five years to reach the stage they were at now. You could have passed a golf ball through them. He explained that he had to apply a lubricant to his lobes every few hours to prevent the skin tissue drying up and cracking. This all seemed far too much effort to me.

When the men in the bright orange jackets finally gave us the go ahead to board, the race was on between us and the other foot passengers who had accumulated. We ran up the flights of stairs, desperately trying to reach the Pullman area before anyone else, as we clearly both knew how uncomfortable the seats were to sleep on, and wanted to claim the small space on the floor in front. We won, and marked out our space by laying our sleeping bags down, then standing guard over our territory as the other passengers arrived and jealously eyed up our beds.

We didn't leave Turkey until after dark which was slightly disappointing, as I had romantic notions of watching it slowly becoming a dot on the horizon. My ticket included four meals at assigned times throughout the 36-hour crossing, the seat numbers due to be fed at any one time were called out over loud speakers. You had to listen carefully because the announcer had a thick accent, and if you missed your time, you missed your meal. There were two Italians at my table, who I quickly became convinced were Mafiosos. They were both dressed expensively and immaculately and constantly taking short intense phone calls. I later realized they were just Italians.

I spent a lot of the crossing sitting outside staring across the choppy sea at the outlines of distant islands just visible on the horizon. Time passed surprisingly quickly considering that there was nothing more than shops and a few arcade machines on board for distraction. During the night my sleep was constantly broken by annoyingly loud and unnecessary announcements coming from the speakers above, telling us things like, "Do not climb over the safety railings".

As we disembarked the next morning, I met up with the Frenchman and we stopped for breakfast in town.

We were amused by the young Italians standing around, the men in their bright pink shirts and slicked-back hair parading around like they were on a fashion shoot, leaning against walls chewing gum and pulling cheesy poses; their female counterparts peacocking down the streets, regularly checking their reflections in shop windows. As far as I could tell though, all this prancing about seemed to be in vain, as they were all too busy worrying about what they looked like to notice anyone else. I was jealous though when a convoy of teenagers on highly polished Vesper scooters cruised past. It was like I had stepped onto the film set of an extremely stereotypical Italian movie. All that was missing was a cluster of fat men with cigars and Tommy guns.

After breakfast I said *bon voyage* to the Frenchman, and headed for the train station. There I boarded a train to Milano and spent much of the journey engrossed in a book which meant I hardly noticed the scenery as we sped through central Italy. I only had an hour in Milano before I boarded another train to Paris that evening. I had just enough time to run out of the station and find a shop selling bottles of olive oil, the one souvenir my mum had requested I should bring back. Olive oil purchased and back in my seat, I set off for my overnight journey to the French capital.

Although I was woken a few times during the night by a guard checking my train ticket, I was aware that since crossing the border from Iran to Turkey, not one single person had asked to see my passport. I spent slightly longer in Paris than I had in Milano, but only by half an hour, and couldn't even find a viewpoint from where I could see the Eiffel tower. I then boarded a train to Calais.

Arriving at Calais train station I was rather concerned that I didn't seem to be able to see the sea and there was nothing else around the station but fields. Confused, I asked one of the few remaining taxi drivers where the port was. He laughed hard, and when he recovered told me that the sea was still 20 miles from the train station, and the only way to get there was by taxi or car. This created a problem, as I had withdrawn the last of my funds in Milano and estimated that I only just had enough money to reach London. I couldn't afford a private taxi for 20 miles, and so I started walking. I had covered more than 10 long miles before I was able to stop a passing car and beg a lift. The family who picked me up kindly went out of their way to drop me right outside the P&O booking office, where I hung around for a few hours as it was cheaper to get a ferry after 9pm.

It was close to midnight when my ferry finally departed for England. I was excited to be heading home and spent ages in the shop on board reading the English newspapers and chatting to the cashier who didn't complain about my failure to buy anything. I visited the duty-free shop and took a gamble with my remaining funds by buying a crate of 24 Stella Artois. For months I had imagined what it would be like to arrive back in England and see the White Cliffs of Dover creep in to view. Sadly, it was dark when we arrived and I couldn't see a thing, but the feeling as I walked down the gangplank back on to British soil was immense and hearing the shouts of the English dockworkers was music to my ears. I couldn't stop grinning. As I approached the customs officers in my Pakistani trousers and Afghan hat with a crate of Belgian beer under my arm, I expected to have my passport checked at the very least, and probably get searched, but they were far too busy drinking tea, and simply waved me straight through without a second glance.

I found an old-fashioned red telephone box and called my friend Tom who lived in London, to ask if he fancied picking me up. Unfortunately, it was a Saturday night, and all he was able to offer me was a drunken welcome home. Knowing that there would be no more trains or buses until the following morning, I wandered around trying to figure out my next move. Walking the streets of Dover, I felt more insecure and on edge than I had been anywhere on my whole trip. Groups of asylum seekers huddled in doorways, some giving off a sense of anger with nothing to lose, others simply looking disheartened and disappointed that Britain's streets were not in fact paved with gold.

It was not the asylum seekers that I really feared though, it was the groups of drunken Englishmen who were hanging around outside closed chip shops and in car parks. Now that I was back in my own country, I immediately tuned in to that sixth sense for knowing who was trouble and who wasn't, just by looking at them. I hadn't had these worries for the last few months I guess, because I didn't know what your stereotypical troublemaker looked like in Tibet or Tehran. Ignorance is bliss, as they say.

I thought it best to find the train station and shelter somewhere safe until daylight. I stopped a passing man to ask which way it was to the train station, but he kept his eyes glued to the ground and walked on, before stopping abruptly, and clearly uncomfortable with the whole situation, hastily pointed me in the right direction.

I had forgotten how inhibited and reserved the English were and reminded myself that I was going to have to be less forward if I was going to fit back in with English society.

Arriving at the train station, I was sure I was being followed, and given that the station was in a cul-de-sac, I quickly ducked around the side of the building and hid in between two Portakabins. I was getting out my sleeping bag and preparing for a long wait, when I heard footsteps coming closer to where I was. I could still hear shouts and general noise coming from the surrounding streets, but I remained quiet and didn't move. Then from the corner of the building, a torch beam lit me up.

"Come out now!" a voice demanded. I did as instructed and was relieved to see it was two railway officials.

"I'm waiting for the first train, and just need a place to sleep safe until morning," I explained.

"Yeah, not the safest of places to be hanging around at this time of night," said one.

"We saw you on the security camera." They told me to gather up my stuff, and then they took me to the platform and showed me a bench.

"We're on duty until noon. Sleep well, son."

I was on the first train to Waterloo the next morning and I loved every minute. I stared at the people getting on and off at the different stops, taking in their clothes and staring at the latest high street fashion, which I was slightly alarmed to see meant a lot of men in pink shirts and ties. As we rolled through town after town, I took great pleasure in reading the oversized number plates on the English cars, and watching the milkmen doing their rounds. I read and re-read all the advertisements aboard the train, simply pleased to be able to understand the words around me again. Of course, I was just as much a spectacle to the other passengers on the train, and when they thought I wasn't looking, they all stared at me, which made me feel something of an outcast in my own country.

At Waterloo station I found I didn't have enough money for my final train ticket. I had budgeted well all the way from Malaysia and now, seven stops from home, I was broke, namely due to the 20 cans of beer I had in my bag, having been unable to resist the discounted prices of duty free.

I caught the train anyway, making sure that I sat in the back carriage, furthest away from the guard, and spent half the time gawping out of the window like I'd never seen London before, and half the time glancing down the carriage for ticket inspectors.

I made it to Teddington station without incident and it felt strangely familiar stepping down on to the platform. I spotted the friendly curly-haired station guard who had worked there for as long as I could remember, and used to shout at me for riding my BMX down the stairs. He recognized me and perhaps assuming that I had been off at university asked, "Home for the holidays, are you?"

"Sort of," I said.

"Behave yourself," he grinned, before heading back inside his little den-like office.

I'd cleverly managed to time my long-awaited homecoming with my family going on holiday, so on the doorstep of home I had to dig down deep into the bottom of my pack to recover my door keys. I opened the front door and stepped inside the quiet hallway, then dropping my pack on the carpet, headed straight for the fridge.

Five minutes later I was sitting on the sofa eating chocolate and staring incoherently at the EastEnders omnibus. I didn't recognize any of the characters and the plot was a total mystery. I kicked off my boots and cracked open a can of Stella and thought about the 26,000km detour I'd taken to be there, then I thought, *I think I will go back to Thailand.*

Acknowledgements

Thank you to Simon – wherever you are – the best travelling companion ever!

Thank you to Nigel and the Khao Lak Family. Thank you to Stevie for getting me started on this project, so sorry you never saw it completed. Thank you to Kate Ross for her advice, encouragement and editing. Thank you to Regine for making sense of my route.

Thank you to all those I met along the way who helped me, guided me, showed me kindness and hospitality. So many, some I never even knew their names.